BERNARD WILLIAMS is remembered as one of the most brilliant [...] philosophers of the past fifty y[...] respected as a moral philosop[...] began to write about politics in [...] way in the early 1980s. Ther[...] stream of articles, lectures, and other major contributions to issues of public concern—all complemented by his books on ethics, which have important implications for political theory.

This new collection of essays, most of them previously unpublished, addresses many of the core subjects of political philosophy: justice, liberty, and equality; the nature and meaning of liberalism; toleration; power and the fear of power; democracy; and the nature of political philosophy itself. A central theme throughout is that political philosophers need to engage more directly with the realities of political life, not simply with the theories of other philosophers. Williams makes this argument in part through a searching examination of where political thinking should originate, to whom it might be addressed, and what it should deliver.

Williams had intended to weave these essays into a connected narrative on political philosophy with reflections on his own experience of postwar politics. Sadly he did not live to complete it, but this book brings together many of its components. Geoffrey Hawthorn has arranged the material to resemble as closely as possible Williams's original design and vision. He has provided both an introduction to Williams's political philosophy and a bibliography of his formal and informal writings on politics.

Those who know the work of Bernard Williams will find here the familiar hallmarks of his writing—originality, clarity, erudition,

(continued on back flap)

In the Beginning Was the Deed

In the Beginning Was the Deed

REALISM AND MORALISM IN
POLITICAL ARGUMENT

Bernard Williams

Selected, edited, and with an introduction
by Geoffrey Hawthorn

PRINCETON UNIVERSITY PRESS

PRINCETON AND OXFORD

Copyright © 2005 by Princeton University Press
Published by Princeton University Press, 41 William Street,
Princeton, New Jersey 08540
In the United Kingdom: Princeton University Press,
3 Market Place, Woodstock, Oxfordshire OX20 1SY

Library of Congress Cataloging-in-Publication Data

Williams, Bernard Arthur Owen.
In the beginning was the deed : realism and moralism in
political argument / Bernard Williams ; selected, edited,
and with an introduction by Geoffrey Hawthorn.
p.   cm.
Includes bibliographical references and index.
ISBN-13: 978-0-691-12430-8 (cloth : alk. paper)
ISBN-10: 0-691-12430-2 (cloth : alk. paper)
1. Political science—Philosophy. 2. Political ethics. I. Hawthorn, Geoffrey. II. Title.
JA71.W462 2005
320′.01—dc22   2005043379

British Library Cataloging-in-Publication Data is available

This book has been composed in Sabon

Printed on acid-free paper. ∞

pup.princeton.edu

Printed in the United States of America

10   9   8   7   6   5   4   3   2   1

Contents

Preface

Patricia Williams

IT IS SAD, but appropriate, that my final, practical gesture of appreciation and love for Bernard should be to help with the publication of the last three collections of his philosophical writings. *The Sense of the Past: Essays in the History of Philosophy, Philosophy as a Humanistic Discipline,* and *In the Beginning Was the Deed: Realism and Moralism in Political Argument* will be published by the Princeton University Press three years after his death in June 2003. Bernard helped and encouraged me in countless ways in my publishing career, bearing out my conviction that editors in university presses should be judged by their choice of advisers as well as by the authors they publish.

Like many who knew him, I thought Bernard was indestructible— and so, I think, did he! But when he was recovering from the drastic effects of his first bout of treatment for cancer in 1999, we talked for the first, and almost the only, time about what should happen to his papers if he could not finish *Truth and Truthfulness.* Thankfully, that was published in 2002, although he would have expanded it in several ways if time had not seemed so pressing. What I learned from this conversation was that Bernard had no faith in his, or any philosopher's, ability to predict whose work would be of lasting interest to their successors. That was for the future to decide. So, although he was totally against what he called "posthumous laundry lists," he refused to express any other opinion about what should be published after his death. Fortunately for me, he did specify that, although I should handle the practicalities of publishing as I thought fit, he would ask "a young philosopher of gritty integrity and severity of judgement who understood the sorts of things he had been trying to do in philosophy" to keep me on the philosophical straight and narrow. That was Adrian Moore. I am deeply grateful to him for the careful consideration he has given to the complicated, general issues of publication and re-publication, and for his friendship.

Deciding on the content of this particular volume has been a heavy responsibility. It is painful to remember how much Bernard wanted to finish a book on this subject. He worked on it right up to the end. His "voice" comes through strongly in the files and many notes and drafts on his computer. But the goal has been to select from the unpublished material only those papers and lectures Bernard himself would have approved for publication in their unedited form, and without the crucial "linking" material and additional topics he would have incorporated in the more ambitious book he wanted to write. In particular, he planned to relate his work on political theory to his experience of political life in post-war Britain and America.

Geoffrey Hawthorn's contribution to this project is due in small part to that missing "autobiographical" element. Throughout our years in Cambridge, he and Bernard spent many enjoyable hours discussing interests they shared, politics being one of the most important to them both. I owe Geoffrey an enormous debt for devoting so much thought and time to this volume.

I should also like to thank those who advised and commented on the selection: Adrian Moore, of course, and Barry Stroud who has long been my trusted friend and adviser on Bernard's work. Thomas Nagel and Samuel Scheffler also helped to shape this book in crucial ways. Sadly, the notes Bernard made on his numerous discussions with Ronald Dworkin over the years and, in particular, on the seminars they gave together in Oxford, though intelligible, were not in publishable form, nor were Bernard's contributions to the joint seminar he gave with Robert Post in Berkeley. But there are many signposts to their intellectual stimulus and influence.

My heartfelt thanks, also, to Walter Lippincott, the Director of Princeton University Press, and his staff in Princeton and Oxford, whose commitment to Bernard as an author, and to high standards of editing, design, production, and marketing are so appreciated at a time when scholarly publishing faces such complex financial challenges.

. . .

Finally, I should like to acknowledge the publishers who have kindly given their permission to publish material in this volume.

- "In the Beginning Was the Deed" in *Deliberative Democracy and Human Rights*, ed. Harold Hongju Koh and Ronald C. Slye (New Haven: Yale University Press, 1999). © 2000 by Yale University.
- "Pluralism, Community and Left Wittgensteinianism" in *Common Knowledge* 1, no. 1 (Durham: Duke University Press, 1992).
- "The Liberalism of Fear." We would like to thank Wolfson College, Oxford, for kindly allowing us to publish this article.
- "From Freedom to Liberty: The Construction of a Political Value" in *Philosophy and Public Affairs* 30, no. 1 (Oxford: Blackwell's, 2001).
- "The Idea of Equality" in *Philosophy, Politics and Society*, 2nd ser., ed. Peter Laslett and W. G. Runciman (Oxford: Blackwell's, 1962).

- "Toleration, a Political or Moral Question?" in *Diogène* 44, no. 4 (1996). The same article was published by *Diogène* in French, English, and Arabic.

Introduction

Geoffrey Hawthorn

I

Bernard Williams did not start writing in a sustained way about politics until the later 1980s. As he says in the first of the essays in this collection, he was most immediately prompted to do so by his encounters with legal and political theorists in the United States. But it was a natural move. He had long had an interest in issues of public concern in Britain and had engaged with the practicalities of several. The experience had strengthened his conviction that questions of principle could not be considered apart from those of practice, and that the practicalities were in part political. In his moral philosophy, the considerations on the question of how we should live that he had brought together in *Ethics and the Limits of Philosophy* (1985) had clear implications for politics: on where we were answering from and to whom, on the relation in our answers between theory and experience, and on how what we say is "relative" to us.[1] But in the academic conversations he enjoyed in the United States about law and politics, subjects that connect more closely there than they do in Britain with philosophy and each other and public life, he was dismayed. There seemed to be a "Manichaean dualism of soul and body" between the intense moralism of much legal and political theory and the bare realism of the concentration in political science on interests. He was also stimulated along the way by exchanges in Germany with Jürgen Habermas. Williams had motives in plenty to work out his own "ethic of political responsibility."

He took the phrase from Max Weber.[2] He was reflecting on it, however, in very different circumstances and pursued it in an altogether more persuasive way. Weber had been making his point to the Union of Free Students in Munich, in 1919, when the "carnival" of revolution was in full swing in the streets outside. Williams was himself well aware of the perpetual threat in what he thought of as the "only certain universals" of politics: power, powerlessness, cruelty, and fear. But he was thinking in more settled times. He was also thinking more carefully. Weber believed

[1] *Ethics and the Limits of Philosophy* (London: Fontana; Cambridge: Harvard University Press, 1985).

[2] Max Weber, "The Profession and Vocation of Politics," in *Political Writings*, ed. Peter Lassman and Ronald Speirs (Cambridge: Cambridge University Press, 1994), 309–69.

that one had to have a cause, and that responsibility consisted in thinking hard about what might follow from acting on that. But he had a disenchantedly arbitrary conception of how anyone might come to a cause in the first place; had little idea of how, beyond the force of personality, one might bring others to share it; and, apart from warning of the demonic force of violence, did not say what the political responsibility he talked of was, and to whom. For Williams, these were the central questions.

The first question of all in politics, however, Williams makes plain, is Hobbes's question, of how to create order out of mayhem. To Hobbes himself, reflecting on England in the 1640s, the mayhem was in the violence of opposed and uncompromising conviction. In many places, one or another kind of disorder persists. Even where it does not, Williams emphasizes, it can never be presumed to have gone for good. The first question is always with us, and fundamental to all politics. In principle, and, if there are no scruples, in practice also, putting a stop to disorder is not difficult. It requires the effective use of state power. But if there are no scruples, the solution will become the problem. Those subject to state power will lose their freedom, and worse. They will ask what the nature of the state's protection and its price are to be and why, and they will want a reasonable reply. They will make what Williams calls a "Basic Legitimation Demand."

In the modern world, this demand is increasingly met by liberalism. This is an historical fact. But the terms have to be elaborated, and the elaboration has to be justified. This is where Williams departs from other liberal political theorists. They succumb to what he describes in *Ethics and the Limits of Philosophy* as "the temptations of theory." They want to find a terminus ad quem, a rational foundation. This, he argues, is a mistake.

> Theory looks characteristically for considerations that are very general and have as little distinctive content as possible, because it is trying to systematize, and because it wants to represent as many reasons as possible as applications of other reasons. But critical reflection should seek for as much shared understanding as it can find on any issue, and should use any ethical material that, in the context of the reflective discussion, makes some sense and commands some loyalty. Of course that will take things for granted, but as serious reflection it must know that it will do that. The only serious enterprise is living, and we have to live after the reflection; moreover (although the distinction between theory and practice encourages us to forget it), we have to live during it as well. Theory typically uses the assumption that we have too many ethical ideas, some of which may well turn out to be mere prejudices. Our

major problem now is actually that we have not too many but too few, and we need to cherish as many as we can.[3]

There is no terminus ad quem. Liberalism is an historical fact. If there were to be a theoretical justification of it, Williams argues, it would have also theoretically to explain why no one before liberalism could see that reason demanded it. But there is no such explanation. Liberals "spectacularly" lack a theory of error. This aside, if there were to be a wholly theoretical justification, it would be extremely general. In the word he uses to describe such generality in "Modernity and the Substance of Ethical Life," it would be very "thin." And in being thin, it would not do what would also be required of it: that is to say, offer a full and satisfactory account of how we should go on, as Williams often put it, "now and around here." It would not be guided by the world in which we live, and would not be a sufficient guide to our action in this world.[4]

It is nevertheless the case that most of the liberal political theory we have proceeds in this way. It starts with a theoretical justification and proceeds to explain what those who propose it see as its political purchase. Utilitarianism, as he mentions in the first essay here, explains in *Ethics and the Limits of Philosophy*, and has elaborated elsewhere,[5] regards politics as simply the executive instrument of the greatest happiness of the greatest number. Contractualism, in John Rawls's much discussed *A Theory of Justice*, offers moral conditions for co-existence under power, and as Williams explains, Rawls does not in this respect materially change his case in his later *Political Liberalism*.[6] Ronald Dworkin's argument for principles of right, with which Williams engages directly in "Conflicts of Liberty and Equality," offers moral foundations for a just and thereby authoritative rule. Other theories (Williams mentions them in several essays, including "In the Beginning Was the Deed" and "Toleration") start

---

[3] *Ethics and the Limits of Philosophy*, 116.

[4] Williams gives an account of "thin" ethical concepts in "Modernity and the Substance of Ethical Life," 79–80; see also his "Replies" in *World, Mind, Ethics: Essays on the Ethical Philosophy of Bernard Williams*, ed. J.E.J. Altham and Ross Harrison (Cambridge: Cambridge University Press, 1995), 207, and *Truth and Truthfulness: An Essay in Genealogy* (Princeton: Princeton University Press, 2002), 305–6 n. 2; his example in the second is the contrast between the thin "good" and the thick "chastity." He discusses the nature of the contrast and the question of whether thick ethical concepts can be true in *Ethics and the Limits of Philosophy*, 140–45.

[5] J.J.C. Smart and Bernard Williams, *Utilitarianism: For and Against* (Cambridge: Cambridge University Press, 1973), now a classic; and Amartya Sen and Bernard Williams, eds., *Utilitarianism and Beyond* (Cambridge: Cambridge University Press; Paris: Maison des Sciences de l'Homme, 1982).

[6] John Rawls, *A Theory of Justice* (Cambridge: Harvard University Press, 1971); *Political Liberalism* (New York: Columbia University Press, 1993).

with a morally consequential theory of personal autonomy. The theories vary. But each starts from outside politics. The distinctiveness of Williams's alternative, which is to work from the historical fact of the "Basic Legitimation Demand," is that it starts from inside. Only his one principle of criticism may not. This is that if a story is told to justify the advantage of a more powerful group over a less powerful, if the story is professedly believed by the more powerful, and if it is accepted by the disadvantaged only because of the power that the advantaged have over them, then the fact that the disadvantaged accept it does not make it legitimate. At least, if this is a principle that is to work from the inside, we must not only have a way of seeing how "professed" the advantaged are in their belief, but also hope that the disadvantaged themselves can come to see how they have come to accept it.[7]

In presenting the kinds of justification they do, the other liberal theories also pay little attention to the question of whom they are theories for. If we try to answer this question, Williams suggests, we cannot be satisfied. Utilitarians are addressing an undifferentiated public that is undefined by anything but its aggregated desires. Rawls appears to be addressing a set of founding fathers, "just off the boat." Dworkin is addressing a somewhat idealized Supreme Court, reflecting above and apart from the politics of the society for which it is pronouncing. Theorists of the liberal person, starting perhaps from an argument for "autonomy," may be addressing everyone (arguing for a notion, Williams adds, that is produced by the forces that created what they want it to justify).

Some political theorists, taking the point, have attempted to identify the wider audience by extending what they take to be a truth in Wittgenstein. This is that concepts are peculiar to "forms of life," which these Wittgensteinians take to mean conceptually distinct communities. Members of such communities can respond only to ideas that connect to those with which they lead their lives. They will also, these theorists argue, have a sense of these lives as communal and be averse to theories that start from the idea of autonomous individuals. Indeed, they should find such ideas, and any other that is not their own, difficult even to grasp. The implication can be that political theorists have themselves actually to be living the lives of the people they are addressing. Williams could see why he was sometimes taken to be a communitarian of this kind. But he was not. It is a view that tends naturally to conservatism. It is also fanciful. Few if any communities of the kind it imagines still exist. (One can wonder whether they ever have; the kind of "hypertraditional" society that Williams himself invoked in his arguments about ethics, "maximally ho-

---

[7] Williams also discusses the principle in *Truth and Truthfulness: An Essay in Genealogy* (Princeton: Princeton University Press, 2002), from 221.

mogeneous and minimally given to reflection," was a device, and hypothetical.)[8] To suppose that they can, certainly to suppose that they can for
us moderns, is wholly unrealistic. Life is everywhere plural.

Among these everywhere plural societies, there will, in modernity, be
those of a liberal kind. Within these, Williams suggests in "The Liberalism
of Fear," there will be two kinds of audience for political theory. One is
what he calls "the audience." This will comprise those with power and
influence in the state, and other theorists. The other is "the listeners."
These will be the people whom the theory is in part about and for, the
people with whom the theory should connect. In one respect, conventional liberal theories may well connect with both. In being theoretical,
they are general; their generality will be expressed in thin concepts; thin-
ness is the quality of the language of modern administrative rationality;
and as Williams remarked in *Ethics and the Limits of Philosophy*[9] and
says again in "Modernity and the Substance of Ethical Life," moral and
political philosophy has become rather too intimate with that. In another
respect, however, the people the theory is about and purportedly for will
not connect with its arguments at all. They lead their lives with more
particular, "thick" concepts, "world-guided" and "action-guiding." So,
too, when not formulating administrative edicts or themselves theorizing,
will Williams's "audience." In modern societies, we all live our lives with
both, and each can have a bearing on politics. There are layers in our
ethical substance. We live in "ethical federations."

If a theory is to "make sense," in Williams's phrase, to its listeners,
it should connect to the complicated and often far from consistent self-
understandings by which they lead their lives. In listeners' lives, moreover
(in contrast to the lives of a few in the audience, who will have reason to
retreat to refining theory as theory), there are always other people. Other
people have different desires and beliefs, and these will clash. There will
be contests, which is to say, politics. And people know, even if theorists
can forget, that contests in politics are not fundamentally conceptual.
They are about what to do, and political concepts, thick and thin, are
guided by what people do. This is why what Williams calls "standard
relativism" is idle. This is the position that if party A favours Y and party
B favours Z, Y is right for A and Z is right for B. It tells parties what is
right. It is a position for which, as he puts it, we are always either too
early or too late. We are too early if there is no exchange between the
parties, too late if there is. And "exchange" here, as he explains in
"Human Rights and Relativism," can importantly involve political recognition, which becomes politically important when the sides have to find

---

[8] *Ethics and the Limits of Philosophy*, 142–48, 158–59.
[9] Ibid., 197.

a way of living with each other. The only sensible relativism is that of distance. This offers people a judgement they need not make, because it makes no difference to what either side does. The most important truth of all in politics, Williams insists in a phrase of Goethe's, is that "in the beginning" is not the word but "the deed."[10]

> A political theory will seem to make sense, and will to some degree reorganise political thought and action, only by virtue of the historical situation in which it is presented, and its relation to that historical situation cannot be fully realised or captured in reflection. (Any reflection that claims to capture it will itself be grounded in practice.) Those theories and reflections will always be subject to the condition that, to someone who is intelligently and informedly in that situation (and these are not empty conditions), it does or does not seem a sensible way to go on. ("In the Beginning Was the Deed")

No political theory can by itself determine its own application.

II

It was Williams's fascination with application—more exactly, with how to think about what to do "now and around here"—that led him practically to engage with difficult issues in British politics. His essay "The Idea of Equality," included here, led to an invitation to sit on the Public Schools Commission set up by a Labour government in 1965 "to advise on the best way of integrating the public"—that is to say, independent and private—"schools within the state system of education." It was his thoughts both on paper and in a range of talks and broadcasts (to listeners) about how to think about fields of competing values and interests, and how to try to resolve these, that led to his serving on a Royal Commission on Gambling between 1976 and 1978 and to chairing a Committee on Obscenity and Film Censorship between 1977 and 1979. (The arguments that emerged from the second were widely admired in Britain and in demand elsewhere.) After the long interlude of Conservative government in the 1980s and the first half of the 1990s, Williams returned in 1997 to take part in an Independent Inquiry into the 1971 Misuse of Drugs Act. He was also, in the early 1990s, an influential member of the Labour Party's commission on the question that had always interested him of "social" or distributive justice.[11]

---

[10] *Faust*, pt. 1, 1237.

[11] The Public Schools Commission produced two reports, under John Newsom in 1968 and David Donnison in 1970. Royal Commission on Gambling 1976–78, *Report*, Com-

The fact that Williams served on these bodies when Labour was in power, and was a member of one of the party's own commissions when it was not, would seem to say something about his politics. In the 1960s and 1970s, he was indeed close to those, party members and others, on what were variously described as Labour's "democratic socialist" and "social democratic" wings, and, after the creation in the 1980s of a new (and as it transpired, rather short-lived) Social Democratic Party, was sympathetic to that. But he was not a party political man. It was the intellectual interest and human importance of the issues that brought him to work with people in all walks of life who shared his commitment to finding the most reasonable agreement.

It was in the nature of Williams's political conception of philosophical argument in politics that he did not consistently argue for the priority of any particular principle. But although Wittgenstein does not (advisedly, even in refutation) appear in the reports of the inquiries in which he was involved, Williams's reaction to the Wittgensteinians' line of thought was his precept. There may be no incontrovertible ground in philosophy for any starting point in politics. But this does not mean that in order to be able to start from somewhere stable, we have to suppose a single, conceptually coherent community. Nor, he would add in response to Richard Rorty's radical reading, does it licence us to start from anywhere, and we certainly do not get anywhere by gazing in ironical amazement at where we do start. Rather, "once a realistic view of communities is applied, and the categories that we need to understand anyone who is intelligible at all are distinguished from those of more local significance, we can follow Wittgenstein to the extent of not looking for a new foundationalism, but still have room for a critique of what some of 'us' do in terms of our understanding of a wider 'we' " ("Pluralism, Community and Left Wittgensteinianism").

What it was to follow this precept comes out with particular clarity in Williams's essays here on toleration, an issue that occupied him as much as any, and censorship. In a plural society there are many values and interests, and a range of corresponding behaviors. Many conflict. Some might be shown to cause actual harm and induce a wider fear. Some will offend. Others will do neither. Some will be expressed in private, others publicly. Some may be practicably restrained; others may not. Some will unavoidably challenge the authority of the state; others will not. Beyond what he regarded as the most basic of the "legitimation demands" in liberalism,

mand Paper 7200 (London: HMSO, 1978). Bernard Williams, ed., *Obscenity and Film Censorship: An Abridgement of the Williams Report* (Cambridge: Cambridge University Press, 1981). Commission on Social Justice, *Social Justice: Strategies for National Renewal*, The Borrie Report (London: Vintage, 1994).

that the state should protect its citizens from fear, it is "hard," he writes, "to discover *any* one attitude" to toleration "that underlies liberal practice." If therefore we are to have "a humanly acceptable legitimate government under modern conditions" ("Toleration, a Political or Moral Question?"), conditions which include, among other things, our pluralities, we shall need a degree of "double-mindedness." We will have to accept that faced with any particular situation for which we want to find a reasonably agreed decision, we may need to favour more than one value and make more than one kind of argument.

If this is plain in many of the political questions that arise within a single state, it is even plainer when we consider those that go across state boundaries. One such, which became pressing in the 1990s, is of whether, and if so how and when, to intervene to provide "humanitarian" relief to others. In a characteristically penetrating move at the end of a lecture, included here, that he gave on the subject in Oxford, he outlines the ways in which unavoidably political considerations will constrain a simple response by one country to suffering in another, and then invites the listener to think the constraints away. Imagine, he suggests, the ideal instrument for those who believe that we should intervene: a non-governmental organization guided by dedicated, independent, and internationally respected figures of ability and good judgement, funded by limitlessly generous billionaires, commanding adequate forces, and for these reasons sufficiently prestigious and effective to face down any state that might want to resist it. It would overcome all the difficulties, except one: who would such a body answer to? If we suggest governments or associations of governments, we are back to politics. If the organization can ignore governments (and a United Nations that is compromised by governments), we might suggest "the moral consciousness of humankind." The implausibility makes the point. It is no answer. We are indeed back to politics: that is to say, to contests with others in which the suffering of those in other countries will at best be one issue among many, and one which it may not always be sensible to put first.

Williams was unusual enough in taking the politics in political thought seriously. He was very unusual indeed in being able so clearly to see, and then so brilliantly and persuasively to explain, where on any matter what combination of ethical argument and political realism made sense. And he engaged. If he could sometimes see himself "largely . . . reminding moral [and political] philosophers of truths about human life which are very well known to virtually all adult human beings except moral [and political] philosophers," as "a kind of flying mission to a small group isolated from humanity in the intellectual Himalaya" ("The Liberalism of Fear"), it does not follow that many other human beings have so powerfully explained what these truths, and truth itself, were. And then made a difference.

III

Williams was working on his next book to the very last moment. It was to have been on politics. His thoughts toward it had developed in the conversations that he greatly valued with his friends in political philosophy, Thomas Nagel, Thomas Scanlon, Amartya Sen, Samuel Scheffler, and Charles Taylor, in a seminar with Robert Post in Berkeley, and in another that he led with Ronald Dworkin for several years in Oxford, occasions celebrated for their excitement and intellectual pleasure. But even in the sense that Williams gave to the word, the book would not have been on theory alone. He intended to reflect more widely on the ways in which his thinking about politics had been affected by his experiences in the political, intellectual, and artistic life of post-war Europe and America.

It will not be only those who knew him who regret not having this book. It would have said much about the place of politics in life. But we do have the lectures and essays in which he was extending some of his ideas for it. I have included all the more substantial of these here. Only one does not date from the later 1980s and 1990s. This is "The Idea of Equality," which first appeared in 1962, has been reprinted several times, and is still unsurpassed. I include it to illuminate the complexity in one aspiration that in "Conflicts of Liberty and Equality," Williams considers against the complexity in another to show what is at issue in aspiring to both.

Williams left only the briefest indication of how he would arrange the more general issues in the book he had in mind. In ordering the essays, I have relied on this, on the judgements of others, most especially of Patricia Williams, and on my own. There are repetitions, but these play different parts in different arguments, and the whole conveys the cumulative force of Williams's lines of thought in a way that no one piece alone can do. Those who know his previous work will know what they are looking for. Those who do not will find a generally accessible and often delightfully witty account of the shape and direction of liberal political thought more generally in the past thirty-five years; Williams is often brief, but he is acute and wonderfully lucid on those with whom he disagreed, and, even at his funniest, always fair. Most important, they will find an original voice in modern political theory: in my opinion, the wisest, most sensible, and most attractive of all.

I have left the pieces as Williams did, adding only a few references. In just two cases have I cut a few paragraphs from one which he repeats in another. "Realism and Moralism in Political Theory," "From Freedom to Liberty," "The Idea of Equality," and "Conflicts of Liberty and Equality" are to varying extents written in a relatively formal, philosophical manner. "Modernity and the Substance of Ethical Life," "The Liberalism of Fear," "Human Rights and Relativism," and "Humanitarianism and the Right to Intervene" are texts of lectures. "In the Beginning Was the Deed," "Pluralism, Community and Left Wittgensteinianism," "Toleration," "Censorship," and "Truth, Politics, and Self-deception" were written (or rewritten) as essays.

In the Beginning Was the Deed

ONE

Realism and Moralism in Political Theory

TWO MODELS OF POLITICAL THEORY

I start with two rough models of political theory (or philosophy: the distinction is not important here) with respect to the relation of morality to political practice. One is an *enactment* model. The model is that political theory formulates principles, concepts, ideals, and values; and politics (so far as it does what the theory wants) seeks to express these in political action, through persuasion, the use of power, and so forth. This is not necessarily (although it is usually) a distinction between persons. Moreover, there is an intermediate activity which can be shared by both parties: this shapes particular conceptions of the principles and values in the light of the circumstances, and devises programmes that might express those conceptions.

The paradigm of a theory that implies the enactment model is Utilitarianism. Unless it takes its discredited Invisible Hand form (under which there is nothing for politics to do except to get out of the way and get other people out of the way), this also presents a very clear version of something always implicit in the enactment model, the panoptical view: the theory's perspective on society is that of surveying it to see how it may be made better.

Contrast this with a *structural* model. Here theory lays down moral conditions of co-existence under power, conditions in which power can be justly exercised. The paradigm of such a theory is Rawls's. In *A Theory of Justice* (*TJ*) itself, the theory also implied a certain amount about the ends of political action, because of implications of applying the Difference Principle: though, interestingly, even there it was presented less in terms of a programme, and more in terms of a required structure. In *Political Liberalism* (*PL*) and the writings that led up to it, this aspect is less prominent.[1] This is because Rawls wants to make a bigger gap than *TJ* allowed between two different conceptions: that of a society in which power is rightfully exercised (a well-ordered society), and that of a society that meets liberals' aspirations to social justice. (This distinction may imply various others: human/political/economic rights etc.)

---

[1] John Rawls, *A Theory of Justice* (Cambridge: Harvard University Press, 1971); *Political Liberalism* (New York: Columbia University Press, 1993).

Differences between these two models are of course important. But my concern here is with what they have in common, that they both represent the priority of the moral over the political. Under the enactment model, politics is (very roughly) the instrument of the moral; under the structural model, morality offers constraints (in *TJ*, very severe constraints) on what politics can rightfully do. In both cases, political theory is something like applied morality.

This is still true in Rawls's more recent work. He indeed says that "in *TJ* a moral doctrine of justice, general in scope, is not distinguished from a strictly political theory of justice" (*PL*, xv), and he sets out to articulate a political conception. But he also says, revealingly, "such a conception is, of course, a moral conception" (*PL*, 11); it is one that is worked out for a special subject, the basic structure of society. Its further marks are that it is independent of a comprehensive doctrine, and that it marshals ideas implicit in the public culture of a democratic society. The supposedly political conception, then, is still a moral conception, one that is applied to a certain subject matter under certain constraints of content.

Rawls holds that the stability of a democratic pluralistic society is, or should be, sustained by the moral psychology of citizens living within an overlapping consensus (*PL*, 141). There must be a question whether this is an appropriate or plausible answer: it is a matter of history, or political sociology, or some other empirical inquiry. But in any case, Rawls is not merely giving an answer to the question of stability in terms of citizens' morality; he is giving a moral answer. This comes out in his repeated claim (for example, *PL*, 147) that the conditions of pluralism under which liberalism is possible do not represent "a mere *modus vivendi*." Rather, the basis of co-existence, and the qualities elicited by these conditions, include the highest moral powers, above all a sense of fairness. Rawls contrasts "a mere *modus vivendi*" with the principled basis of his own pluralism, and he takes it to cover, not only a Hobbesian standoff of equal fear, but also equilibria based on perceptions of mutual advantage. That these options are grouped together implies a contrast between principle and interest, or morality and prudence, which signifies the continuation of a (Kantian) morality as the framework of the system.[2]

I shall call views that make the moral prior to the political, versions of "political moralism" (PM). PM does not immediately imply much about

---

[2] The very phrase "a mere *modus vivendi*" suggests a certain distance from the political; experience (including at the present time) suggests that those who enjoy such a thing are already lucky. There is also an interesting question, which I do not pursue here, about how we are supposed to think about the emergence of the conditions of pluralism. Rawls seems committed to thinking that they constitute not just one historical possibility among others (still less, the calamity suggested by communitarian nostalgia), but a providential opportunity for the exercise of the highest moral powers.

the style in which political actors should think, but in fact it does tend to have the consequence that they should think, not only in moral terms, but in the moral terms that belong to the political theory itself. It will be familiar how, in various ways, PM can seek to ground liberalism. I shall try to contrast with PM an approach which gives a greater autonomy to distinctively political thought. This can be called, in relation to a certain tradition, "political realism." Associated with this will be a quite different approach to liberalism. (This is related to what the late Judith Shklar called "the liberalism of fear," but I do not develop that aspect of it here.)[3]

THE FIRST POLITICAL QUESTION

I identify the "first" political question in Hobbesian terms as the securing of order, protection, safety, trust, and the conditions of cooperation. It is "first" because solving it is the condition of solving, indeed posing, any others. It is not (unhappily) first in the sense that once solved, it never has to be solved again. This is particularly important because, a solution to the first question being required *all the time*, it is affected by historical circumstances; it is not a matter of arriving at a solution to the first question at the level of state-of-nature theory and then going on to the rest of the agenda. This is related to what might count as a "foundation" of liberalism.

It is a necessary condition of legitimacy (LEG) that the state solve the first question, but it does not follow that it is a sufficient condition. There are two different sorts of consideration here. Hobbes did, very roughly, think that the conditions for solving the first problem, at least in given historical circumstances, were so demanding that they were sufficient to determine the rest of the political arrangements. In this sense, he did think that the necessary condition of LEG was also the sufficient condition of it; someone who disagrees with this may merely be disagreeing with Hobbes on this point.

If one disagrees with Hobbes, and thinks that more than one set of political arrangements, even in given historical circumstances, may solve the first question, it does not strictly follow that the matter of which arrangements are selected makes a further contribution to the question of LEG, but it is entirely reasonable to think that this can make a contribution, and that some, but only some, of such arrangements are such that the state will be LEG.

---

[3] Judith Shklar, "The Liberalism of Fear," in *Liberalism and the Moral Life*, ed. Nancy Rosenblum (Cambridge: Harvard University Press, 1989), 21–38, and Williams's essay under the same title here.

Even Hobbes, of course, did not think that a LEG state could be identical with a reign of terror; the whole point was to save people from terror. It was essential to his construction, that is to say, that the state—the solution—should not become part of the problem. (Many, including Locke, have thought that Hobbes's own solution does not pass this test.) This is an important idea: it is part of what is involved in a state's meeting what I shall call the Basic Legitimation Demand (BLD).

THE BASIC LEGITIMATION DEMAND

Meeting the BLD is what distinguishes a LEG from an ILLEG state. (I am not concerned with cases in which the society is so disordered that it is not clear whether there is a state.) Meeting the BLD can be equated with there being an "acceptable" solution to the first political question. I shall say some more about what counts as "acceptable."

It is important, first, to distinguish between the idea of a state's meeting the BLD, and its having further political virtues (e.g., its being a liberal state). I mean that these are two different *ideas*, and in fact I think there manifestly have been, and perhaps are, LEG non-liberal states. However, this does not exclude the possibility that there might be circumstances in which the only way to be LEG involved being liberal. This relates to the question of extra conditions on LEG, and, as I said, I shall come back to this.

I shall claim first that merely the idea of meeting the BLD implies a sense in which the state has to offer a justification of its power *to each subject*.

First, one or two definitions:

(a) For these purposes, the subject of a state is anyone who is in its power, whom by its own lights it can rightfully coerce under its laws and institutions. Of course this is not satisfactory for all purposes, since a state can claim too many people, but I shall not try to pursue this question. I doubt that there is any very general answer of principle to the question of what are the proper boundaries of a state.

(b) "What someone can fear" means what someone would reasonably be afraid of if it were likely to happen to him/her in the basic Hobbesian terms of coercion, pain, torture, humiliation, suffering, death. (The fear need not necessarily be of the operations of the state.)

(c) Call being disadvantaged with regard to what one can fear, being "radically disadvantaged."

Suppose a group of subjects of the state—within its borders, required to obey its officials, and so forth—who are radically disadvantaged relative to others. At the limit, they have virtually no protection at all, from the operations of either officials or other subjects. They are no better off than enemies of the state. There may be something that counts as a local legitimation of this. But is it LEG? Is the BLD satisfied?

Well, there is nothing to be said *to this group* to explain why they shouldn't revolt. We are supposing that they are not seen as a group of alien people captured within the boundaries of the state. (The citizens of ancient Sparta regarded the Helots openly as enemies, and in at least one period, the Spartan officials, on taking office, renewed a declaration of war against them. The frequent Helot "revolts" were thus simply attempts to fight back.) We suppose, contrary to this, that there is an attempt to incorporate the radically disadvantaged group as subjects. I propose that in these circumstances the BLD, to this extent, has not been met.

So we have:

(a) Mere incompetence to protect a radically disadvantaged group is an objection to the state.

(b) The mere circumstance of some subjects' being de facto in the power of others is no legitimation of their being radically disadvantaged. This implies that slavery is imperfectly legitimated relative to a claim of authority over the slaves: it is a form of internalized warfare, as in the case of the Helots.

It may be asked whether the BLD is itself a moral principle. If it is, it does not represent a morality which is prior to politics. It is a claim that is inherent in there being such a thing as politics: in particular, because it is inherent in there being first a political question. The situation of one lot of people terrorizing another lot of people is not per se a political situation: it is, rather, the situation which the existence of the political is in the first place supposed to alleviate (replace). If the power of one lot of people over another is to represent a solution to the first political question, and not itself be part of the problem, *something* has to be said to explain (to the less empowered, to concerned bystanders, to children being educated in this structure, etc.) what the difference is between the solution and the problem, and that cannot simply be an account of successful domination. It has to be something in the mode of justifying explanation or legitimation: hence the BLD.

The answer is all right as far as it goes, but more needs to be said about how a demand for justification arises, and how it may be met. One thing can be taken as an axiom, that might does not imply right, that power itself does not justify. That is to say, the power of coercion offered simply as the power of coercion cannot justify its own use. (Of course, the power to justify may itself be a power, but it is not merely *that* power.)

This principle does not itself determine when there is a need for justification (for instance, it does not imply that a Hobbesian state of nature violates rights). It does do something to determine, when there is a demand for justification, what will count as one. We cannot say that it is either a necessary or a sufficient condition of there being a (genuine) demand for justification, that someone demands one. It is not sufficient, because anyone who feels he has a grievance can raise a demand, and there is always some place for grievance. It is also not a necessary condition, because people can be drilled by coercive power itself into accepting its exercise. This, in itself, is an obvious truth, and it can be extended to the critique of less blatant cases. What may be called *the critical theory principle*, that the acceptance of a justification does not count if the acceptance itself is produced by the coercive power which is supposedly being justified, is a sound principle: the difficulty with it, of making good on claims of false consciousness and the like, lies in deciding what counts as having been "produced by" coercive power in the relevant sense.

However, one sufficient condition of there being a (genuine) demand for justification is this: A coerces B and claims that B would be wrong to fight back: resents it, forbids it, rallies others to oppose it as wrong, and so on. By doing this, A claims that his actions transcend the conditions of warfare, and this gives rise to a demand for justification of what A does. When A is the state, these claims constitute its claim of authority over B. So we have a sense in which the BLD itself requires a legitimation to be given to every subject.

There can be a pure case of internal warfare, of the kind invoked in the case of the Helots. There is no general answer to what are the boundaries of the state, and I suppose that there can in principle be a spongiform state. While there are no doubt reasons for stopping warfare, these are not the same reasons, or related to politics in the same way, as reasons given by a claim for authority. In terms of rights, the situation is this: first, anyone over whom the state claims authority has a right to treatment justified by the claim of LEG; second, there is no right to be a member of a state, if one is not a member—or, at any rate, no such right that follows from just this account; third, there is no claim of authority over enemies, including those in the situation of the Helots. In virtue of this last point, such people do not have a right of the kind mentioned in the first point. However, crimes against stateless persons are surely crimes, and Helot-like slavery surely violates rights, and this will require a more extended account in terms of the desirable extent of living under law (and hence of the political). However, the significant cases for the present problems are those in which the radically disadvantaged are said to be subjects and the state claims authority over them.

To Liberalism

However, this will not exclude many legitimations which will not be satisfactory from a liberal point of view. How do we get to liberalism?

Liberals will, first, raise the standards of what counts as being disadvantaged. This is because they raise their expectations of what a state can do; moreover they adopt, perhaps because they are in a position to adopt, more demanding standards of what counts as a threat to people's vital interests, a threat in terms of the first problem itself; they take more sophisticated steps to stop the solution becoming part of the problem. They recognize, for instance, rights of free speech; in the first instance, because it is important that citizens and others should know whether the BLD is being met.

Liberals will also add at least the following:

(a) Rationalizations of disadvantage in terms of race and gender are invalid. This is partly a question of how things are now, but it also reflects the fact that only some rationalizations are even intelligible. Those associated with racism, and the like, are all false or by everyone's standards irrelevant. It is also important that acceptance of them by the dominating party is readily explained, while their being accepted by the dominated is an easy case for the critical theory principle.

(b) Hierarchical structures which generate disadvantage are not self-legitimating. Once the question of their legitimacy is raised, it cannot be answered simply by their existence (this is a necessary proposition, a consequence of the axiom about justification: if the supposed legitimation is seen to be baseless, the situation is one of more coercive power). In our world, the question has been raised (this is an historical proposition).

We can say at this point that liberalism imposes more stringent conditions of LEG; that non-liberal states do not now in general meet the BLD. This can be seen in the light of the point just made, that when the "legitimations" of hierarchical states are perceived to be mythical, the situation approximates to one of unmediated coercion.

Summary of Considerations about the BLD

The claim is that we can get from the BLD a constraint of roughly equal acceptability (acceptability to each subject); and that the BLD does not represent morality prior to politics. But we get beyond this to any distinctively liberal interpretation only given further assumptions about what counts as legitimation. It will be seen that these further conditions contain rejections of some things that certainly have been accepted as legitimations in the past. Moreover, they refer to demands for legitimations where no such demands were made in the past.

So the general position can be summarized:

(a) We reject PM, which claims the priority of the moral over the political. This is to reject the *basic* relation of morality to politics as being that represented either by the enactment model or by the structural model. It does not deny that there can be local applications of moral ideas in politics, and these may take, on a limited scale, an enactment or a structural form.

(b) At the basic level, the answering of the "first" question does involve a principle, the BLD. The approach is distinguished from that of PM by the fact that this principle, which comes from a conception of what could count as answering a demand for justification of coercive power, if such a demand genuinely exists, is implicit in the very idea of a legitimate state, and so is inherent in any politics. The satisfaction of the BLD has not always or even usually, historically, taken a liberal form.

(c) Now and around here the BLD together with the historical conditions permit only a liberal solution: other forms of answer are unacceptable. In part, this is for the Enlightenment reason that other supposed legitimations are now seen to be false and in particular ideological. It is not, though it is often thought to be, because some liberal conception of the person, which delivers the morality of liberalism, is or ought to be seen to be correct.

(d) Inasmuch as liberalism has foundations, it has foundations in its capacity to answer the "first question" in what is now seen, granted these answers to the BLD, as an acceptable way. Insofar as things go well, the conceptions of what is to be feared, of what is an attack on the self, and of what is an unacceptable exercise of power, can themselves be extended. This may indeed be explained in terms of an ethically elaborated account of the person as having more sophisticated interests, which may involve, for instance, a notion of autonomy. This account might be, or approximate to, a liberal conception of the person. But this is not the foundation of the liberal state, because it is a product of those same forces that lead to a situation in which the BLD is satisfied only by a liberal state.

This picture will help to explain two things. First, one can invoke a liberal conception of the person in justifying features of the liberal state (they fit together), but one cannot go all the way down and start from the bottom.[4] Second, it sheds some light on the important fact that liberalism has a poor account, or in many cases no account, of the cognitive status of its own history. PM has no answer in its own terms to the question of why what it takes to be the true moral solution to the questions of politics, liberalism, should for the first time (roughly) become evident in European culture from the late seventeenth century onward, and why these truths have been concealed from other people. Moralistic liberalism cannot plausibly explain, adequately to its moral pretensions, why, when, and by whom it has been accepted and rejected. The explanations of the various historical steps that have led to the liberal state do not show very persuasively why or how they involved an increase in moral knowledge; but from here, with our conception of the person, the recognition of liberal rights indeed looks like a recognition.

THE NATURE AND POINT OF THE CONCEPT OF LEG

It may help to explain the idea of LEG that I am using if I relate it briefly to some ideas of Habermas, with whom I am partly, but only partly, in agreement. First, there is the basically sociological point, that the legitimations appropriate to a modern state are essentially connected with the nature of modernity as the social thought of the past century, particularly that of Weber, has helped us to understand it. This includes organizational features (pluralism, etc., and bureaucratic forms of control), individualism, and cognitive aspects of authority (*Entzauberung*). I have already referred to the last. To make my view even cruder than it is anyway, it could be expressed in the slogan LEG + Modernity = Liberalism, where the ambiguities of the last term serve to indicate a range of options which make political sense in the modern world: they are all compatible with the *Rechtstaat*, and they vary depending on how much emphasis is put on welfare rights and the like.

Second, my rejection of PM, though not in quite the same terms, is shared with Habermas; I, like him, reject the derivation of political LEG from the formal properties of the moral law, or from a Kantian account of the moral person (though he makes more of the concept of autonomy than I do, and I shall come to that, on the subject of representation). Equally, though I have not stressed the point here, I reject as he does what he calls

[4] The same difficulty is making itself felt in reverse, when Michael Sandel (*Liberalism and the Limits of Justice* [Cambridge: Cambridge University Press, 1982]) rejects the liberal theory of the state because he rejects the liberal account of the person, but nevertheless finds it very hard to detach himself from many features of the liberal state.

an "ethical" derivation, that is to say, a civic republican conception of the polity based on neo-Aristotelian or similar considerations.[5]

Taking these two points together—the facticity of modern societies and the refusal of a mere moral normativity—I can agree with Habermas also in trying to situate these issues "Between facts and norms."[6] Moreover, this is not merely a verbal agreement: the project of taking seriously in political theory an understanding of what modern social formations are is very fundamental. However, we clearly have different ideas of how a space is to be found between facts and norms. Habermas uses discourse theory; in my case what does this work is the all-purpose concept of LEG (together with the associated idea of its specific historical determinations).

However, Habermas's conceptions of legitimacy carry stronger universalistic implications than does the notion of LEG that I am using. So let me say some more about this notion; in particular, to locate it between facts and norms.

If, very roughly speaking indeed, LEG + Modernity = Liberalism, this gives no ground for saying that all non-liberal states in the past were ILLEG, and it would be a silly thing to say. It may be asked, in fact, what the point, or content, is of wondering whether defunct political orders were LEG. Political moralism, particularly in its Kantian forms, has a universalistic tendency which encourages it to inform past societies about their failings. It is not that these judgements are, exactly, meaningless— one can imagine oneself as Kant at the court of King Arthur if one wants to—but they are useless and do not help one to understand anything. The notion of LEG, however, distinguished from the idea of what we would now find acceptable, can serve understanding. It is a human universal that some people coerce or try to coerce others, and nearly a universal that people live under an order in which some of the coercion is intelligible and acceptable, and it can be an illuminating question (one that is certainly evaluative, but not normative) to ask how far, and in what respects, a given society of the past is an example of the human capacity for intelligible order, or of the human tendency to unmediated coercion.

We can accept that the considerations that support LEG are scalar, and the binary cut LEG/ILLEG is artificial and needed only for certain purposes.[7] The idea is that a given historical structure can be (to an appropriate degree) an example of the human capacity to live under an intelligible order of authority. It makes sense (MS) to us *as such a structure*. It is vital that this means more than it MS. Situations of terror and tyranny

---

[5] One can reject the Rawlsian priority of the right without going all the way to this: compare Dworkin, who tries to rewrite proceduralism in terms of the good life.

[6] Jürgen Habermas, *Between Facts and Norms: Contributions to a Discourse Theory of Law and Democracy*, trans. William Rehg (Cambridge: MIT Press, 1996).

[7] In the contemporary case, related to (but not identical with) the question of recognition.

MS: they are humanly entirely familiar, and what the tyrant is doing MS (or may do so), and what his subjects or victims do MS. The question is whether a structure MS as an example of authoritative order. This requires, on the lines already explained, that there is a legitimation offered which goes beyond the assertion of power; and we can recognize such a thing because in the light of the historical and cultural circumstances, and so forth, it MS to us as a legitimation.

"MS" is a category of historical understanding—which we can call, if we like, a hermeneutical category. There are many difficulties of interpretation associated with it, for example whether there are not some historical constellations of belief which altogether fail to MS. (We are probably wise to resist that conclusion: as R. G. Collingwood says, "we call them the Dark Ages, but all we mean is that we cannot see.") The point is that these are general problems in historical and more broadly social understanding.

One can say, as I have said, that "MS" is itself an evaluative concept; certainly, it is not simply "factual" or "descriptive." This is part of the general theory of interpretation, and I cannot address it here. What it certainly is not, is *normative*: we do not think, typically, that these considerations should guide our behaviour, and there is no point in saying that they ought to have guided the other people's behaviour, except in exceptional cases where there was a clash of legitimations, of which, in the light of the circumstances, one more MS (as it seems to us) than the other.

But when we get to our own case, the notion "MS" does become normative, because what (most) MS to us is a structure of authority which we think we should accept. We do not have to say that these previous societies were wrong about all these things, though we may indeed think, in the light of our *entzaubert* state, that some of what MS to them does not MS to us because we take it to be false, in a sense that represents a cognitive advance—a claim which carries its own responsibilities, in the form of a theory of error, something which PM in its current forms has spectacularly tended to lack.

In any case, there is no problem about the relation between the "external" and non-normative "MS" that we apply to others, and the "MS" we use about our own practices, which is normative: this is because of the hermeneutical principle, which is roughly that what they do MS if it would MS to us if we were them. In the light of this, it would be actually inconsistent to deny that when we apply "MS" to ourselves, we have a normative notion what MS. The same follows for LEG; what we acknowledge as LEG, here and now, is what, here and now, MS as a legitimation of power as authority; and discussions about whether it does MS will be engaged, first-order discussions using our political, moral, social, interpretive, and other concepts. Much of the time, in ordinary life, we do not discuss whether our concepts MS, though, of particular ones, we may. Mostly, the fact that we use these concepts is what shows us that they MS.

The Concept of the Political

I have not done much to define the concept of the "political" that I have been using. In particular, it may be unclear how it is related to a realist conception of political action. It will probably be clear that my view is in part a reaction to the intense moralism of much American political and indeed legal theory, which is predictably matched by the concentration of American political science on the coordination of private or group interests: a division of labour which is replicated institutionally, between the "politics" of Congress and the principled arguments of the Supreme Court (at least as the activities of the Supreme Court are primarily interpreted at the present time). That view of the practice of politics, and the moralistic view of political theory, are made for each other. They represent a Manichaean dualism of soul and body, high-mindedness and the pork barrel, and the existence of each helps to explain how anyone could have accepted the other.

I want a broader view of the content of politics, not confined to interests, together with a more realistic view of the powers, opportunities, and limitations of political actors, where all the considerations that bear on political action—both ideals and, for example, political survival—can come to one focus of decision (which is not to deny that in a modern state they often do not). The ethic that relates to this is what Weber called *Verantwortungsethik*, the ethic of responsibility.

Rather than trying to give a definition of the political, which would certainly be fruitless, let me end by giving two applications—ways in which thinking "politically" changes the emphasis as contrasted with what I have called PM. One relates to the conduct of political thought, and specifically political theory itself; the other to the way we should think about other societies.

PM naturally construes conflictual political thought in society in terms of rival elaborations of a moral text: this is explicit in the work of Ronald Dworkin. But this is not the nature of opposition between political opponents. Nor can the elaboration of one's own position take this form. (It is helpful to consider the idea of the "ideal" or "model" readers of a political text. PM typically takes them to be utopian magistrates or founding fathers, as Plato and Rousseau did, but this is not the most helpful model now.[8] They are better seen as, say, the audience of a pamphlet.)

We can, after all, reflect on our historical situation. We know that our and others' convictions have to a great degree been the product of previ-

---

[8] Dworkin is addressing a Supreme Court of the United States unencumbered with the historical circumstances that actually affect it.

ous historical conditions, and of an obscure mixture of beliefs (many incompatible with one another), passions, interests, and so forth. Moreover, the joint outcome of these things has often been that political schemes had perverse results. We can now see to some extent how these convictions came about, and why they worked if they did and didn't work when they didn't; and we would be merely naive if we took our convictions, and those of our opponents, as simply autonomous products of moral reason rather than as another product of historical conditions. Even in the very short term, a minority conception can become mainstream or vice versa, and there can be significant changes in what counts as a conceivable or credible option. This does not mean that we throw our political convictions away: we have no reason to end up with none, or with someone else's. Nor does it mean that we stare at our convictions with ironical amazement, as Rorty suggests. But we do treat them as political convictions which determine political positions, which means, for one thing, that we acknowledge that they have obscure causes and effects.

It also means that we take certain kinds of view of our allies and opponents. Even if we were utopian monarchs, we would have to take into account others' disagreement as a mere fact. As democrats, we have to do more than that. But remembering the points about the historical conditions, we should not think that what we have to do is simply to argue with those who disagree: treating them as *opponents* can, oddly enough, show more respect for them as political actors than treating them simply as arguers—whether as arguers who are simply mistaken, or as fellow seekers after truth. A very important reason for thinking in terms of the political is that a political decision—the conclusion of a political deliberation which brings all sorts of considerations, considerations of principle along with others, to one focus of decision—is that such a decision does not in itself announce that the other party was morally wrong or, indeed, wrong at all. What it immediately announces is that *they have lost*.

Reflection on history should also affect our view of those who agree with us, or seem to do so, or may come to do so. One important political activity is that of finding proposals and images that can reduce differences (just as, in other political situations, it may be necessary to play them up). What people actually want or value under the name of some given position may be indeterminate and various. It can make a big difference, what images we each have of what we take ourselves all to be pursuing.

All these are platitudes about politics, and that is just the point: liberal political theory should shape its account of itself more realistically to what is platitudinously politics.

The same general point, in a different form, applies to our attitude to certain other societies. To some extent, we may regard some contemporary non-liberal states as LEG. This is different from Rawls's point, that

we can recognize as well-ordered some non-liberal (e.g., theocratic) societies with which we have certain kinds of principled differences which are
limited in certain particular ways (e.g., that they accept the freedom of
religion). The present point concerns what turns on regarding them as
LEG or not. The idea of "LEG" is normative for us as applied to our own
society; so it is also normative in relation to other societies which co-exist
with ours and with which we can have or refuse to have various kinds of
relations: they cannot be separated from us by the relativism of distance.
So there can be practical consequences of applying or withholding "LEG"
in the contemporary world. Since these consequences must be responsibly
considered, they must be considered politically. An important aspect of
thinking about this lies in political realist considerations about the stability of such states. For instance:

(a) With whom does the demand for justification arise? It will be a
    significant question, who does and who does not accept the current
    legitimation.
(b) If the current legitimation is fairly stable, the society will not any-
    way satisfy the other familiar conditions on revolt.
(c) The objections to traditional hierarchical setups are typically based
    in part on the mythical character of the legitimations. Faced with
    the criticism of these myths, increasing information from outside,
    and so on, non-liberal regimes may not be able to sustain them-
    selves without coercion. They will then begin to encounter the basic
    legitimation problem.
(d) This will also apply to what come to be seen as targets of the *critical
    theory principle*, accepted social and institutional understandings
    which increasingly come to appear, now, as more subtle forms of
    coercion.

It will be seen that the more significant the factors (c) and (d) become,
the more coercion may become overt, and the more this happens, the
more reason there will be for concern at the level of the BLD. So nothing
succeeds like success, with liberal critique as much as anything else. This
is one sound application of a general truth (which is important to politics,
but not only to politics), the truth discovered by Goethe's Faust: *Im Anfang war die Tat*, in the beginning was the deed.

Modernity and Political Representation

Faust's axiom—perhaps we can indeed call it Goethe's axiom—applies
much more widely in these matters. It applies, for instance, to the question

of how much, at what level, can be determined by social and political theory with regard to modern states: in particular, how far idealized conceptions of political relations should play a part. I should like to end with a particular application of that question, to the matter of political representation. This also raises, I think, a possible area of disagreement with Habermas.

It goes without saying that Habermas has offered very deeply and broadly elaborated work on the possibilities of the modern state and what might contribute to its legitimation. My few remarks or suggestions in no way seek to address most of the issues he has elaborated, nor am I competent to do so; the role of law, notably, in the understanding of the modern state is a central concern of his on which I have nothing special to offer. Much of this work, it seems to me, fits together with the kind of structure I have suggested. For instance, it seeks to show *in what ways* the conditions of modernity—the facticity of modern societies—demand or impose certain conditions on LEG. It shows how some kinds of legal order and not others, and some understandings of a legal order, MS to us. It therefore has a practical and progressive possibility. What I have said here does not directly have such consequences, except in the possible improvement of the way in which we, in particular lawyers, think about such questions. This is because mine is a very general sketch at a very high level of generality. But I salute thought that does yield such consequences, and I agree in this respect with a criticism that Habermas has made of Rawls, that Rawls identifies no *project* with regard to the establishment of a constitution— it appears only in the role of the non-violent preservation of basic liberties that are already there.

However, Habermas wants to show something else at the level of the most basic theory: that there is an internal relation between the rule of law, the *Rechtstaat*, and deliberative democracy.

Now certainly I agree—it is a manifest fact—that some kind of democracy, participatory politics at some level, is a feature of LEG for the modern world. One need look no further than the worldwide success of the demand for it. Any theory of modern LEG requires an account of democracy and political participation, and of course such an account may take its place in a programme of improvement. We *may* be able to say: the *point* of democratic political participation in relation to our conception of LEG is such-and-such, and developing our institutions and practices in such-and-such ways is what will further MS in terms of what in this area MS to us.

Now Habermas develops this part of his account at a very deep level, in relation to the discourse theory. It would not be to the present point for me to try to engage with the details of his argument. My question concerns the kind of argument that this yields; specifically, whether it does not situate itself a great deal nearer—too near indeed—to the moral rather than the facts. Habermas writes, "[I]t must be reasonable to expect [participants in the political process] to drop the role of the private subject. . . . The combination [of facticity and validity] requires a process of law-making in which the participatory citizens are *not* [his emphasis] allowed to take part simply in the role of actors oriented to success."* So the concept of modern law harbours the democratic ideal, and we derive, more or less, an ideal associated with Kant and Rousseau, while going beyond the merely moral formalism of Kant and—roughly speaking—the ethical and communitarian over-enthusiasm of Rousseau.

But what is this "are not allowed to"? It cannot be blankly normative. Suppose, one is bound to say, that they do? It may be replied: it will defeat the point. But what if it does? And how can we be sure, in the light of the possibility, what the point really is? It may be said, alternatively: it cannot work—in other words, the system will break down, and the political process will begin to lose significance in relation to other activities and the life world.

I want to say at this point two things: if that is so, then it will show itself, and we shall have a manifest social or political problem for which we shall have to mobilize ideas which already MS to the public and might move toward possible political action. Second, it will be only one of many conflicts about what the processes of political participation can be hoped to yield under conditions of modernity. There are needs that people have which seemingly can be met only by more directly participatory structures; but equally, there are objectives which are notoriously frustrated by these, and other aims which are at least in competition with them, and considerations which raise doubts about the extent to which any procedures can be really participatory anyway.

No transcendental or partly transcendental argument—one might say, more generally, theoretical argument—could serve to resolve these conflicts.

My own view is that the minimum requirements of participatory democracy as an essential part of modern LEG are delivered at a fairly straightforward and virtually instrumental level in terms of the harms and indefensibility of doing without it. What is delivered at that level can only speciously be represented in Kantian and Rousseauian terms as either expressions of autonomy or of *self*-government. To represent it as such may lead to cynicism: while it may be no more than utopian to make larger ambitions which might meet these descriptions—and "self-govern-

---

* Editor's note: Williams gave no reference for this quotation, and I have been unable to trace it.

ment" I doubt can be met at all: which is why Rousseau was right to impose impossible conditions on it.

Indeed we should explore what more radical and ambitious forms of participatory or deliberative democracy are possible, which is why I agree that the conditions of LEG in modern states present a progressive project. But how much more is actually possible seems to me a question that belongs to the level of fact, practice, and politics, not one that lies beyond these in the very conditions of legitimacy.

TWO

In the Beginning Was the Deed

CARLOS NINO WAS A BRAVE MAN and an admirable philosopher who did his country notable service and stood against a tyrannical and corrupt regime on the basis of a robust belief in liberal political values and universal human rights. In his own mind and in his life, his philosophy and his political values were intimately linked. His philosophy not only expressed those values, but firmly claimed a certain type of foundation for them. He was deeply opposed not only to those who rejected liberal values but to those, such as Richard Rorty and myself, whom he saw as trying to detach those values from their proper and necessary philosophical base. Even John Rawls was thought to have fallen away in his more recent work from the correct objective of putting human rights on a solid base, one that would have universal application.

As Nino himself recognized, I do not share his faith in that style of legitimation of liberal values.[1] Although I disagree with Nino about the *basis* of his values, I hope here to offer an even more direct link than his own account offers of the connection between such values and a political life.

The human rights that I shall discuss are the most basic ones: those that, as Thomas Nagel put it in his essay in this volume, stand against such things as "the maintenance of power by the torture and execution of political dissidents or religious minorities, denial of civil rights to women, total censorship." Nagel says of these that they "demand denunciation and practical opposition, not theoretical discussion." He also says, a little more surprisingly, that "the flagrant violation of the most basic human rights is devoid of philosophical interest." I do not think that he means that there is no philosophical interest in discussing the basis or status of these most fundamental rights. Moreover, reference to their flagrant violation is not a bad way of recalling what these rights are. Nagel does not disagree, and his point indeed fits in with this: he wants to say that no very elaborate and refined philosophical discussion is needed to establish what these rights are. In this they differ from the issues he addresses, of freedom for hate speech and for pornography and a high level of sexual toleration.

---

[1] I do not think, any more than he did, that my reasons for this, or the position that emerges, are the same as Rorty's.

We differ because I agree with the critics he mentions at the beginning of his essay in wondering whether these are matters of fundamental human rights at all. The fact that elaborate philosophical distinctions are required to define and establish these rights supports my uncertainty. Fundamental human rights, it seems to me, had better get slightly nearer to being what their traditional defenders always took them to be, that is self-evident, and self-evidence should register more than the convictions of their advocates if the claims to human rights are to escape the familiar criticism that they express only the preferences of a liberal culture. This point seems to me all the more telling if they express the preferences of only some liberals. It is simply a fact that many European liberals, fully respectable (I hope) in their liberal convictions, find it a quaint local obsession of Americans that they insist on defending on principle the right to offer any form of odious racist insult or provocation so long as by some argument it can be represented as a form of speech. I should have thought that these were obviously matters of political judgment, above all in telling the difference between the point at which the enemies of liberalism have been given only enough rope to hang themselves, and the point at which they have enough rope to hang someone else. The fact that many trustworthy people elsewhere see it in that light should itself, I think, encourage American liberals to ask whether the powerful personal conviction that Nagel very clearly describes, to the effect that this is not a policy question but a matter of ultimate right, may not be partly the product of a culturally injected overdose of the First Amendment.

On the other matter Nagel discusses, sexuality, I very much agree with him, both with his psychological views and with his policy recommendations in our actual situation. But here also I wonder how much of this can really rest in the territory of fundamental human rights. Just because of the basic truths he invokes, about the power of sexuality, it is unsurprising that many and various conventions obtain in the world, and it must be a matter of judgment, I suppose, and one that to some extent will turn on local cultural significance, to decide where and when an accepted tradition becomes a matter of an unambiguous case of abusive power, which is what I take to be the subject matter of fundamental human rights. No one supposes that the drawing of boundaries is easy in such matters, and for reasons well known in semantics, it is no easier to draw an unambiguous boundary around just the unambiguous cases. I shall say a little more about this at the end. I would like to concentrate, however, on those only too clear and familiar cases of violations of fundamental human rights: torture, assault, and arbitrary power.

Nino's own account of human rights is based on Kantian moral theory. Human rights are derived from moral principles, which could secure agreement and reduce conflict under certain postulated conditions of discussion, conditions which set constraints on what the moral principles can be like.[2] This constructivist enterprise implies a certain conception of the person as someone capable of enjoying these rights; this conception confers a very high value on autonomy. Autonomy, understood as the capacity and opportunity to choose one's own values and way of life without coercion or undue persuasion, is taken as the basis of other values as well, not just in the sense that it is, through the construction, presupposed in the articulation of other values, but because it confers the value on other valuable items ("the source of almost all social value").[3] Nino was prepared to say that the reason why it is wrong to abuse others is that it is an assault on their autonomy: "an individual who is killed, raped, cheated, etc., has less opportunity for choosing and realizing moral standards."[4]

This last idea presents a problem, which comes from the basic disposition of Kantian theories (in direct contrast, here, to utilitarianism) to make the beneficiaries of morality co-extensive with its agents. If the wrong of killing or abusing someone rests in its being an assault on his or her moral autonomy, an inability to be a moral agent will undercut one's protection against being killed or abused. One would hope that the theory could avoid this result without losing its general shape and motivation. However, there is a larger difficulty near at hand: what is involved in being a person in the sense relevant to morality. Nino was very emphatic that he did not want his theory to be seen as a dogmatic derivation of moral principles from some factually given account of what persons are. He thought that this might offend against the is/ought principle, and would in any case expose the theory, with its claim that persons in the relevant sense are equal, to empirical attack. He accordingly stressed the idea that the notion of a person that the theory required was *normative*.[5]

This, in turn, means that persons must be *treated as* autonomous, as capable of freely accepting or rejecting moral positions, and the justification of accepting this normative idea must be, Nino said, that it is implicit in the business of moral reasoning: it is "necessarily assumed when we participate in the practice of moral discourse."[6] Nino directly contrasted this strong approach with Rawls's more recent view that such conceptions are implicit only in certain political practices, those (roughly) of the modern democratic state. Nino's view is stronger perhaps even than Rawls's

---

[2] Nino, *Ethics of Human Rights* (Oxford: Oxford University Press, 1991), 72–73.
[3] Nino, *Ethics of Human Rights*, 139.
[4] Nino, *Ethics of Human Rights*, 141.
[5] Nino, *Ethics of Human Rights*, 36, 112 et seq.
[6] Nino, *Ethics of Human Rights*, 112.

earlier position, and comes nearer to the outlook of Habermas, though Nino himself does not offer any elaborate presuppositional or communication-theoretical argument for it.

There is a problem with the internal economy of this argument. It looks as though the normative conception of the person enjoins us to treat others as possessing equally the powers relevant to autonomy, but one consideration that motivated the normative conception in the first place was precisely a doubt whether people do empirically possess such powers equally. This is, once again, a recurrence of a type of difficulty that Kant encountered, in his dealings with God, for instance, where he seems to be involved in a kind of doublethink; he offers as a regulative idea a conception that seems indistinguishable from a constitutive idea which is false but which we are enjoined to treat as though it were true.

However, I do not want to pursue this line of criticism. I want to ask, rather, where this interlocking set of aspirations is supposed to touch reality. Are the items in the circle rights-principles-moral discourse-person-autonomy-rights merely identified in terms of each other? It will not matter in itself that there is a definitional circle here, if the circle is long and interesting enough, but we do need to identify a place in the world, a practice, which will give the set of concepts a grounding in reality. This is what Rawls does when he identifies something like this as the discourse of modern democratic states. But Nino rejected this approach as relativist, and it is clear that he wanted to get beyond any such idea to something universal. Where did he think he had found it?

I think that the item in this set that he supposed could in principle apply to everyone, and so lead everyone to recognize the force of the other notions, was moral discourse, with its associated ideas of reducing conflict and bringing about agreement.[7] The "social practice of moral discourse"[8] is one that will, properly understood, mobilize these other notions, including the normative conception of the person, in terms of which we can understand human rights.

But then, as so often, the gap between reality and aspiration appears in a new place. Where, among which human beings, under what conditions, do we actually find the social practice of moral discourse? Certainly not universally: some human beings do not even want agreement and the elimination of conflict, or at least its universal elimination, as Nino perfectly well knew and pointed out when condemning "tribalism, nationalism,

---

[7] If Nino hung the circle from the idea of the moral, his project was formally similar to Hare, though it would not share a peculiarity of Hare's theory, that it is supposed to depend on a linguistic point about the word *moral*. On this, see Williams, "The Structure of Hare's Theory," in *Hare and Critics*, ed. Douglas Seanor and N. Fotion (Oxford: Clarendon Press, 1988).

[8] Nino, *Ethics of Human Rights*, 139.

and religious sectarianism."[9] Many who want agreement and co-existence, and indeed enjoy them, do not share the aspirations of autonomy. It is not true that every human group, or every human group enjoying a measure of peace, engages in the "social practice of moral discourse," as that notion is defined in the circle of concepts that delivers the normative conception of the autonomous person and, along with it, human rights.

Of course, any human group living in a moderately stable order under peace shares some set of ethical understandings, some rules and concepts that govern their relations. If these were all tantamount to what Nino called the social practice of morality, everyone would already have implicitly accepted liberalism, at least as an ideal, and one would merely have to spell it out. But this is manifestly not so, and the mere fact that there is so far for the liberal to go, and the fact that societies of the past, as well as recalcitrant societies of the present, have had relatively stable ethical systems which were not based on these presuppositions, make it clear that the practice of morality, in this distinctive sense, is not the only possible basis of peaceful social existence.

Liberals sometimes give the impression that the practice of morality, understood in liberal terms, is the only alternative to an overtly coercive or deceitful regime. When Nino wrote, for instance, "When we resort to the exacting task of discussing the moral merits of a solution instead of availing ourselves of propagandistic, seductive, or coercive means to promote its adoption,"[10] he exploited the idea that morality, and by implication the liberal ideals of autonomy, stand as the only alternative to means which are described in terms that will elicit disapproval from almost anyone except the most ruthless Realpolitiker or nihilist. At another point, the practice of morality in the liberal sense is seemingly equated, as it was by Kant, with the practice of reason itself: "we must accept that there may be some people or societies which do not follow the same practice of moral discourse; that is, that they follow a practice of moral reasoning and discourse which differs in relevant respects from ours. This usually provokes the question, 'What can we do to convince those people?' My answer is 'Nothing.' If there are people who refuse to listen to reasons—depending on what we understand by the word 'reasons'—it is as if they covered their ears. We can induce them or compel them but we cannot convince them."[11] The phrase "depending on what we understand by the word 'reasons' " hangs a little awkwardly in that sentence, no doubt because it registers a discomfort. Can we really suppose, as Kant supposed, that reason itself is liberal reason, and that an ethical practice which is

---

[9] Nino, *Ethics of Human Rights*, 114.

[10] Nino, *Ethics of Human Rights*, 139.

[11] Nino, *Ethics of Human Rights*, 104.

other than the morality of autonomy involves the refusal to listen to reasons at all, the equivalent of covering one's ears? Surely not.

There are indeed universal paradigms of injustice and unreason. They consist of people using power to coerce other people against their will to secure what the first people want simply because they want it, and refusing to listen to what other people say if it goes against their doing so. This is a paradigm of injustice because institutions of justice, wherever and whatever they may be, are intended to stand precisely against this. "Might is not, in itself, right" is the first necessary truth, one of few, about the nature of right. Simply in this form, the universal paradigm excludes many bad things, but it is indeterminate about what it requires: it says not much more than that coercion requires legitimation and that the will of the stronger is not itself a legitimation. It is already clear, however, how long a journey the liberal would have to make to arrive at the conclusion that morality in his sense and its notion of autonomy provide the only real alternative to injustice and unreason. He would have to show that the only considerations that could count as a legitimation were those of liberal consent. In fact—and this is a point I shall come back to—he would have to show something stronger, that only his considerations could even decently be supposed to count as a legitimation. That seems, as it surely is, a wildly ambitious or even imperialistic claim.

It may be said that the liberal's legitimation is the only universal one, or at least the only universal one that is not simply dogmatic. One who believes in a revealed religion with universalistic pretensions has his view of a legitimation which can make coercion just and desirable, but he has the problem that not everyone accepts it, and the coercion will, obviously enough, not be legitimate to those who do not accept it. Only a constructivist solution, it has been thought, can get around this problem. But it does not ultimately get around it. For if it involves a top-down argument from a certain substantive conception of the person, for instance, it will (as Nino noted) have enough in common with dogmatic positions to run into a stand-off with them; liberalism sees persons as free autonomous choosers, and so forth, and religious fundamentalism sees them as something else. If, on the other hand, liberalism makes its conception of the person normative, as Nino wanted it to be, we are back to the point we have already discussed, that the circle of normative notions cannot be forced on to a recalcitrant world; in particular, it cannot be forced on to the world through a certain other element in the circle. Liberalism is no worse off in these respects than any other outlook, but it is not, at any absolutely general level of principle, better off. It may possibly, and for historical reasons, be rather better off now. But it will have a chance of being so only if it accepts that like any other outlook it cannot escape starting from what is at hand, from the kinds of life among which it finds itself. Like everyone else, it must accept the truth that in the beginning was the deed.

This famous line from Goethe's *Faust*, "Im Anfang war die Tat," is known best to philosophers, perhaps, from being quoted by Wittgenstein in *On Certainty*, where it steals into the text rather surreptitiously, in brackets. It follows a passage that says that there are statements about material objects that "form the foundation of all operating with thoughts (with language) . . . they do not serve as foundations in the same way as hypotheses which, if they turn out to be false, are replaced by others." Goethe's line can indeed help us to understand this Wittgensteinian theme, by reminding us in particular that the "primacy of practice" (in a familiar exegetical phrase) is not the primacy of descriptions of practice. It is not that when we represent to ourselves our practices, we can see in that representation a ground of our beliefs. The relation between a practice and a set of beliefs cannot be anything like that of premises and conclusion, or indeed any other relation of two sets of propositions. There could not be a description of our practices which adequately represented the way in which belief was grounded in practice, if only because the understanding of that relation itself would have to be grounded in practice. It follows from this that the powers of reflection on this relation are limited; indeed, that we must rethink what it is for reflection to get anywhere at all. (Those who attempt to recast the later Wittgenstein's philosophy as a theory, or, slightly more reasonably, to accommodate it to philosophy which consists of theory, have not fully grasped this point.)

It is even more important to bear these considerations in mind when we bring Goethe's saying back to politics. Moral and political philosophy supposedly influenced by Wittgensteinian ideas can easily slide into an uneasy communitarian relativism, under which we reflect on our (local) practices and take them as authenticating a way of life for us. This cannot be right. For one thing, no Wittgensteinian argument tells us who, in any given connection, is meant by *we*.[12] The particular passage in *On Certainty* is in fact one of those in which "we" seems to extend itself most generously to anyone who can share a language, that is, to more or less everyone, and the political analogue to this would be, if anything, a Kantian universal constituency of human beings (at least), rather than some community to be identified as consisting of some human beings as distinct from others. Moreover, even if *we* in the political interpretation meant a local *us*, the communitarian interpretation of this runs straight into the point often made by Ronald Dworkin and other liberals, that in any sense

---

[12] I have argued this in "Wittgenstein and Idealism," reprinted in *Moral Luck* (Albany: State University of New York Press, 1993). On Wittgensteinian political philosophy, see "Left Wittgenstein," *Common Knowledge* (New York: Oxford University Press, 1992), 1 [reprinted as chapter 3, below].

in which *we*, this local *we*, have identifiably local practices, one of them consists in criticizing local practices.

What the Wittgensteinian idea does mean for politics is that foundationalism, even constructivist foundationalism, can never achieve what it wants. Any such theory will seem to make sense, and will to some degree reorganize political thought and action, only by virtue of the historical situation in which it is presented, and its relation to that historical situation cannot fully be theorized or captured in reflection. Those theories and relections will themselves always be subject to the condition that, to someone who is intelligently and informedly in that situation (and those are not empty conditions), it does or does not seem a sensible way to go on.

This important negative conclusion is, in my view, basically as far as the Wittgensteinian idea in itself will take us. Given simply this much, it might seem possible that the liberal project could in our circumstances make sense, even in a strongly foundationalist or constructivist form. (The *we* now appropriate to political practices is approaching the Kantian limit.) But this is not really so. For in virtue merely of the Wittgensteinian idea, the foundationalist project cannot in the end do what it really wants to do, and since that is both true and (granted these sorts of considerations) now evident, the liberal project, *in this particular form*, does not in fact any longer make sense. Moreover, Goethe's saying, not now as recruited by Wittgenstein but in its own right, reminds us how far such a project falls short of making sense. For political projects are essentially conditioned, not just in their background intellectual conditions but as a matter of empirical realism, by their historical circumstances. Utopian thought is not necessarily frivolous, but the nearer political thought gets to action, as in the concrete affirmation of human rights, the more likely it is to be frivolous if it is utopian, a truth that Nino, a man with a serious political life, well understood. Those circumstances almost always are created not by our thought but by other people's actions. It follows, in fact, that whether our thoughts even make political sense depends to an indefinite degree on other people's actions.

Some of those actions are bad ones. The circumstances in which liberal thought is possible have been created in part by actions that violate liberal ideals and human rights, as was recognized by Hegel and Marx, and, in a less encouraging spirit, by Nietzsche. Equally, some are good actions that have gone ahead (as a later account will put it) of prevailing interpretations and changed the background in which interpretations are understood. Exceptional action gets ahead of theory, and theory, or other less formally organized modes of political speech and persuasion, can get ahead of ordinarily accepted practice. But there is no way in which theory can get all the way ahead of practice and reach the final determination of what can make sense in political thought; it cannot ever, in advance, determine very securely what direction might count as "ahead." Very powerful political discourse can of course be proleptic and help to create the conditions it foresees. Liberal discourse itself has had considerable success in this, but it is a way that is markedly different from the ways in which liberalism typically sees itself, and there is good reason to think that its continued success, now, may require a better, more Wittgensteinian and, more important, Goethean self-understanding.

This returns us to human rights. There is, I said earlier, a universal paradigm of injustice. What in a given historical context will count as injustice will of course depend on what counts there as a legitimation of constraint of power used by the stronger, and this in turn involves questions of who is stronger and in what respects, of what count as the interests of the weaker, and so forth. The most basic violations of human rights are indeed self-evident: they are abuses of power that almost everyone everywhere has been in a position to recognize as such. An extreme contrast with these are cases in which it is predictably contested, and a recognizable matter of political decision, what the exact limits of legitimate constraint may be; I suggested earlier that the control of pornography and setting boundaries between political expression and harassment fell into this class.

The most significant and difficult area falls between these extremes. This contains cases in which a style of legitimation that was accepted at one time is still accepted in some places but no longer accepted in others. These notably include, now, theocratic conceptions of government and patriarchal ideas of the rights of women. Should we regard practices elsewhere that express such conceptions as violations of fundamental human rights?

I must make clear that I am not raising here any relativist issue. The question does not involve the manifestly confused notion that these ideas might be somehow right for those that hold them and not for those who do not. Let us grant that such supposed legitimations have no sound support. The question is whether we must then think of these practices as violations of human rights. A short argument will say that they must be, as involving coercion without legitimation. But this is a bit short. For one thing, there is an issue of how much manifest coercion is involved, and that is why the situation is worse in these respects if opponents of the theology are silenced or women are forced into roles they do not even think they want to assume. Simply the fact that this is so makes the situation more like the paradigm of injustice. How far it will have come to be like that paradigm is one of those matters of the historical environment which I have already mentioned. Up to a point, it may be possible for supporters of the system to make a decent case (in both senses of that helpful expression) that the coercion is legitimate. Somewhere beyond that point there may come a time at which the cause is lost, the legitimation no longer makes sense, and only the truly fanatical can bring themselves to believe it. There will have been no great change in the argumentative character of the legitimation or the criticisms of it. The change is in the historical setting in terms of which one or the other makes sense.

Much of this, of course, is equally true of a liberal regime taking steps against anti-liberal protestors. It is precisely because this is so that it is a crucial, and always recurrent, matter of political judgment, how much rope a given set of protestors may be given. (A corollary of Goethe's saying is that there can be an important question of whose *Tat* should be *im Anfang*.)

Suppose, then, that the theocratic regime, or the subordinate role of women, is still widely accepted in a certain society, more or less without protest. Then there is a further question: to what extent this acceptance, though it does not produce a genuine legitimation, nevertheless means that, as I put it earlier, it can be decently supposed that there is a legitimation. An important consideration, as the Frankfurt tradition has insisted, is how far the acceptance of these ideas can itself be plausibly understood as an expression of the power relations that are in question. It is notoriously problematic to reach such conclusions, but to the extent that the belief system can be reasonably interpreted as (to put it in improbably extreme terms) a device for sustaining the domination of the more powerful group, to that extent the whole enterprise might be seen as a violation of human rights. Without such an interpretation, we may see the members of this society as jointly caught up in a set of beliefs which regulate their lives and are indeed unsound, but which are shared in ways that move the society further away from the paradigm of unjust coercion. In that case, although we shall have various things to say against this state of affairs, and although we see the decline of these beliefs as representing a form of liberation, we may be less eager to insist that this way of life constitutes a violation of human rights.

The charge that a practice violates fundamental human rights is ultimate, the most serious of political accusations. In their most basic form, violations of human rights are very obvious, and so is what is wrong with them. Moreover, in their obvious form, they are always with us somewhere. It is a mark of philosophical good sense that the accusation should not be distributed too inconsiderately, and in particular that theory should not lead us to treat like manifest crimes every practice that we reject on liberal principle, even if in its locality it can be decently supposed to be legitimate. It is also a question of political sense how widely the accusation should be distributed. As always, that consideration can cut both ways. It may be politically helpful in certain circumstances to exaggerate the extent to which a practice resembles the paradigms of injustice. As always in real political connections, there is a responsibility in doing such a thing: in order for the practice to come to be seen as resembling manifest crimes, it will almost certainly have to be made to change in actual fact so that more are committed.

Whether it is a matter of philosophical good sense to treat a certain practice as a violation of human rights and whether it is politically good sense cannot ultimately constitute two separate questions. This is because of the basic truth represented in Goethe's verse, that no political theory, liberal or other, can determine by itself its own application. The conditions in which the theory or any given interpretation of it makes sense to intelligent people are determined by an opaque aggregation of many actions and forces. A few of those actions are political actions. A few, a very few, may be the actions of theorists, whether acting politically, like Nino, or like him and the rest of us, as theorists.

THREE

Pluralism, Community and Left Wittgensteinianism

THE MOST POWERFUL CONTRIBUTION to Anglo-American political philosophy in this century has been that of John Rawls, and like most people discussing this subject now, I shall start from his work. The central idea of Rawls's theory is to model the demands of a conception of social justice by the fiction of contracting parties making a rational choice under ignorance. We are to imagine people choosing a social system without knowing what particular role or position they will occupy in it. These people, in their assumed state of ignorance, are represented as disinterested toward one another and as making what is roughly speaking a self-interested choice. This combination of self-interest and ignorance is equivalent, in effect, to impartiality on the part of an informed agent. If ordinary, informed people have a sense of social justice or fairness, they will be in effect willing to think about what they would choose behind "the veil of ignorance," as Rawls calls it, and willing to stick to those conclusions in actual life.

There are many deep analogies between these ideas and a characteristically Kantian approach to morality. The willingness to take oneself behind the veil of ignorance and conduct this kind of thought experiment is analogous to the disposition which Kant identified as fundamental to morality, the disposition to conceive of oneself as both a citizen and a legislator of a republic of equals. Rawls does not think, as Kant did, that the project of engaging oneself to this morality of justice is implicit in the very conception of being a rational agent. However, he does suppose that the dispositions of justice lie very close to a proper understanding of the self, and that a story of psychological fulfillment for the individual would embrace the dispositions of justice as his theory characterizes them. This is one way in which Rawls's theory, even though it insists that questions of what is right or just must come before questions of what is a good or satisfying human life, does have implications about what such a life will be. It will be a life shaped by a sense of justice, and the questions of justice are ones that it is natural for human beings living together to want to answer.

In his original book, Rawls did, very broadly, tend to agree with Kant in a further matter, namely that this was a universal theory of social justice: that is to say, that it was perfectly appropriate to think of any human beings anywhere as arriving at some such conceptions. This made the theory universalistic in a strong sense which associates it with the outlook of the Enlightenment. In more recent work, however, Rawls has rather moved away from this to a position well expressed by the title of one of his articles, "Justice as Fairness: Political not Metaphysical." Under this conception, he sees his idea of justice as particularly appropriate to a modern society, "a modern society" being conceived of as technically advanced, democratic, and, above all, pluralistic. This emphasis does not only limit the ambitions of the original theory. It also rewrites its basis. The idea of procedural justice was of course always contained in Rawls's theory, in the sense that the just society was defined in terms of what would emerge from a certain hypothetical discussion, namely that behind the veil of ignorance. But the new emphasis brings out a way in which the procedural aspects of the theory are not simply confined to a hypothetical discussion behind a fictional veil of ignorance. Under the new emphasis, the whole theory, the whole way of going about things—including the appeal to the veil of ignorance—recommends itself as a solution to a characteristically modern problem, namely that of negotiating fairly the conditions of coexistence of people who have very diverse conceptions of the good. The procedural motions of fairness no longer characterize merely the theoretical content of the theory (structuring, in particular, the situation behind the veil of ignorance) but apply also to the kind of social reality which is likely to embrace such a theory in the first place.

However, this new emphasis does at the same time still preserve, and indeed even underscores, the idea that living with a sense of justice is natural to human beings. It is very central to Rawls's more recent ideas that the adoption of the scheme of the well-ordered society by parties who have to live together with diverse conceptions of the good—the adoption, that is to say, of justice as fairness as an appropriate way of life under pluralism—this procedure is not merely a *pis aller*. (Here he emphatically differs from many other contractual theorists, such as Hobbes.) To live under some such system does itself express an important dimension of the human personality. This aspect of the theory throws an interesting light on the new developments which emphasize the idea that justice as fairness is a particular answer to some peculiar problems of modernity. If justice as fairness does particularly well express certain fundamental aspects of human personality; and if it is a characteristic response to the conditions of pluralism rather than a timeless demand on all human agents living in any society anywhere; then the right conclusion will be that the conditions of pluralism particularly well express fundamental aspects of the human personality. This view itself, interestingly, seems not so much Kantian as characteristic of some other liberal views, such as those of John Stuart Mill. If the idea is very strongly pressed—more strongly pressed than it has been by Rawls—then it would itself imply a certain conception of modernity to which Mill was well disposed: that at least so far as its pluralism is concerned, it represents a form of progress from societies which, in contrast to the typically modern condition, were held together by some more unifying and concrete conception of the good itself, and not merely by procedural arrangements for negotiating the coexistence of different conceptions of the good.

Rawls's enterprise has of course been criticized from many different directions. I shall leave aside criticisms from Utilitarians, which seem to me less interesting. More significant have been criticisms from what has been called, very broadly and perhaps not very helpfully, a communitarian direction. I have in mind here criticisms that have been made, among others, by Charles Taylor, by Alasdair MacIntyre, and (under the influence of Charles Taylor) by Michael Sandel in a book directly critical of Rawls's theory. Indeed I myself have been associated with some strains in these criticisms, though for reasons that I shall mention later, I am resistant to being classed with those who deserve in any strong sense the communitarian label. Some of the criticisms relate to the theory's conception of what human beings are like. It is said that the picture of the moral agent presented by Rawls is too resolutely abstract; the Rawlsian person is concerned in the first instance only with certain primary goods of a nonethical kind, and is capable of thinking of himself or herself in abstraction from any concretely given social or historical situation. Further, Rawls's emphasis on the primacy of the right over the good has been read as implying that a sense of justice is the primary moral sentiment. It is fair to say that Rawls himself in many places seeks to counteract the more severe consequences of this kind, but critics still insist that people who really fitted Rawls's conception would think of themselves, on the lines of traditional liberal theory, simply as individuals who were bearers of desires, individual projects and rights, to which in turn corresponded duties; other forms of bonds or social solidarity would be secondary to these.

These critics stand to Rawls much as Hegel and his followers stood to Kant. Their criticisms, like those of the Hegelians, have political and social consequences as well; but, again as with the Hegelians, it is not agreed what the consequences are. Charles Taylor tends to agree with certain things that Rawls says about modern society, including the value of certain aspects of pluralism and of the Enlightenment emphasis on individual rights, while holding that Rawls's explanation or understanding of this situation is too impoverished and does not allow enough for other aspects of the ethical consciousness. Alasdair MacIntyre, on the other hand, is certainly opposed to modern society in almost all its forms, and occupies a position radically opposed to liberalism. In the case of Michael Sandel, I must say that I find it quite hard to discover whether or not he believes that the ethical powers which he most esteems, and which he finds insufficiently honored in Rawls's theory, would be better expressed in a more homogeneous and traditional society. The rhetoric of his criticism is on the strongest Right Hegelian lines, but some of his political preferences seem distinctly to the Left of that.

It is easy to see why there should be a problem at this point. Rawls's theory, and particularly its more recent developments, directs itself to certain characteristics of a modern society, in particular its pluralism, and tries to give an account of how that pluralism might be related both to schemes of social justice, and to the moral capacities of its citizens. As I said, it has to tread quite a delicate path between thinking, on the one hand, that the pluralistic character of modern societies is in fact among their disadvantages, and that the conception of justice as negotiating a fair coexistence between different conceptions of the good represents a kind of second-best answer; and thinking, on the other hand, that the pluralism of modern societies brings out what is in fact the best in human beings, namely a capacity for impartial fairness and toleration, and therefore itself represents a desirable human social condition.

This ambivalence is not simply a difficulty for Rawls's theory. It is rather a very real ambivalence that faces all of us: these philosophical problems represent familiar disquiets of modernity. On the one hand, there are characteristics of modern societies, such as their pluralism, their ideology of toleration, and their emphasis on at least the ideal of justificatory discursive discussion, which are well expressed in a philosophy that emphasizes procedural justice and fair coexistence, rather than privileging any other substantive conception of what makes life worthwhile. On the other hand, such a philosophy seems untrue to a great deal of human experience, and tends to reduce the conception of the ethical powers of human beings to too thin a basis. This is so in at least two senses. The fundamental moral power, the sense of justice, is too abstracted from other affections, commitments, and projects that make people what they are or at least make their lives what they are. At the same time, it seems to introduce an element of dissociation or alienation at the social level, inasmuch as widely diverse conceptions of the good have to be seen under the sign of toleration, to such an extent that one has to be very deeply committed to one's own conception of the good, while at the same time regarding very different ones as tolerable within a framework that is held together by a form of citizenship motivated by the sense of fairness and not much more. Since these conflicting aspirations do act on many of us, the fact that they show up so strongly in current philosophy suggests the encouraging conclusion that philosophy is at least to this extent in touch with reality.

Rawls allows more than his critics sometimes admit to the other side of the argument, and gives an answer of very considerable fineness even if one does not entirely agree with it. The communitarians, on the other hand, find it difficult to avoid a simpler and more straightforwardly reactionary answer, to the effect that a culturally more homogeneous society, where fewer questions were asked and there was a higher degree of traditional social solidarity, would be a better state of affairs, and that the pluralism of modernity represents, in effect, varying degrees of disintegration. Taylor tries fairly hard to avoid that conclusion; MacIntyre on the other hand seems happy to embrace it.

My contribution to the philosophical debates has been to some extent that of making myself a nuisance to all parties. Inasmuch as I have tried to make a nuisance of myself to the Kantian, and also to the Utilitarian, party, I have found myself cast from time to time as a communitarian. I resist that description for political reasons, and because of the often undisguised element of nostalgia which seems to hang over its aspirations. The whole debate is, in a sense, rather too familiar. The responses of both Left and Right Hegelians to Kant in the nineteenth century already powerfully expressed the yearning (radical in the one case, conservative in the other) for a life that would have a greater ethical density, a more thickly shared sense of community, than was offered, it seemed, by modernity and its most progressive philosophy, critical liberalism. This yearning, at least in philosophy, hardly ever took simply the form of unqualified nostalgia for an imagined past of traditional solidarity. It was always associated in some way with a desire to preserve the reflective freedom and self-consciousness that had issued in and from the Enlightenment; or, at the very least, associated with an assumption that at some level it would be preserved. The Left or radical tendency wanted a society that somehow would embody at once solidarity and criticism, tradition and freedom, familiarity and adventurous variety; the Right was happier to settle for a more traditional style of consciousness for most citizens, reserving the critical sense of the contingency of these arrangements to an elite, perhaps, or at the limit, to the theorist himself. Some of these nineteenth-century positions are being expressed again in the current discussions. Can we get beyond them?

The oppositions between (broadly) "Kantian" and (broadly) "communitarian" thinkers are often expressed, particularly by the Kantians, in terms of the possibility, and the basis, of critique. If there is some general and abstract framework of principles of justice, such as Rawls's theory, local practices and traditions can be criticized, at least to the extent that they stand opposed to toleration and the fair acceptance of diversity; but if we emphasize only the local significances of a densely structured traditional existence, there may seem to be no point of leverage for criticism.

Particularly as things have recently gone, this form of controversy has been rather distorted by the fact that, faced with an Anglo-American consensus that has been in good part liberal, the various "Hegelian" theorists have themselves appeared in the role of critics, urging us to change our aspirations in a communitarian direction. (Indeed, this is not only a recent phenomenon: since all Hegelian positions represent to some extent the desire to recover something supposedly absent from modernity, they have always tended to be more oppositional than anyone would be in the world they themselves would best like.)

There is one important philosophical position which has been deployed for Right Hegelian purposes, in this contemporary sense, and which, taken in that way, makes it mysterious, not only how critique can be legitimate, but how it can even intelligibly exist. This is the later philosophy of Wittgenstein. This philosophy (which, together with Heideggerian and other influences, has contributed to the outlook of Richard Rorty) is very strongly opposed to foundationalism in every area of thought and experience. Whether in mathematics, in our ordinary language, or in ethics, everything equally is a matter of practice, of what we find natural. It is mistaken, on this picture, to try to ground our practices, whether ethical or cognitive; we must rather recognize that our way of going on is simply our way of going on, and that we must live within it, rather than try to justify it. This philosophy, in its rejection of the "abstract," may itself remind us of a kind of Hegelianism, though without, of course, Hegel's systematic pretensions or his historical teleology. But if so, it has been, up to now, very much of the Right variety: despite the efforts of some of his followers, the tendency of Wittgenstein's influence has been distinctly conservative.

The point may be put in a number of different ways. When the later philosophy of Wittgenstein has been applied to the social sciences, it has been thought to yield conservative conclusions because of its holism, which may have much the same consequences as the similarly holistic doctrine of functionalism did in social anthropology. Each practice, seen as part of a form of life, plays its own role in such a way that its suppression or criticism must involve the distortion of the functioning whole. Again, the point can be put in terms of gradualism. Even if you do not think that the Wittgensteinian picture encourages an extravagantly organic picture of the synchronic state of society, it certainly encourages the view that changes in our thought and practice must essentially be piecemeal if they are to be comprehensible at all, and not merely arbitrary: even if society as a whole is not one organic item, each conceptual tendril in the interwoven mass is itself a living thing and can be directed in a certain way only if that is the way in which, in that context of social vegetation, it finds it easy to grow. Or again, for those who dislike biological analogies, much the same point may be put in terms of consensus. On this picture of things, to understand anything is to share in understanding, and nothing sustains understanding or knowledge except a shared social practice. The redirection of an ethical term, or more generally, the radical departure from an ethical practice, looks as though it will be merely arbitrary unless it can carry at least a substantive body of agreement with it; indeed, some critics of the picture might say that even this is a kindly understatement, and that the consequence of the picture is that no change in practice can comprehensibly occur unless it has already occurred—that is to say, it cannot occur at all except by magic.

Yet another way in which the picture may seem to be conservative is that it involves an undiscriminating acceptance of whatever conceptual resources of the society actually exist. Moral philosophy, in its more radical moods, hopes to be able to put some existing ethical concepts out of business by showing that their implications are unacceptable from its preferred perspective; but if no such leverage can appropriately be applied, there seems no way in which any of the existing ethical ideas can be killed off. The most that might happen, perhaps, is that some might die out, but if this happens, it presumably does so for reasons that are, as it were, opaque to philosophy. The Wittgensteinian picture itself insists that conceptual change is likely to be closely associated with any social change there is, but it is unclear how an understanding of either could be particularly accessible to philosophy: even conceptual change is likely to be represented, in this perspective, as a matter of brute facticity.

It is at this point that a certain paradox in the view begins to emerge. If all social phenomena equally are just whatever they are, merely part of this interwoven net of practices, then all of them equally will be opaque to philosophical criticism. But the Wittgensteinian philosopher is himself criticizing something, if only the practices of ethical theorists and other philosophers who misunderstand the proper nature of our thought. In the case of Wittgenstein himself, this point does not really apply very directly, because so much of his later philosophy consisted of a criticism of himself, and of philosophy itself inasmuch as it had a hold upon him. But to those who regard Wittgensteinian ideas as making a contribution to an ongoing discourse of philosophy, the point does apply, and it applies even more to social philosophers of a conservative tendency who have taken up Wittgensteinian ideas in order to justify their conservatism. For they will wish to criticize not just the misconceptions of philosophy, but the aspirations of radicals, and there is a paradox in their doing so on the basis of such a philosophy. According to this philosophy itself, all that philosophy can do is to remind us how our ethical ideas are rooted in our ethical practice; but (as Ronald Dworkin has repeatedly emphasized) part of our ethical practice consists precisely in this, that people have found in it resources with which to criticize their society. Practice is not just the practice of practice, so to speak, but also the practice of criticism.

If we reject foundationalism, we have to recall (as Hegel did and Wittgensteinians typically do not) that our form of life, and hence, more particularly, our ethical concepts and thoughts, have a history, and that a society such as ours is conscious of that fact. Not every society can think about its ethical life in historical or social categories, but it is a salient feature of literate, and most particularly of modern, societies that they embody a conception of their own institutions and practices, and of the ways in which these differ from those of other societies.

The force of this point is not readily recognized by Wittgensteinian philosophers. This comes out particularly if one considers their use of the expressions "we" and "our." When Wittgensteinians speak of "our" form of life, they characteristically use that expression in what linguistics calls an inclusive rather than a contrastive way: the "we" represents not us as against others, but an "us" that embraces anybody with whom we could intelligibly hold a conversation. It is obvious why this should be appropriate to matters of meaning and of understanding, and why also it is plausible to say in those connections that we have no way of standing outside "us." But we cannot simply take this idea over into ethical and social thought, if "our" way of life is to be that way of life within which you and I live and find particular meaning in our lives; since that form of life is precisely not the form of life of other human beings who have lived within some ethical system or other. It is, for one thing, the life of a distinctively modern society, and that is very different from other lives that have been lived, and no doubt from other lives that will be lived in the future.

There are two points here that it is very important for moral philosophy to remember together. It must realize that we can understand from the inside, as anthropologists understand, a conceptual system in which ethical concepts are integrally related to ways of explaining and describing the world. At the same time, it must be conscious that there are alternatives to any such system, and that there is a great deal of ethical variety. A well-known feature of modern life—one that directly contributes to the disagreements between Rawls and his critics which I have discussed—is that it actually brings into the substance of ethical life the consciousness of this very diversity, and requires one to live some kind of ethical life while conscious not only that alternatives to it have existed in different social circumstances at different times and places, but also that alternatives to it may exist at our own door. Moreover, it is the case that our own ethical ideas come from very various sources.

Once we regard the ethical life we now have as a genuinely historical and local structure, one that is peculiarly self-conscious about its own origins and potentialities, we shall have less temptation to assume that it is a satisfactorily functioning whole; and we shall be more likely to recognize that some widely accepted parts of it may stand condemned in the light of perfectly plausible extrapolations of other parts.

The correct conclusion is not that foundationalism is necessary for social critique. What we are left with, if we reject foundationalism, is not an inactive or functionalist conservatism that has to take existing ethical ideas as they stand. On the contrary, once the resultant picture of ethical thought without foundationalism is made historically and socially realistic, in particular by registering in it the categories of modernity, it provides a possibility of deploying some parts of it against others, and of reinterpreting what is ethically significant, so as to give a critique of existing institutions, conceptions, prejudices, and powers.

So far as critique is concerned, there seems no reason why non-foundationalist political thought, characterized in the way that Wittgenstein's philosophy suggests, should not take a radical turn. There could be, one might say, a Left Wittgensteinianism. The disposition of most of his followers not to go in this direction is due to their refusal to think in concrete social terms about the extent of "we." In Wittgenstein's own work, because of his principal preoccupation with problems of language, meaning, and knowledge, it may often not make too much difference whether the "we" refers to one cultural group or tribe as contrasted with another, or rather extends to everyone with whom we might intelligibly speak; or where it does make a difference, the correct understanding can be easily extracted. But in political and ethical matters of pluralism and community, these are the differences that matter to the exclusion of almost everything else, and the right understanding cannot be uncontentiously extracted. Once a realistic view of communities is applied, and the categories that we need to understand anyone who is intelligible at all are distinguished from those of more local significance, we can follow Wittgenstein to the extent of not looking for a new foundationalism, but still leave room for a critique of what some of "us" do in terms of our understanding of a wider "we."

The emphasis that this discussion has given to questions of toleration and critique of course accords with the traditional concerns of liberal theory; it also provides a familiar home for the labels, perhaps increasingly unhelpful, of "Left" and "Right." But any such discussion depends on an assumption, not only of liberal theory but of almost all political philosophy, that we are concerned with questions of how one society should be structured and ruled—of how people in one society, under a government, should live. With the exception of some considerations of global justice, third-world poverty and development, most political philosophy continues to address problems of justice and legitimacy within one society or state, and this concentration is taken for granted in formulating the issues of pluralism. It is not in the least surprising that this should be so, for both historical and theoretical reasons.

More specifically, it is not surprising that American philosophers should think about these problems in terms of a large and complexly pluralist society with an elaborate system for identifying individual rights. They have already had their war to preserve the Union, a war that involved very obviously both the identity claimed for a local culture, and some definite individual rights. But in many other parts of the world, such as Eastern Europe and parts of what used to be Soviet Asia, what is at issue at the present time is precisely the integrity of states, and questions of what kind of society can reasonably claim a political identity. In relation to these problems, theories that tell us how to run a pluralist state simply beg the question.

It may be said, in admittedly very simplistic terms, that (whatever the practical difficulties) it is not impossible to extend pluralist theory to cover such cases. If a culturally homogeneous group within an existing state wishes to secede, and it could do so without severely damaging the interests of the others, then it should have the right to do so. Here, they may seem to be a benevolent alliance of liberal and communitarian opinion, the liberals resisting the coercion of these individuals, and the friends of community applauding their desire to live as a culturally individual society. But this happy agreement may be very fragile. First, the breakaway state is likely, in any real case, itself to include some minorities. It can be argued that those who claimed the right to set up the breakaway state did so in the name of a minority culture, and, in the merest consistency, must allow the expression of cultural identity by people who now form a minority among them. But apart from the well-attested fact that the previously persecuted are not often very sensitive to this kind of argument, the argument itself is not very strong. What the breakaway group claimed, after all, was the right to set up a culturally homogeneous state. This may commit the breakaway state to accepting the right of some minority to do the same thing, if they can; but if the minority cannot do that, it does not necessarily commit the new state to respect their rights to cultural self-expression, in the middle of what was precisely intended to be a culturally unitary state.

Another reason why the apparent accord between liberals and communitarians on the right of cultural secession may not be very robust is that pluralist liberals in the original formation may be concerned, not just with the rights of potential minorities in the breakaway state, but with the rights of individuals who belong even to the seceding culture: the culturally homogeneous society may contain people (women, for instance) whom the pluralist liberals see as disadvantaged by the separatist cultural system. Such a view would have put a strain on their pluralist toleration in the original situation; indeed, interference by a liberal government in the supposed interests of individuals who belong to the cultural group is just the kind of thing that could encourage the break from a pluralist state.

Faced with these conflicts, it is hard to see how political philosophy could attain some neutrally acceptable view of them. It is not even clear whether either liberal pluralist theory or its opponents can produce a clear answer derived from their own principles. The liberals will have to advance from the mere idea of fair coexistence in a society, to the stronger views that have been part of their Enlightenment legacy, which claim the absolute value of individual autonomy and self-determination against the values of traditionalist cultural homogeneity. It may be hard to support such a substantive conception of individual rights without taking the path which Rawlsian liberalism has resisted, of putting a conception of a desirable human life before, or at least on a level with, a theory of the right. The communitarians, on the other hand, will have to consider, more clearly than they have been disposed to do, how far their affirmations of the value of cultural solidarity can go once they are freed from the disapproved, but perhaps rather welcome, limitations imposed by a liberal consensus. In particular, they must consider how important it is to the affirmation of that solidarity that it is expressed in one society, and that that society should constitute one state. The Wittgensteinians, certainly, have nothing merely from their own resources that could help one to think about such issues—it is only too obvious that these are questions that involve who is to count as "we."

In the meantime, we have to look, as always, not so much to political theory, of whatever kind, as to the economic and political forces that surround these conflicts. The line between a politics of legitimate community, and blank tribalism, is going to be held, if at all, by the influence of a world commercial order and that of the only powers at the present time—themselves liberal powers—which are in a position, through international agencies, to enforce solutions. Writing as the smoke rises from Croatia, I see no great reason to suppose that the outcomes of these conflicts will be rapid, painless, or reasonable.

FOUR

Modernity and the Substance of Ethical Life

WE ARE MET to discuss the relations of ethics to modern life. When such a subject is proposed, the discussion almost always turns to ethical discontent with modern life, to the feeling that the modern world is, from an ethical point of view, peculiarly problematical or unsatisfactory. That feeling may not be altogether wrong. But it makes a great deal of difference how such feelings are brought to bear on the discussion, and how we understand ethical discontent itself. I should like first to say something about this.

There have been complaints about the ethical state of the modern world as long as there has been a modern world. Indeed, there have been such complaints as long as there has been a world conscious that it was later than, and different from, some other world; that is to say, as long as there has been social life self-consciously placed in time. One of the very earliest documents of Western literature, Hesiod's *Works and Days*, already richly displays many of the materials of cultural and ethical nostalgia that in one form or another have been current ever since.

As that example shows, the nostalgic consciousness does not have to locate itself determinately in what we would regard as metric historical time. As is well known, the Golden Age, for Hesiod, was earlier than his own time, but no determinate number of years earlier; even though, so far as his own time itself was concerned, he thought (as surely all human beings have thought) that if something really happened earlier than today for instance, if we can remember its happening then it happened some number of days ago. The consciousness of metric historical time involves the application of that local thought to a generalized, recursive, "earlier," and that application is inescapable once a group of people have the idea that they are the successors of temporally overlapping groups of people, each of whom thought of their own time in terms of successive days. But once people think of themselves and their predecessors in those terms, the character of ethical nostalgia must change. To think of past people in these terms implies that it is merely a matter of temporal perspective whether they are "they" or earlier members of "us."[1] This by no means

---

[1] Williams considers further implications of this change in "What Was Wrong with Minos?," in *Truth and Truthfulness: An Essay in Genealogy* (Princeton: Princeton University Press, 2002), 149–71.

excludes ethical nostalgia, but it does rule out the archaic kind of nostalgia under which earlier times were, in their superiority to the present, insuperably other. (Although the idea of metric historical time emerged two millennia earlier, there is an analogy here to the Galilean revolution of thought by which the heavenly bodies came to be seen at once as at various determinate distances from the earth, and as composed of the same kind of matter.)

The nostalgia that succeeds the more deeply mythological version must have more negotiations with history; it must, for instance, be prepared to consider the question of whether the earlier should have been better than the later. If the thought is that the later is always worse than the earlier, a special kind of explanation is needed—one, obviously enough, that explains why things continuously get worse. Such an explanation would provide the inverse of what is needed by a doctrine of progress. However, it is not typical of ethical nostalgia to take the stance of explicitly claiming that the later is always worse than the earlier, and there is an asymmetry here between characteristic forms of ethical nostalgia and doctrines of progress. Theories of progress necessarily take the general view, and their explanations, such as they may be, correspond to the general view: they invoke models of learning, or climbing, or accumulation. Such theories and the explanations that go with them may be worthless, but they have no problem, as such, with locating themselves in metric historical time.

Ethical nostalgia, on the other hand, even when it has given up the deeply archaic outlook, is still resistant to the general view. It is more tied to "now" and "then" than to "later" and "earlier," and it is grounded in an experience that resists recursive generalization, the familiar experience of simply finding something inferior to something else. This experience does not inevitably, or even naturally, lead to the general thought "every present is worse than each earlier past." On the contrary, the discovery that people have always, or very often, had such experiences, tends to undermine the authority of the experience, and hence the nostalgia itself. For theories of progress, on the other hand, it would even be encouraging to discover that people had always believed in it. It is not essential that this should have been so, but the theories do have to find explanations of why it has not been so. Those explanations will, once again, no doubt be fanciful, but they operate within the structure of metric historical time, while ethical nostalgia, even when it has detached itself from the deep mythology of archaic times, retains a mythological aspect; it is naturally resistant to thinking of itself in terms of the structure of metric historical time.

This feature of ethical nostalgia, which shows up in its structural asymmetry from the ideas of progress, is significant when one considers the most important current version of it. This is the version in which complaints about "the modern" relate, not just to what happens to be more recent rather than less recent, but to a specific and unique historical epoch in which we live, that of modernity. "Modernity" in this sense claims to be a genuinely historical category, which organizes both explanations and phenomena to be explained; the idea that the modern world is immensely different from any previous historical formation is often said to be the founding thought of sociology. In relation to the category of modernity, ethical nostalgia takes a special, and superficially less mythological, form. Its characteristic disposition simply to treat the present as unique is transformed into an historical claim, that modernity is unique; its typical resistance to thinking about its own relation to history is replaced by a specific claim about history.

Just because of this transformation, however, it acquires a new vulnerability to reminders that it is indeed a recurrent phenomenon: its increased engagement with historical time means that it has to take those reminders seriously. Its complaints about the ethical condition of modernity and its explanations of the phenomena about which it complains are weakened if what it says about the supposedly unique situation of modernity is just a version of what it has been saying about each contemporary situation throughout its long life.

Its complaints will be weakened even if the phenomena of which it complains really are characteristic of modernity. It is generally agreed that modernity is marked by the decline of traditional patterns of authority, and by secularization. (I mean this merely in the sense of the substitution of secular for religious conceptions and institutions, not in the sense of the "secularization thesis," criticized by Blumenberg, to the effect that the leading ideas of modernity are secular versions of religious ideas.)[2] Ethical nostalgia, particularly in its most immediately conservative forms, will seize on these phenomena as part or cause of what is bad in the modern world. But, at the same time, those complaints are the most familiar expressions of traditional ethical nostalgia; already in antiquity the decline of parental and other authority, and the neglect of the gods, have been central to the repertoire of those who praise times past at the expense of the present.

Those people are not necessarily wrong. But if their repertoire is notably the same as the traditional repertoire, we have no particular reason to think that they are right; in particular, we have no reason to think that they are right because we share, if only in certain moods, their experience of nostalgia.

[2] Hans Blumenberg, *The Legitimacy of the Modern Age*, trans. Robert M. Wallace (Cambridge: MIT Press, 1983).

Moreover, we should be distrustful of their accounts of the past. One important example concerns the supposed ethical effects of religious belief. Here it is important, in my view, to make two distinctions. One is a distinction between a religious outlook, on the one hand, and simply an acceptance of the divine on the other. The scholar who interestingly said that there is no less religious poem than the *Iliad* is not refuted by our pointing out that the *Iliad* is full of gods. The second distinction, more immediately important here, is to be drawn between the social facts of secularization and a supposed consequence about motivation. It can scarcely be denied that the modern view of the world is more secular than that of, say, seventeenth-century Europe. (It is another question whether that change is as permanent and irreversible as has often been believed.) One consequence of this is that in describing, or trying to arouse, approved motivations, people make fewer appeals to religious authority, sanctions, or institutions. In one sense, then, it follows that people rarely now have a kind of motivation that they used to have, a motivation characterized in religious terms. But it does not follow that just in virtue of that, they are less motivated to act in the approved ways. There seems in fact a good deal of evidence that the efficacy of ethical motivations has not much to do with the religious or non-religious character of their expression. In this respect, as in many others, the picture of the past as better-ordered, more disciplined, more homogeneous than the present, may well be a fantasy; and in this case, as in all others, there is no substitute for a truthful recovery of the past. (It is an ironical reflection that some contemporary movements of thought, concerned to expose ethical nostalgia and similar outlooks as ideological, at the same time disempower themselves by denying that there can be such a thing as a truthful recovery of the past.)

In any case, the most important points here go beyond questions of whether the complaints and explanations of ethical nostalgia are true or not. It is rather that ethical nostalgia and its formative experiences have to be abandoned before one can even properly formulate the questions.

At best, ethical nostalgia mistakes a problem for a solution. I say "at best," because there may be no problem, beyond its own problem of accepting the unfamiliar. But even when there is a problem, even if there is something in the thought that there is now a new level of ethical disorder or uncertainty, no solution could be conjured merely from the sense that things are not as they used to be. All that ethical nostalgia can generate from its own resources is, literally, reaction. Reactionary aspirations necessarily share the mythological aspects of the nostalgia; just as nostalgia looks back to an indeterminate or fictional place, so what it yearns for is an impossible journey. Unfortunately, this does not mean that there is no such thing as reactionary politics, or that reactionary thoughts leave everybody as stationary as they would be if they were sitting in something they imagined to be a time machine. What it does mean is that reactionary politics cannot be what it pretends to be, namely a practice which may indeed need to deploy coercive force, but only in order to turn the ship around. It proposes, rather, an ongoing ship the direction of which is concealed by a regime of coercive force.

If ethical nostalgia reached no further than everyday discussion or the commonplaces of conservative columnists, it might not be so important. But it reaches further than that. It has affected some important political philosophy of this century, including, interestingly, some that has purported to be among the most radical. The results are literally pathetic, and doubly so when to the emptiness of the nostalgia is added the self-importance of philosophy. The proper role of philosophy in these matters is something I shall touch on later, but we should bear in mind from the beginning how extraordinary the presuppositions are of the sage who claims on philosophical grounds insight into our ethical plight, and pretends on the basis of reflections on Being, for instance (to take one notably indecent example), to tell busy or impoverished people what is wrong with the modern world.

Granted ethical nostalgia reaches a long way, one needs to go some way to get away from it. A useful rule seems to me to be this: when thinking about the relation of ethical thought to the modern world, start with concepts that in themselves involve the minimum of ethical commitment. To many people, this will immediately seem a positivist proposal, relying on some spurious distinction of fact and value. In fact, I reject that distinction in anything like the form that it takes in positivism, and it is not needed here; all that is needed is the much more modest idea that it will be useful to start, if we can, with characterizations of the modern world couched in terms that are acceptable to a range of people with differing ethical outlooks on it. This may encourage us to try to understand the modern world before we address the question of the relations to it of ethical thought. One important consequence of this is that it helps to leave open the relation of philosophy itself to such inquiries, something that is merely ignored or taken for granted by many philosophical theories on these matters. In case anyone still thinks that the motivations of this approach are positivist, and that it aims at a "scientific" account that leaves out all evaluations, it is worth recalling the point I have already touched on, that values are already deeply involved in the ways in which we should understand critiques of the modern world. These critiques run the risk of being not merely intellectually empty and unrealistic, but pathetic, pretentious, evasive, or deceitful as well.

Two concepts very relevant to describing the present state of things in relation to ethics are those of the "public" and the "private." At this present moment—that is to say, in the 1980s, a very brief period relative to the modern world as identified by the theory of modernity—it is notable that, in one sense, the boundaries of the public have been retreating in favour of the private, for instance by the "privatization" of hitherto public industries or institutions; the growth of insurance-funded health schemes as opposed to a national tax-based system; the encouragement of entrepreneurs, and so forth. Some such developments appear to be affecting the Eastern bloc as well as the West. Their future, and indeed their correct description, seem to me still very unclear, and that extends to the sense in which privatization really involves the private; in Britain, for instance, when the government sells off a nationalized industry, some private persons indeed buy shares in the resultant company, but no one even pretends that they acquire much control over it. But in any case, I mention this area only to contrast it with what I principally have in mind, which is the question of the extent to which events and actions of considerable ethical significance are governed by regulations which are publicly declared and debated. In this sense, the extent of the public is growing, and this is so even if the institutions in question—hospitals, for instance—are, in terms of the first contrast, private institutions.

When I say that the extent of the public is growing, one thing I mean is that decisions that used to be made in private on the grounds of individual ethical belief are now made by public institutions on the grounds of promulgated regulations. But it is not simply a question of the same decisions being made now in different places by different people. In many cases, public institutions enter the question because they, and they alone, offer possibilities that did not exist before, possibilities which generate new decisions. This is overwhelmingly true in medicine. Death used to be something that happened, more or less, at whatever time it happened; doctors tried to postpone it and were forbidden to cause it. They always had to make accommodations with those simple rules, in the light of their own outlook and those of their patients and their patients' relatives. If people are dying at home, and a physician is coming to see them, and the physician has any human contact with the patient and his or her relatives, then that may be to some extent how it still goes; but that is an increasingly rare conjunction of circumstances these days. Because of technological advance, possibilities exist and decisions are required that did not present themselves before. Moreover, they present themselves in public institutions, hospitals and clinics, and what happens in those is properly a matter of public concern. This means, in turn, that these practices have to be regulated by principles that can be publicly stated; and that means that they cannot be very indefinite, or too heavily dependent on the individual's sense of what is individually appropriate.

This importantly alters the nature of the ethical judgement involved in such matters. What has happened in some places is that the presence of ethical argument in these decisions has itself been institutionalized, in the form of supposed experts in medical ethics who are appointed to take part in discussions of the rules and of decisions about particular cases. This performs a number of functions: it enables ethical considerations to be presented in an institutionally recognizable form, parallel to a consultant's expertise, and as a secular alternative, or addition, to religious opinions (which themselves are now typically expressed in more secular terms). The presence of authorities on medical ethics also helps to guard against lawsuits. To some philosophers, it will seem that it is the fulfilment of an Enlightenment dream, the regulation of ultimate questions by the institutional embodiment of systematic ethical reason. To others, however, including myself, that view seems a clear example of what Nietzsche called the reversal of effects and causes: these procedures represent, rather, a conception of ethical reason that it itself formed by the requirements of bureaucratic organizations.

You need to accept some startlingly strong presuppositions if you are to believe in these practices on their own terms. The supposed experts receive their qualifications by taking certain courses in philosophy, in particular in ethical theory and associated devices of casuistry. It is obvious that someone may acquire an excellent Ph.D. in such topics and yet be someone whose judgement you would not trust on anything. To believe in these practices on their own terms, you have to believe that what matters most to regulating issues of life and death, beyond medical expertise, is skill in manipulating theories, rather than any other human characteristic; and it is hard to see why anyone should believe that. People are forced to believe it—or rather, forced to forget that they need to believe it—by the demands made by a publicly answerable institution that has to make decisions about the most intimately significant human issues.

It is natural to translate the extension of the public, in these senses, into an extension of the "political"; if certain subjects become increasingly a matter of public, explicit, regulation, then they are seemingly the proper concern of politics. But if the relations are changing between the public and the private, it is equally true that there are changes in the conception of the political and of its importance. The matters in question here, if they are going to be regulated by law, are going to be regulated, as things now are, at a national level, and it is the politics of the nation-state that remain primarily important. Yet many very important matters obviously transcend the nation-state, and the most that the politics of individual states can achieve is to encourage or discourage the possibility of international solutions, solutions which have to be reached on the basis either of widely shared values and objectives, or else at the level of bargaining. At the same time, some agencies, such as multi-national corporations, have greater international power, in certain fields, than any nation-state has; and while those fields may be limited, they are probably of greater relevance to the development of human life than the power, which still largely rests with nation-states, to coerce or annihilate other states.

The sense that technical or commercial considerations often have more determinative power than the policies of states applies within states as well. The current contraction of state functions in favour of "private" entrepreneurs, to which I have already referred, cannot go on indefinitely, and may reverse itself, but there is a more general tendency, to distrust the capacity of states to bring about ethical transformations of society, and this may prove more enduring. Scepticism about the practical and ethical consequences of *les grands récits* that have been enacted in the past century here meets the sense of the declining effectiveness of the nation-state. Whether states seem to have the power to shape society ethically or whether they do not, it seems that they will not succeed in doing so, and so it is better that they should not try.

If these extremely schematic thoughts are at all correct, then it is a significant characteristic of the modern world, a direct product of its distinctive modernity, that many ethical issues become matters for public regulation and institutional discussion, while at the same time a traditional place for the principled discussion of public matters, the politics of the nation-state, seems to be declining in importance, or at least in its credibility as a vehicle of ethical discussion. This may appear to present a conflict, or double difficulty; but I shall suggest at the end of these remarks that the second phenomenon may in fact conceivably help us in overcoming some consequences of the first.

As we explore some consequences of these phenomena for ethical thought, it will be helpful to consider first how they bear on something that is not identical with ethical thought, and indeed is not always even an example of it, namely ethical theory (the sort of thing in which the experts in medical ethics are typically trained). I take ethical theory to be an intellectual structure such as Kantianism or various versions of Utilitarianism, which has characteristically sought to achieve three ends. (1) It has sought to systematize ethical thought and to reduce it to some basic principles and concepts. One particular path that this process takes is that theory regards as basic very general or abstract ethical concepts such as "deceit"—what may be called "thin" ethical concepts—and uses these to explain or, more significantly, to replace "thick" concepts with a relatively high descriptive content, such as "brutality" or "treachery." (2) Theory seeks to provide a personal morality. Various ethical theories have differing ambitions in this respect, as in others; the differences show up both in how much they seek to control, and in how direct their control is meant to be. Thus some ethical theories may try to lay down only restrictive principles of right, while others, such as Utilitarianism, have ambitions to dictate an entire system of value. These are differences of ethical scope. But some well-known manifestations of Utilitarianism, in particular, do not intend each agent all of the time to conduct his or her life by Utilitarian reasoning, which is intended rather to justify other, perhaps more traditional, patterns of reasoning for private use. In such a case, the control of the theory is indirect, but it is still intended, by these indirect means, to control everything. (3) Differences in ambition apply also to the third aim of ethical theory, which is to produce a public or political morality. In this area, however, it is more typically the extent of the control, rather than the degree of its directness, that gives rise to the differences between different theories. Though theorists are not always very open on the subject, the idea of indirect control seems less commonly employed at this level.

I have elsewhere criticized these various pretensions of ethical theory. In particular, I have argued that the underlying idea of objective (1), that rationality itself requires ethical thought to be systematized in this way, is baseless; so far from trying to eliminate or reduce all "thick" concepts in the name of rationality, we should try to hold on to as many as we can. This relates also to objective (2), the aim of ethical theory to provide a private morality. The familiar (originally Hegelian) criticism of modern ethical reflection that it is too abstract and theoretical to provide any substance to ethical life is well taken, and it is precisely the use of "thick" ethical concepts, among other things, that contributes to a more substantive type of personal ethical experience than theory is likely to produce.

This insistence of theory on reducing ethical thought to "thin" concepts is, I believe, itself an example of something that I have already mentioned, the disposition to construe the requirements of certain kinds of public justification as themselves the criteria of ethical rationality. Public justification does not in itself inevitably imply the use of "thin" concepts; in a very homogeneous traditional society—assuming that it does allow some relevant contrast between public and private—public justification may deploy "thick" ethical concepts that figure equally in private practice. Modern societies, however, are characteristically more pluralistic. Moreover, their conception of public legitimacy is one that encourages institutions to behave as though society were pluralistic, and to adopt styles of justification that are more procedural, or appeal to notions of welfare or consensus that are less committal and less ethically distinctive than "thick" concepts. There is a political argument for public justifications to take these forms, and to deploy, correspondingly, "thin" concepts. So if public justification does make the increasing demands that I have already suggested, then there are forces (though they are not well understood by ethical theory itself) that work in favour of what ethical theory wants, the replacement of the "thick" by the "thin" at the public level.

If, further, these categories are inadequate to provide any great substance to personal ethical experience, as I have also suggested, then there is a divergence between the requirements of a personal ethic and a public morality, in the sense of the discourse in which it is most natural to discuss the public regulation of ethically sensitive matters. I take this to be a genuine problem of ethical thought in the modern world, one that transcends mere ethical nostalgia for an imagined homogeneous past world. Ethical theory has tried to bypass this problem; by combining ambitions (2) and (3), it has sought to bring private and public moralities together. But ignoring the problem has not solved it, and these attempts have manifestly not succeeded: and to the extent that Utilitarianism, in particular, has resorted to indirect methods of control in the private and not in the public sphere, and thus attempted to get the best of both worlds, its attempts have been either unintelligible or politically extremely suspect, implying the presence of a manipulative Utilitarian elite.

We can hope to make sense of ethical thought in relation to the modern world only if we give up, along with other ambitions of ethical theory, the attempt to find one set of ideas that will represent the demands of ethics in all the spheres to which ethical experience applies. We must then try to find some better ways in which we can have the best of both worlds. In some way, we must aim to cherish as best we can a range of ethical concepts of the more substantive kind; these will differ, no doubt, to some extent, from place to place and group to group. At the same time we may recognize, possibly in virtue of some of these ideas themselves, such as certain conceptions of justice, the need that decisions taken by public bodies may have to be argued about and justified in more abstract, procedural terms, with a "thinner" ethical content.

Simply to embrace some such formula, however, cannot take us far. In itself, it may lead merely to a distinction between public and private as paralleling a distinction between "thin" and "thick," and that is a place that modern reflection has visited only too often before. To get further, we would have to go beyond any absolute distinction between public and private, and think in terms of a structure in which (notably in contrast to the aims of traditional ethical theory) public justification did not try to justify what it was doing to everybody, or every possible person; it would justify it, so far as possible, within its own ethical constituency. This would mean that while its arguments would necessarily have procedural features, the basis of the considerations it took into account could borrow more from the distinctive ethical experience of its constituency, and not fall back merely on the most general and "thin" considerations. The more general and purely regulatory the functions, the larger the appropriate constituency, but also the discourse of "right" and the appeal to thin notions of the good would to that extent be more appropriate.

Such a speculation would lead us to the idea of a kind of ethical federation, with denser ethical considerations being deployed at more local levels, and "thinner," more procedural, notions applying at higher levels: though it is very important, as I shall suggest below, that "local" here should not be taken in a purely geographical sense. I do not know whether such an entirely schematic picture could be given social substance. One arrives at such a picture from the need to meet the characteristic problem that I have described as presented to ethical thought by the modern world: that one kind of ethical concept and thought seems necessary to a substantive ethical experience, but many ethically important issues must be discussed in a public discourse that typically, particularly in a pluralistic society, uses other and "thinner" concepts. There exist various schemata that embody respectively the "thick" and the "thin": the virtuous republic model, on the one hand, and on the other the Kantian and the Utilitarian constructs, the association of individual right, and the welfare machine. All, for different reasons, have been found inadequate to the modern world. The present speculation marks the spot for a further possibility, which in some form or other is certainly required.

These ideas themselves, and the scepticism I mentioned earlier about the powers of the state ethically to transform society, imply that it is unlikely that a theoretical or prophetic blueprint for such ethical institutions will be forthcoming; they are more likely to be generated, historically, by the need for them. However, it is relevant to recall here the other phenomenon I mentioned as characteristic of present developments, the decline in ethical importance of the nation-state. The power and significance of this institution have encouraged theorists, as the ideal of the good encouraged Aristotle, to seek for a theory that would serve both aims (2) and (3), those of an individual and a political morality. The idea has been that the territory of legal control, and the sphere of significant ethical life, should be the same. The consequences drawn from this have been different for different theories, as I have already suggested: very roughly, for Hegelians and theorists of the virtuous republic, the aim has been to give the state a substance comparable to that of individual life, while with Utilitarians (at least of the more direct persuasion) it has been the other way around. The present suggestion is that we should give up this assumption and concentrate on unities of ethical experience between groups of people who are less than the population of a state—the more familiar pluralist picture—but also on groups that cross its boundaries. Particularly with modern forms of communication, a "constituency" of persons need not live contiguously to one another.

This is only a gesture to the direction in which one might think. But if it is true, as I have suggested, that there is more than one genuine feature of the modern world that does give rise to novel difficulties for ethical thought, transcending the familiar reactions of ethical nostalgia, it may also be true that the difficulties do not merely sum to a greater difficulty but may turn out to help in solving one other.

FIVE

The Liberalism of Fear

IT IS AN HONOUR and a special pleasure to give a lecture in honour of my friend Isaiah Berlin. I have known him for more than forty years. I still recall the first occasion on which I spoke to him. It was after an under-graduate lecture, in the East Schools, then as now presenting problems of audibility. Berlin had been talking about the polarity or contrast principle, and Thales. I made a pushy objection.

There is something appropriate about that occasion. Berlin was deny-ing (admittedly in a rather untypical context) that everything is one thing. It is odd that I should have been disagreeing, although not that I should have been disagreeing with him. I have managed to do that on various occasions: on the relative appeal of the operas of Rossini and Wagner, for a start. We have also disagreed on certain philosophical matters. It is odd rather that I should have been disagreeing on *that*. One of our strongest intellectual affinities was in our distrust of system: our commitment to non-reducibility, to pluralism, to conflicts of values, our general fox-like dispositions. I recall a remark made to me by Stefan Körner, which I found a compliment, after a paper on moral conflict: "You said it's all a mess, and it is all a mess."

There is a problem with this kind of view: how does one carry on the subject—the subject, that is to say, of philosophy? I had a conversation recently with Michael Stocker, an American philosopher of similar tem-per. We were in the bar of a melancholy modern hotel in a melancholy run-down city in upstate New York. After one glass of bourbon, we agreed that our work consisted largely of reminding moral philosophers of truths about human life which are very well known to virtually all adult human beings except moral philosophers. After further glasses of bourbon, we agreed that it was less than clear that this was the most useful way in which to spend one's life, as a kind of flying mission to a small group isolated from humanity in the intellectual Himalaya.

Fifty or sixty years ago, there was a more general problem than this about the identity and survival prospects of philosophy. There seemed to be three analytical options. The first was positivist. This required one to act like the character in the film *La femme Nikita*, Victor le nettoyeur, cleaning up after and around natural science. The second was Wittgen-steinian, which in some forms became what Karl Kraus said psychoanalysis was, the disease of which it was itself the cure, but to which the most authentic witness was the master himself, who regarded the subject as an academic enterprise with complete contempt and periodically retired from it altogether. The third was the option offered by Berlin's friend J. L. Austin, who coined the memorable phrase "linguistic phenomenology" but did not live to distinguish in his work between a phenomenology guided by language, which is what a lot of philosophy is, and an activity of which the point is less clear: the phenomenology of the use of language itself, the tracing of the shudder of an exquisite distinction.

These very general problems barely exist now, in such forms. Philosophy has regained a confident institutional identity, in some cases in rather scientistic forms. There is, admittedly, some "end of philosophy" talk, but that is about the end of the philosophy outside (broadly) analytic philosophy. Other and more specific problems, however, do exist, such as that about the identity of moral philosophy and, I suggest, a different problem about the identity of political philosophy.

Berlin dealt with the problems of that earlier time at a relatively early age by, as he puts it, getting out of philosophy. This is not altogether true, although he did get out of it as it was then understood. The turn to intellectual history gave him something more satisfying to do than that philosophy, something closer to human idiosyncrasy. But it also in fact provided a way of continuing philosophy by other means. It registered the point that political philosophy requires history. This is a point better recognized now, and certainly better recognized than it is with regard to moral philosophy, where I believe it is also true.

But it is not altogether registered even now. In a curious way, it is concealed in the work of two notable political philosophers who both accept it but for quite opposite reasons are not taken to express it. One is Berlin himself, who led people to agree with him that he got out of philosophy, so that his work is taken to be history and not philosophy, and reasonably so, since a lot of it consists of history.

The other is John Rawls, who has only more recently said emphatically that the elaborate reflections of *A Theory of Justice* are reflections for a particular time and apply to a particular political formation, the modern pluralist state. His work is taken to be philosophy rather than history, and reasonably so, since most of it consists of philosophy and very little of it looks like history. But it does presuppose, and now explicitly, an historical story.

The idea that this end of philosophy—at least, of political philosophy and (I claim) moral philosophy—has close relations with history overlaps with a more ambitious view held by a consistently underestimated Oxford philosopher, R. G. Collingwood. The trouble with Collingwood's kind of commitment is that it requires one to know some history. My two associates in the view I am sketching are Alasdair MacIntyre and Charles Taylor. They are both Roman Catholics, though of different sorts. I used to find this a disquieting fact but no longer do so. All three of us, I could say, accept the significant role of Christianity in understanding modern moral consciousness, and adopt respectively the three possible views about how to move in relation to that: backward in it, forward in it, and out of it. In any case, we all assume some historical commitments, they on a more ambitious scale than I, and perhaps there is a rather nervous competition for who writes the most irresponsible history.

There is a double relation of political philosophy and history. One can put the first in terms of a sense of the past and a sense of the present. The sense of the present, of course, also involves a sense of the past. Another way of putting it would be distinguish what you are talking about (Berlin) and whom you are talking to (Rawls). The second is the question of the audience of political philosophy. Any work of any consequence in the subject raises the question of who is being addressed. Who does the author suppose needs to know this philosophy, and for what purpose?

This point arises also with moral philosophy. In that case, this is one thing that particularly presses the question, on which I have insisted, of the point of ethical theory: who needs such a theory? What for? What relation might it have to someone's life? But that is not the sort of question to be pressed with political philosophy. With political philosophy, there may indeed be some clearer answers about what some kinds of theory might do in some kinds of circumstances. But we have to be clear about these circumstances.

I am going to suggest later that the idea of the audience of a work of political philosophy is complex, in a way that is very relevant to an understanding of what political philosophy might and might not achieve. But that is for later, since I want to approach it through an example which is indeed the subject that I principally want to discuss. This is a certain style of liberalism, the liberalism of fear.

> For this liberalism, the basic units of political life are not discursive and reflective persons, nor friends and enemies, nor patriotic soldier-citizens, nor energetic litigants, but the weak and the powerful. And the freedom it wishes to secure is freedom from the abuse of power and the intimidation of the defenceless that this difference invites. . . . The liberalism of fear . . . regards abuses of public powers in all regimes with equal trepidation. It worries about the excesses of official agents at every level of government, and it assumes that these are apt to burden the poor and the weak most heavily. The history of the poor compared to that of the various elites makes that obvious enough. The assumption, amply justified on every page of political history, is that some

agents of government will behave lawlessly and brutally in small or big ways most of the time unless they are prevented from doing so.[1]

These are the words of the late Judith Shklar, who invented the phrase "the liberalism of fear." She died, relatively young, and at the height of her powers, two years ago. She was professor of government at Harvard. She was a splendid person and an admirable scholar. She was a friend of mine and Berlin's; indeed her family, like his, came from Riga. Her views, as you can already see, are not unlike Berlin's in certain respects, although the political implications of "the liberalism of fear" and the ideas associated with "negative liberty" are in several respects different. The liberalism of fear makes fewer presuppositions, if any, about moral pluralism, and has stronger implications about a pluralism of powerful institutions.

The liberalism of fear is "entirely nonutopian," and it differs from other forms of liberalism in that respect. Shklar separates it from two in particular. The first is the liberalism of natural rights. This was the reference to "energetic litigants": "the liberalism of natural rights envisages a society composed of politically sturdy citizens, each able and willing to stand up for himself and others." There is a contrast, equally, with the liberalism of personal development. "Morality and knowledge can develop only in a free and open society. There is even reason to hope that institutions of learning will eventually replace politics and government."

It would not be unfair to say that these two forms of liberalism have their spokesmen in Locke and John Stuart Mill respectively, and they are of course perfectly genuine expressions of liberal doctrine. It must be said, however, that neither one of these two patron saints of liberalism had a strongly developed historical memory, and it is on this faculty of the human mind that the liberalism of fear draws most heavily. The most immediate memory is at present the history of the world since 1914. In Europe and North America, torture had gradually been eliminated from the practices of government, and there was hope that it might eventually disappear everywhere. With the intelligence and loyalty requirements of the national warfare states that quickly developed at the outbreak of hostilities, torture returned and has flourished on a colossal scale ever since. We say "never again," but somewhere someone is being tortured right now, and acute fear has again become a common form of social control. To this the horror of modern warfare must be added as a reminder. The liberalism of fear is a response to these undeniable actualities and therefore concentrates on damage control.[2]

[1] Judith Shklar, "The Liberalism of Fear," in *Liberalism and the Moral Life*, ed. Nancy Rosenblum (Cambridge: Harvard University Press, 1989), 27, 28.
[2] Ibid., 26–27.

The liberalism of fear has its own founding fathers and heroes. Montaigne, for one, himself scarcely a liberal, but someone whose scepticism against fanaticism and sense of the impositions of cruelty put him in this line. Montesquieu, Constant. It is a fine lineage.

A good deal can follow within the ambit of the liberalism of fear. Rights, for instance, in the first instance because entrenched rights are one necessary protection against the threats of power. But it will inevitably be said that not enough follows from it. It is negative: the old liberal idea that the only enemy is the state. Or again it will be said that either what it requires can be taken for granted; or if not, it is obvious enough but represents only a minimum basis.

These are serious and familiar criticisms. Before we can assess them, we have to consider what the theory, indeed what any such theory, is for. This brings us back to the question of the audience of a given piece of political philosophy, a notion which I said was complex. We have to distinguish between, on the one hand, people who may be expected or hoped actually to read and be influenced by such a text, and the people or person whom, in terms of its content, it purports to address. We are familiar with a distinction, particularly with respect to the novel, between the author and the narrator. (This is a distinction not unknown in philosophy. Consider for instance the differences between the *Meditations* and the *Discourse on Method*.)

What I have in mind is a second-person analogue to that. The second-person analogue to the author comprises the people actually expected to read the text, the audience. The second-person analogue to the narrator, the person purportedly addressed, is the listener. There are several traditional types of listener to works of political philosophy. One is a prince, who is being told what to do or how to conduct himself. Another is a concerned citizenry, which may be the citizenry in general, as in the case of Paine's *Common Sense*, or some set of them, as in the case of Burke's address to the electors of Bristol. As in one of these examples, *Common Sense*, a pamphlet, the audience and the listener may coincide: the text is explicitly directed to just the people who may be expected to read it. If every text were like that, there would be no point in the distinction, but it is not so. In Burke's case, the listeners, the electors of Bristol, constitute part of the audience. (A similar case on a grander scale is a papal address which has the faithful as its listeners but is directed to a wider audience.)

The distinction will actually be more helpful if we extend the idea of the listener a bit from those whom the text addresses in the second person to people to whose particular attention the text will, if properly understood, be best taken to be directed, in terms of what it actually says. Thus Machiavelli's *Prince* is not addressed vocatively to a prince; it does not, as it were, take the form of a letter to one. But it can be read as a third-personal version of such a thing, a text which is presented as something which a prince would specially profit from reading. Its intended actual audience, of course, is something else again. They consist of the people whom Machiavelli thought could be instructed in the nature of politics and its relations to virtue by reading a text which says those things about princes in a way that purports to provide instruction to a prince.

One might include under a similar conception some examples of what might be called founding father political philosophy. Perhaps there are texts which explicitly claim to address such people in the second person. More commonly, they figure as people in such a situation likely to benefit from such a text. Rawls's *A Theory of Justice* is to some degree like this. It is about such people, of course, in a particularly fanciful situation. But rather as *The Prince* presents itself in a way that seems especially designed to help princes, so *A Theory of Justice* presents itself in such a way that could best help such people to go about their business. Its audience, of course, Rawls must hope, is the concerned and well-disposed citizenry of a modern pluralist state. The question then immediately arises why those people should interest themselves in a text that presents itself in this way: why should this audience interest itself in a text addressed to that kind of listener? Rawls has an answer to this: that those founding, indeed Pilgrim, fathers, the listeners, are the audience's own Kantian selves.

If we confine ourselves to the present time, and to what is indeed political philosophy, and we leave out the many items which are professional exercises of various kinds, the audience is almost always supposed to be the public at large: the public, indeed, in some cases—but not typically in American cases—of more than one state. The aim of addressing such a diffuse public is a diffuse effect, an effect of diffusion: the influence of ideas of which, in a very Millian spirit, Keynes wrote at the end of the *General Theory*: "[T]he ideas of economists and political philosophers, both when they are right and when they are wrong, are more powerful than is commonly understood. Indeed, the world is ruled by little else. Madmen in authority, who hear voices in the air, are distilling their frenzy from some academic scribbler of a few years back. I am sure that the power of vested interests is greatly exaggerated compared with the gradual encroachment of ideas. Not, indeed, immediately, but after a certain interval."[3]

But if this is the intended audience, there is a question of whether the text presents itself as though this were, equally, the listener. The answer to this is very often, perhaps more often than not, no. Above all, the text seems to address itself to the attention of someone who has *power*, who could enact what the writer urges on him. A particular example of this is

---

[3] J. M. Keynes, *The General Theory of Employment, Interest and Money* (London: Macmillan, 1939), 383.

where the reader seems (as in the writing of Ronald Dworkin) to be a constitutional court: the argument seeks to persuade the listener that a certain set of provisions would be the best and most harmonious interpretation of a set of values that the writer and listener are taken to accept. Similarly with some at least of founding father literature: the reader is being told how best he or she can start from the ground up, perhaps not in a state of nature, but at least having just got off the boat.

Maybe such political philosophers do think of an audience who might coincide roughly with these powerful listeners: by the processes that Keynes referred to, or more directly, their writings might come to Supreme Court justices, or ministers short of ideas for policy, or legislators. If so, this perhaps makes some sense of the fact that they address an empowered listener when in fact that audience will for the most part be unempowered. But it will make less sense of the fact that they address an empowered and very patient listener with a great appetite for argument and very few political restrictions on what he can do. Supreme Courts and founding fathers have fewer purely political restrictions on what they do than politicians generally do. It is typical of such political philosophy that the *others* are not there.

This is related to the absence from much political philosophy of any sense of political contest, which has been noticed in a recent book by Bonnie Honig, who notes incidentally that there are some who have been able to resist, in part, this influence: among others "Stuart Hampshire (who gets there via Machiavelli) . . . Stanley Cavell (via Emerson), Michael Walzer (via Rousseau) . . . Isaiah Berlin (via John Stuart Mill), Bernard Williams (via Isaiah Berlin)."[4]

The displacement of politics is not merely the effect of the listener's being taken to be empowered. For consider *The Prince*. This explicitly has an empowered listener, if not directly addressed. But it hardly leaves out the politics relevant to his situation. This is because it addresses itself precisely to the politics of his situation, above all to the question of how he should remain empowered. The relation between listener and audience which alienates politics from political philosophy rather involves this: that such political philosophy deals in ideals, or natural rights, or virtue, and also addresses a listener who is supposedly empowered to enact just what such considerations enjoin. And no actual audience, no audience in the world, is in that situation, not even the Supreme Court.

The liberalism of fear can be construed as having any one of the traditional listeners: prince, citizens, founding fathers. There is no reason why it should not be addressed to a listener conceived of as empowered,

---

[4] Bonnie Honig, *Political Theory and the Displacement of Politics* (Ithaca: Cornell University Press, 1993), 14.

though it is likely to express some anxiety about how much notice will be taken of what it says. But even when it is so conceived, it does not displace politics, because like *The Prince*, but in a contrasting sense, it serves to remind its listener of the existence of politics. Like *The Prince*, it takes seriously power and the surrounding distributions and limitations on power in any given situation. It is a close relation of Machiavelli (in that incarnation, not in his virtuous republic persona); very roughly, it has the same sense of what is important and is on the other side.

The liberalism of fear has historically been taken to have such listeners. But when it is so taken, it naturally attracts the traditional criticisms, because what it can be taken to enjoin is the extreme limitation of state power, the message that indeed it has traditionally conveyed. And that will not do for us, now, because it is not state power that we have most to fear. And when we ask what it has to tell legislators who are in that situation, it is less than clear what it has to add.

The liberalism of fear can be taken as having a different and much wider set of listeners: roughly, everybody. Indeed, its relations to its listeners and its audience are the reverse of the other traditional options. Its listeners, unusually, form a much larger group than its expected audience. It speaks to humanity. And it has a right to do this, a unique right, I think, because its materials are the only certainly universal materials of politics: power, powerlessness, fear, cruelty, a universalism of negative capacities. What it offers or suggests in any given situation depends on that situation: it depends, in particular, on the politics of that situation. The liberalism of fear, once more like its natural counterpart, *The Prince*, does not displace politics, but is understood only in the presence of politics, and as addressing its listeners in the presence of their politics.

One consequence of the fact that the liberalism of fear's listeners are not empowered figures of a given state, or the founding fathers of a possible state, is that it has no inbuilt restriction of its concerns to a given state, such as a nation-state. Of course, the liberalism of fear offers an account of *politics*, and since political power is largely conceived in terms of the nation-state—and little can be done, as Presidents Carter and now Clinton have discovered, even by a powerful state to curb outrages elsewhere—much of the concerns of the liberalism of fear at any given time will have to stay at home. But that is, so to speak, an externality, and recognized as such by the liberalism of fear. It is therefore all the more timely, for the politics of now are manifestly to a diminishing degree those of the nation-state. The centres, certainly, of economic power are international.

The traditional criticism, that the liberalism of fear stands for the normative limitation of state power, is under this emphasis misconceived. By its genuine universalism, and its awareness of politics, it is better placed to recognize the actual limitations of state power than are political theories addressed to listeners assumed to be, within a given state, at the relevant level (the level set by the theory) omnipotent.

But certainly, there is a politics of the relatively happier and better ordered society, and the question raised by the traditional critics must be faced, of what if anything the liberalism of fear has to say to people so placed. Even if we read the liberalism of fear as not trying to say that its concerns are not all the concerns of politics, but those that must be attended to first, there remain questions of what should be attended to second, when what must be attended to has been, at least to a decent extent, locally attended to. Liberalism, one might hope, would have something to say now. Indeed, this is the point at which the liberalisms of rights and virtues for the first time have something to say: Rawls's minimum conditions. This fits the condition of their assumed listeners.

Well, one thing that the liberalism of fear does is to remind people of what they have got and how it might go away. As Shklar said: "To those American political theorists who long for either more communal or more expansively individual personalities, I now offer a reminder that these are the concerns of an exceptionally privileged liberal society, and that until the institutions of primary freedom are in place these longings cannot even arise. Indeed the extent to which both the communitarian and the romantic take free public institutions for granted is a tribute to the United States, but not to their sense of history."[5]

There is a real lesson here. As Stephen Holmes has admirably shown in "The Permanent Structure of Anti-liberal Thought," the language of communitarian opponents of liberalism, themselves perhaps of a most respectable kind, can bear an unnerving resemblance to that of Carl Schmitt or Gentile.[6] In our own country, a more demure and less theoretical temper combines with large reserves of resentment, individual and national, to yield another but again disquietingly familiar tone on the anti-liberal right, the tone of Vichy.

But the liberalism of fear is not confined to uttering warnings and reminders. If indeed primary freedoms are secured, and basic fears are assuaged, then the attentions of the liberalism of fear will move to more sophisticated conceptions of freedom, and other forms of fear, other ways in which the asymmetries of power and powerlessness work to the disadvantage of the latter. There is much to be said about how these processes of extension and sophistication should work. In particular, the fears that are most basic in human terms do not map neatly onto fears that are most basic in political terms. This is the point that has always been urged by

---

[5] "The Liberalism of Fear," 35–36.
[6] Stephen Holmes, "The Permanent Structure of Anti-liberal Thought," in Rosenblum, *Liberalism and the Moral Life*, 227–53.

radicals and revolutionaries against the liberalism of fear and other kinds of moderate liberalism: the *erst kommt das Fressen* principle, the conception of freedom as freedom from—from unemployment and want and so on. These are indeed aims which any modern state will seek to forward by political means. But its unsuccess as such does not necessarily show that it is a despotic government, whereas its misuse of its own powers or its failure to curb people's use of their powers to subordinate others is directly that, for that is what the state first is.

Similar ideas have to be pursued in relation to freedom. The basic sense of being unfree is being in someone else's power, and that in the basic sense implies that what you do is directed by another person's intentions even if you do not want to do those things. (Note how this conception coincides neither with "negative" nor with "positive" freedom.) But things that people reasonably fear are often side effects, not the product of intentions directed at them; and they may be more severe in their impact than the direction aimed at them, or the direction aimed at others to help in curing the first people's situation. This is not a necessary problem for the liberalism of fear unless it is construed as a complete political doctrine for all circumstances. It does not have to think that freedom, in particular freedom defined narrowly by the political, is the only value that matters.

There is room for general, philosophical reflection on these themes. But the particular arguments that carry forward liberal policies in particular situations must be not just practically but conceptually a matter of those circumstances. This is the truth in anti-universalism, insisted on by some of liberalism's opponents. The liberalism of fear can combine this with its own universalism. It does so in the form of its constant reminder of the reality of politics, that there is a political reality out there.

Relatedly to that, the approach of the liberalism of fear is bottom-up, not top-down. Just as it takes the condition of life without terror as its first requirement and considers what other goods can be furthered in more favourable circumstances, it treats each proposal for the extension of the notions of fear and freedom in the light of what locally has been secured. It does not try to determine in general what anyone has a right to under any circumstances and then apply it. It regards the discovery of what rights people have as a political and historical one, not a philosophical one.

It asks, too, how secure what has been secured is. It is disposed not to be too sanguine about that, particularly since it remembers to look beyond national boundaries. It is conscious that nothing is safe, that the task is never-ending. This part of its being, as Judith Shklar said, is resolutely nonutopian. But that does not mean that it is simply the politics of pessimism which has not collapsed into the politics of cynicism. In the words that Shklar quoted from Emerson, it is very importantly the party of memory. But it can be, in good times, the politics of hope as well.

SIX

Human Rights and Relativism

WE HAVE A GOOD IDEA of what human rights are. The most important problem is not that of identifying them but that of getting them enforced. The denial of human rights means the maintenance of power by torture and execution; surveillance of the population; political censorship; the denial of religious expression; and other such things. For the most gross of such violations, at least, it is obvious what is involved.

I am going to discuss the case in which the violations are committed by governments or quasi-governments (e.g., a movement which controls part of a territory). There is a borderline between these cases and others in which government has lost control and the infringements are committed by bandits, warlords, and so on. It is important to the theory of this subject (and more generally to the theory of politics) that this is a borderline which is not always very clear. This is because government is in the first instance the assertion of power against other power.

I identify the "first" political question (in the manner of Thomas Hobbes) as the securing of order, protection, safety, trust, and the conditions of co-operation. It is the "first" political question because solving it is the condition of solving, indeed posing, any other political question. It is not (unhappily) first in the sense that once solved it never has to be solved again. Because a solution to the first political question is required *all the time*, the character of the solution is affected by historical circumstances: it is not a matter of arriving at a solution to the first question at the level of state-of-nature theory and then going on to the rest of the agenda. It is easy to think of the political in those terms, particularly in countries which have been long settled and whose history has not been disrupted by revolution or civil war. Rather more surprisingly, it is the standard picture in the United States, which has not been long settled, and whose history has been spectacularly disrupted by civil war.

The point, however, is not that in any country, at any moment, the basic question of recognizing an authority to secure order can reassert itself. It is obvious that in many states most of the time the question of legitimate authority can be sufficiently taken for granted for people to get on with other kinds of political agenda. But it is important to remember the elementary truth that even in settled circumstances the political order does rest on the legitimated direction of violence; and also that even in settled states, the nature of the legitimation, and what exactly it will legitimate, is constantly, if not violently, contested.

There is another, equally obvious, truth. In the history of the world, there have been quite a number of settled states in which people have got on with their business in conditions of relative order, but there have been few liberal states. Since any state that maintains a stable political order must offer its citizens some legitimation of its power, there have been many legitimations in the history of the world which were not liberal legitimations. In fact, at the present time, many of the states that display a settled and effective political order are, more or less, liberal states. But this is not universally true now, it has certainly not been true in the past, and it is only on the basis of a world-historical bet of Hegelian dimensions that we believe, if we do believe, that it will continue to be true in the future.

The idea of a legitimation is fundamental to political theory, and so to the discussion of human rights. The situation of one lot of people terrorizing another lot of people is not a political situation; it is, rather, the situation which the existence of the political is in the first place supposed to alleviate (replace). If the power of one lot of people over another is to represent a solution to the first political question, and not be itself part of the problem, *something* has to be said to explain (to the less empowered, to concerned bystanders, to children being educated in this structure, etc.) what the difference is between the solution and the problem; and that cannot simply be an account of successful domination. It has to be something in the mode of justifying explanation or legitimation. Our conceptions of human rights are connected with what we count as such a legitimation; and our most basic conceptions of human rights are connected with our ideas of what it is for the supposed solution, political power, to become part of the problem. Since—once again, at the most basic level—it is clear what it is for this to happen, it is clear what the most basic violations of human rights are. In the traditional words of the Catholic Church, the most basic truth on this matter is *quod semper, quod ubique, quod ab omnibus creditum est.*

This is true only of the most basic human rights. Some other items that have been claimed to be human rights are much more disputed. However, we do need to make a distinction here. In many cases where there is a disagreement about whether people have a human right to receive or to do a certain kind of thing, at least one of the parties doubts whether the thing in question is even a good thing.[1] This is so with arguments about the right to have an abortion, for instance, or to consume pornography. I shall come back to disagreements of this kind.

---

[1] Both may do so, as when a liberal defends people's right to go to hell in their own way.

However, there is another kind of disagreement, in which nobody doubts that having or doing the thing in question is good: the question is whether people have a *right* in the matter. This above all arises with so-called positive rights, such as the right to work. Declarations of human rights standardly proclaim rights of this kind, but there is a problem with them. Nobody doubts that having the opportunity to work is a good thing, or that unemployment is an evil. But does this mean that people have a right to work? The problem is: against whom is this right held? Who violates it if it is not observed? One understands why it is said that this is a matter of right. Unemployment is not just like the weather or an approaching asteroid: government action has some effect on it, and with that goes an idea of governmental responsibility (an idea which has both risen and sunk in my lifetime). But even if governments accept some responsibility for levels of employment, it may not be possible for them to provide or generate work, and if they fail to do so, it is not clear that the best thing to say is that the rights of the unemployed have been violated.

I think that it may be unfortunate that declarations of human rights have, though for understandable reasons, included supposed rights of this kind. Since in many cases governments cannot actually deliver what their peoples are said to have a right to, this encourages the idea that human rights represent simply aspirations, that they signal goods and opportunities which, as a matter of urgency, should be provided if it is possible. But that is not the shape of a right. If people have a right to something, then someone does wrong who denies it to them. I shall concentrate on cases in which this is really what is claimed.

• • •

Philosophers often say that the point of their efforts is to make the unclear clearer. But they may make the clear unclear: they may cause plain truths to disappear into difficult cases, sensible concepts to dissolve into complex definitions, and so on. To some extent, philosophers do do this. Still more, they may seem to do it, and even to seem to do it can be a political disservice. So it is very important that the clear cases should remain clear, and in this talk, I shall try to keep them so. Moreover, I want to emphasize the importance of thinking politically about human rights abuses, and I hope that this may at any rate emphasize reality at the expense of philosophical abstraction. Admittedly, the arguments that lead even to this are philosophical and perhaps will display philosophical abstraction. But that is the ineliminable consequence which follows from a philosopher's discussing the subject at all.

Not all rights are "human rights"—some are conferred by or are consequences of positive law, by contract and so on. Also, as I have already said, there are human goods the value of which is perhaps not best expressed in terms of rights. There are indeed clear cases of human rights, and we had better not forget it. But in addition to all these there are demands which would be claimed to be rights by many people in a modern liberal or near liberal state such the United States, which would not be recognized in many other places. They resemble the clear cases of human rights in this sense, that their basis is not positive law but a moral claim which is taken to be prior to positive law and is invoked in arguments about what the positive law should be. Examples include equality of treatment between the sexes; the right of a woman to have an abortion; a terminally ill patient's right to assisted suicide; freedom for publication of pornography. (I am not suggesting that all these will turn out to be on the same level.)

· · ·

The outlook of liberal universalism holds that if certain human rights exist, they have always existed, and if societies in the past did not recognize them, then that is because either those in charge were wicked, or the society did not, for some reason, understand the existence of these rights. Moreover, liberal theory typically supposes that universalism simply follows from taking one's own views about human rights seriously. Thomas Nagel has said: "Faced with the fact that [liberal] values have gained currency only recently and not universally, one still has to decide whether they are right—whether one ought to continue to hold them. . . . The question remains . . . whether I would have been in error if I had accepted as natural, and therefore as justified, the inequalities of a caste society."[2] But does this question remain? Here is where the crucial distinction comes in. Nagel is absolutely right to say that the liberal, if he really is a liberal, must apply his liberalism to the world around him (Nagel is keen to resist the force of Robert Frost's joke, that a liberal is a man who will not take his own side in an argument). Nagel rightly says, too, that if one knows that few people in the history of the world have been liberals, this does not itself give one a reason to stop being a liberal. If there are reasons for giving up liberalism, they will be the sorts of considerations which suggest that there is something better, more convincing, or more inspiring to believe instead. In this, I entirely agree with Nagel.

But how far does this extend? Does it follow, as Nagel also puts it, that "presented with the description of a traditional caste society I have to ask myself whether its hereditary inequalities are justified"? Many of us will agree that if we are presented *with such a society*, we may have to ask

[2] *The Last Word* (New York: Oxford University Press, 1997), 104.

ourselves this question. But is it really just the same if we are presented with the *description* of such a society—one long ago, let us suppose, belonging to the ancient world or the Middle Ages? Of course, thinking about this ancient society, I can ask myself Nagel's question, but is it true that the force of reason demands that I must do so, and what does the question mean? "Would I have been in error if I had accepted its inequalities as justified?"—would *who* have been in error? Must I think of myself as visiting in judgement all the reaches of history? Of course, one can imagine oneself as Kant at the court of King Arthur, disapproving of its injustices, but exactly what grip does this get on one's ethical or political thought?

The basic idea that we see things as we do because of our historical situation has become over two hundred years so deeply embedded in our outlook that it is rather the universalistic assumption which may look strange, the idea that, self-evidently, moral judgement must take everyone everywhere as equally its object. It looks just as strange when we think of travel in the opposite direction. Nagel expresses very clearly a powerful and formative assumption when he says, "To reason is to think systematically in ways anyone looking over my shoulder ought to be able to recognise as correct." *Anyone*? So I am reasoning, along with Nagel, in a liberal way, and Louis XIV is looking over our shoulder. He will not recognize our thoughts as correct. Ought he to?—or, more precisely, ought he to have done so when he was in his own world and not yet faced with the task of trying to make sense of ours?

Of course, it does not matter very much, in itself, whether we get indignant with Louis XIV, but one familiar reason for not doing so is that if we don't, we may do better in understanding both him and ourselves. Nagel's outlook poses a question which it cannot answer: If liberalism is correct and is universal in the way that Nagel takes it to be, so that the people of earlier times had ideas which were simply in the light of reason worse than ours, why did they not have better ideas? Kant had an answer, in terms of a theory of enlightenment. Hegel and Marx had other and less schematic answers. All of them accepted a progressive view of history. In the sciences and technology, a progressive history can indeed be sustained, in terms of the explanations we can give of scientific development. Perhaps ethical and political thought can join in a history of progress, as Hegel and Marx supposed, but there is a large and now unfashionable task to be discharged by those who think so. I would say that such theorists lack a "theory of error" for what they call correctness in moral thought: unlike the situation with the sciences (or at least, what I and most scientists—as opposed to certain sociologists of science—take to be the situation with the sciences), there is in the moral case no story about the subject matter and about these past people's situation which explains why those people got it wrong about that subject matter. But we do not need to press the formulation in terms of a theory of error. It is enough that these theorists lack an explanation of something which, surely, cries out for one.

Why is it important to make these distinctions between our attitudes to the past and to the present? The reason is that it is tempting to argue in the following way: if one does not think of one's morality as universally applicable to everyone, one cannot confidently apply it where one must indeed apply it, to the issues of one's own time and place. Some people do seem to think that if liberalism is a recent idea and people in the past were not liberals, they themselves should lose confidence in liberalism. This is, as Nagel says, a mistake. But why does the queasy liberal make this mistake? I think that it is precisely because he agrees with Nagel's universalism: he thinks that if a morality is correct, it must apply to everyone. So if liberalism is correct, it must apply to all those past people who were not liberals: they ought to have been liberals, and since they were not, they were bad, or stupid, or something on those lines. But—the queasy liberal feels, and to this extent he is right—these are foolish things to think about all those past people. So, he concludes, liberalism cannot be correct. That is the wrong conclusion; what he should do is give up the universalist belief he shares with Nagel. That does not mean, as Richard Rorty likes to suggest, that we must slide into a position of irony, holding to liberalism as practical liberals, but backing away from it as reflective critics. That posture is itself still under the shadow of universalism: it suggests that you cannot really believe in liberalism unless you hold it true in a sense which means that it applies to everyone.

So I agree, very broadly, with the outlook expressed by the British philosopher R. G. Collingwood (who died in 1942 and is still grossly underestimated in Britain), when he said that the question whether we might prefer to live in a past period because we think it better "cannot arise," because "the choice cannot be offered." "We ought not to call [the past] either better than the present or worse; for we are not called upon to choose it or to reject it, to like it or dislike it, to approve it or condemn it, but simply to accept it."* I said I agreed with this "very broadly"; in particular, I agree with Collingwood's emphasis on what one can affect in action, and I shall come back to that. But I do not agree that there are no judgements that one can make about the past; I am going to claim that there are some that one must be able to make. But it does mean that one isn't compelled to extend all one's moral opinions, in particular about rights, to the past; and in particular it means that one needn't suppose

---

* Editor's note: Williams gave no reference for this quotation, and I have been unable to trace it.

that if one doesn't so extend them, one has no right to them at all, as applied to the present world.

. . .

So is this relativism? One can call it a kind of relativism, if one likes, and I have myself called such a position "the relativism of distance." But it is very importantly different from what is standardly called relativism. Standard relativism says simply that if in culture A, X is favoured, and in culture B, Y is favoured, than X is right for A and Y is right for B; in particular, if "we" think X right and "they" think X wrong, then each party is right "for itself." This differs from the relativism of distance because this tells people what judgements to make, whereas the relativism of distance tells them about certain judgements which they need not make. But more basically, as soon as standard relativism is applied to any case that goes beyond the relativism of distance—that is to say, to any case that is not distant—it is completely useless.

The reason for this is that the distinction on which relativism hangs everything, that between "we" and "they," is not merely given, and to erect it at a certain point involves a political decision or recognition. Standard relativism arose first in the Western world in the fifth century BC, when Greeks reflected on their encounters with peoples who were, very significantly, identified as not Greeks. It was in part, perhaps, a reaction against the sense of superiority that the Greeks typically brought to that distinction, and I think it is no accident that the paradigm expression of the distinction between nature and culture, which contributed to relativism, referred to the despised enemy: "fire burns the same in Persia as it does here, but what counts as right and wrong is different."

In something of the same way, modern relativism has complex relations to colonialism. Some colonialists thought that native peoples should be forced or encouraged to adopt European outlooks. Others thought that some peoples should be treated in that way, and others (more or less) left alone. Again, there were places in which some practices were suppressed—a notorious example was suttee in India—while other practices were not. Anti-colonialists thought that European powers should leave everyone alone. But every one of these outlooks transcends the outlook of standard relativism, even the last: to say that it is better for them to be left alone by us is not at all the same as to say that what they think is right for them and what we think is right for us.

Now, after colonialism, we still have to work out our relations with various societies, and standard relativism still cannot help us. Confronted with a hierarchical society in the present world, we cannot just count them as them and us as us: we may well have reason to count its members as already some of "us." For standard relativism, one may say, it is always too early or too late. It is too early, when the parties have no contact with each other, and neither can think of itself as "we" and the other as "they." It is too late, when they have encountered one another: the moment that they have done so, there is a new "we" to be negotiated.

So far as human rights in the contemporary world are concerned, standard relativism is an irrelevance—as it is, in fact, everywhere. The relativism of distance, on the other hand, in many though not all respects, is a sensible attitude to take. It applies to the past (to the extent that it does) for the reason that Collingwood implied, because the past is not within our causal reach. So far as human rights are concerned, what matters is what presents itself in our world, now. In this sense, the past is *not* another country: if it were just another country, we might have to wonder what to do about it.

In fact, as I have said, there are some judgements we can make about the past. There are very many, such as that Caligula seems to have been a singularly nasty man and Cicero notably self-important, and we should not forget all those: they are connected with our capacity to understand the past at all. But for the present purpose, we need to emphasize a particular kind of judgement which we can, indeed must, make about the past: those that we make in virtue of what I called the first question of politics, the question of order, and the danger related to that question, that the solution may become part of the problem. The categories of an ordered as opposed to a disordered social situation, disorder which is at the limit anarchy, apply everywhere; correspondingly, so do the ideas of a legitimate political order, where that means, not necessarily what we would count now as an acceptable political order, but what counted then as one. There simply is a social and historical difference between a medieval hierarchical state, for instance, and an area controlled by a band of brigands. Everywhere, universally, at least this much is true, that might is not per se right: the mere power to coerce does not in itself provide a legitimation.

· · ·

This means, as I said at the beginning, that there are conceptions, which apply everywhere, of what it is for the solution to have become the problem, for the supposedly legitimate order to approximate to unmediated coercive power. This applies to the past, and, more relevantly, it applies to the present. Under such a conception we recognize the most blatant denials of human rights, torture, surveillance, arbitrary arrest, and murder: the world of Argentina under the junta, the story, only partly ever to be told, of those who disappeared.

Of course, it goes without saying that such cases are near some slippery slopes. There are other states which are uncomfortably like this, but which may be able to make a rather better case for their activities. Thus what is in its own terms a legitimate order may use what we would regard as cruel and unusual punishments; it is significant that, not surprisingly, they make no secret of this. They or others may use, rather less openly, ruthless methods against subversives or threatening revolutionaries. Are such measures in themselves violations of human rights? If they are, are they violations justified by emergency?

Of course, there is always room for argument about cases, but the point here is that it is clear what the argument is about. Any state may use such methods in extremis, and it is inescapably true that it is a matter of political judgement, by political actors and by commentators, whether given acts are part of the solution or of the problem. Liberal states make it a virtue—and it is indeed a virtue—to wait as long as possible before using such solutions, because they have the constant apprehension that those solutions will become part of the problem. Liberal states are well regarded, and rightly so, for showing this restraint. They should be less well regarded, as the writings of Carl Schmitt may remind us, if they turn this into the belief that the only real sign of virtue is to wait too long.

These cases, I think, are not conceptually very complicated. They indeed involve complexity and danger in deciding what is needed when, and these are matters of historical and sometimes personal luck. Conceptual complications multiply when one is concerned with a different case, that in which a style of legitimation that was accepted at one time is still accepted in some places but no longer accepted in others. I said earlier that the past is not causally within our reach. However, the contemporary world is certainly within the reach of the past, and the influences of the past include, now, theocratic conceptions of government and patriarchal ideas of the rights of women. Should we regard practices elsewhere that still express such conceptions as violations of fundamental human rights?

I should repeat that this is not a question to be put in terms of the standard relativist theory. We should have left behind us by now the manifestly confused notion that we cannot possibly talk about violations of human rights in such a case because these practices must be right for them, though they are not right for us.

We must ask, first, what is actually happening? Let us grant, as a condition of the problem, that we do not accept the local legitimation. It may depend on a religious story which we reject, either in its entirety or, perhaps, in the way it is used to legitimate the current forms of political power. (It is particularly important to remember this second possibility when, as in the case of Islam, some critics offer only a relentless Westernized secularism to oppose a rigidly autocratic theocracy; Islam itself has more resources than this old saga suggests.) In any case, we reject the legitimation of the theocrats. The question is whether we must then think of these practices as violations of human rights. A short argument will say that they must be: since the legitimation is unsound, the practices involve coercion without legitimation. But this is rather too short. For one thing, there is an issue of how much manifest coercion is involved, and that is why, very obviously, the situation is worse in these respects if opponents of the religion are silenced or women are forced into roles they do not even think they want to assume. Simply the fact that this is so makes the situation more like the paradigm of rights violation, of the solution becoming part of the problem.

How far it will have come to be like that paradigm is in good part a matter of fact and understanding. Up to a certain point, it may be possible for supporters of the system to make a decent case (in both senses of that helpful expression) that the coercion is legitimate. Somewhere beyond that point there may come a time at which the cause is lost, the legitimation no longer makes sense, and only the truly fanatical can bring themselves to believe it. There will have been no great change in the argumentative character of the legitimation or the criticisms of it. The change is in the historical setting in terms of which one or the other makes sense.

Much of this, of course, is equally true of a liberal regime taking steps against anti-liberal protestors, and it is one that revolutionaries often rely on. It is precisely because this is so that it is a crucial, and always recurrent, matter of political judgement, how much rope a given set of protestors may be given.

Suppose, then, that the theocratic regime, or the subordinate roles of women, are still widely accepted in a certain society, more or less without protest. Then there is a further question, to what extent this fact, granted it does not rest on a genuinely credible legitimation, nevertheless means that, as I put it earlier, it can be decently supposed that there is a legitimation. Here it seems to me an important consideration, as the Frankfurt tradition has insisted, how far the acceptance of these ideas can itself be plausibly understood as an expression of the power relations that are in question. It is notoriously problematical to reach such conclusions, but to the extent that the belief system can be reasonably interpreted as (to put it in improbably simple terms) a device for sustaining the domination of the more powerful group, to that extent the whole enterprise might be seen as a violation of human rights. Otherwise, without such an interpretation, we may see the members of this society as jointly caught up in a set of beliefs which regulate their lives and which are indeed unsound, but which are shared in ways that move the society further away from the paradigm of unjust coercion. In that case, although we shall have various things to say against this state of affairs, and although we may see the decline of these beliefs as representing a form of liberation, we may be less eager to insist that its way of life constitutes a violation of human rights.

The charge that a practice violates fundamental human rights is ultimate, the most serious of political accusations. In their most basic form, violations of human rights are very obvious, and so is what is wrong with them: unmediated coercion, might rather than right. Moreover, in their obvious form, they are always with us somewhere. It is a mark of philosophical good sense that the accusation should not be distributed too inconsiderately, and in particular that our theories should not lead us to treat like manifest crimes every practice that we reject on liberal principle and could not accept here—especially if in its locality it can be decently supposed to be legitimated. It is also a question of *political* sense, how widely the accusation should be distributed. Of course it can be politically helpful in certain circumstances to exaggerate the extent to which a practice resembles the paradigm violations of human rights, in order that it should be seen to do so. As always in real political connections, there is a responsibility in doing such a thing: in order for the practice to come to be seen as resembling manifest crimes, it will almost certainly have to be made to change in actual fact so that more of them are committed.

Whether it is a matter of philosophical good sense to treat a certain practice as a violation of human rights, and whether it is politically good sense, cannot ultimately constitute two separate questions. The first question that we have to ask, I said, is: what is actually going on? Which includes: how is it to be interpreted? It is on the answers to this that our judgements must depend, not on any deployment of general relativistic categories.

The second question is: what, if anything, can we do about it? It should be obvious that this must be on every occasion a political question. The term "political" in such connections tends to be associated simply with matters of national interest or trade policy and the like. Or again the political is understood in internal terms, of how intervention or its opposite will go down at home. These are certainly considerations that are not irrelevant to the political. Max Weber in *Politik als Beruf* distinguished between an ethic of responsibility and an ethic of commitment, and it was his point that the former is still very much an ethic. But many do not see this point, and I was interested to find it made very firmly by Roman Herzog, in the first of a series of articles on human rights published in *Die Zeit*:

Bei der Verwirklichung des Ziels kommt es aber auch auf Pragmatismus an. Das klingt in deutschen Ohren oft kompromisslerisch oder gar heuchlerisch. In Wirklichkeit ist ein Pragmatismus, der auch darauf achtet, wie das für richtig erkannte Ziel möglichst weitgehend realisiert werden kann, alles andere als das, und auf keinen Fall darf er einfach mit Opportunismus gleichgesetzt werden.[3]

[To realize one's aim is to take pragmatism seriously. To a German ear, this can smack of compromise, even hypocrisy. Nothing could be further from the truth. Nor will the true pragmatist be tempted to opportunism. He will understand the nature and importance of the end, and see clearly and without emotion how most effectively to achieve it.]

Franklin D. Roosevelt famously said of Somoza, the ghastly dictator of Nicaragua, "He is a Son of a Bitch, but he is our Son of a Bitch." This can, on some occasions, be the correct attitude. Again, the habitual saying of a less revered American president, "How will it play in Peoria?" can be a responsibly democratic question. But the main point is that the political does not simply exclude principle; it includes it, but many other things as well. Because the question "What should we do?" can only be a political question, there is not much that can be said in general about it at an ethical or philosophical level. But let me end with two sets of outline remarks.

I have said that a violation of basic human rights approximates to unmediated coercion. We are likely to think that, other things being equal (which is a large qualification) and supposing there are some things we can do, there is more reason to do something if the violation is gross. Why should this be so? Well, (1) what is happening is worse. (2) In other cases, it is more likely that intervention will make it worse. (3) If the case is one which looks less like unmediated coercion, the victims may not think they are victims, and then intervention may be difficult to distinguish from ideological imperialism. But, most basically, (4) the nearer to the paradigm the violations are, and the more the state is part of the problem, the nearer the situation may be to that of a state apparatus being at war with its own people. The reimposition of a solution, the stopping of such a war, can be a better justification for intervention than ideological disagreement.

My second and last set of remarks concerns freedom of speech and information. Denial of this freedom is widely perceived as a significant human rights violation. Yet it may not be overtly very coercive, particularly if it is efficient enough. It hardly seems at all a case of what I have called the solution being part of the problem. Some liberals will say that denial of free expression is very deeply coercive, and attacks the individual's interests just as radically as violence attacks his physical being, because it attacks his interests, in John Stuart Mill's famous words, as a

---

[3] September 6, 1996.

progressive being. But if we say this, we shall need a theory of the human person more ambitious than any invoked in the present account of basic human rights—a theory in terms of liberal autonomy.

More ambitious, such a theory will also be more disputable. It seems to me sensible, both philosophically and politically, to make our views about human rights, or at least the most basic human rights, depend as little as possible on disputable theses of liberalism or any other particular ideology. We should rely, so far as we can, on the recognition of that central core of evils (*quod semper, quod ubique, quod ab omnibus . . .*); together with our best critical understanding of what may count now as a legitimation; together with what in modern conditions is implied by these recognitions.

It is in this last connection that I would bring in the rights to freedom of expression and communication. They are indeed basic, but not because their denial is coercive relative to a distinctively liberal conception of the individual's interests. Rather, freedom of speech is involved in making effective any criticism of what a regime is doing, in relation to any reasonable conception of the individual's interests. Neither the citizens themselves nor anyone else can answer the question "What is actually going on?" without true information and the possibility of criticism. Liberals may think that this is an excessively instrumental account of the freedom of speech, and indeed it is, relative to the elaborations of that value, its extensions and defences, which are appropriate to the political agenda of a settled liberal state. But the instrumentalist account is better for an account of free speech as a basic human right, and for the criticism of states that constrain that right.

We are concerned, as I have repeatedly said, with the contemporary world, with what actually exists. One encouraging feature of that world is that free speech tends to be internationally infectious. By the same token, that other question which comes up when rights are violated— "What shall we do?"—is clearer: encouragement of information, denunciation of censorship, and the like, can be legitimately and often effectively achieved. It gets very hard for states to complain that others are insisting on informing their citizens. Moreover, it gets harder for them to stop the information. Modern communications technology can contribute negatively to human rights observance: by making surveillance more powerful; and also, less obviously, by reducing the serious discussion of politics, and creating an international din of rubbish in which nothing critical or serious can be distinctly heard. But without doubt it also makes a positive contribution against secrecy, the control of information, and the suppression of criticism. In doing that, it equally makes a contribution against tyranny and unmediated coercion, and against regimes whose operations, rather than solving the problem that politics is there to address, add to it.

SEVEN

From Freedom to Liberty:
The Construction of a Political Value

I. Introduction

My subject is freedom and in particular freedom as a political value. Many discussions of this topic consist of trying to define the idea of free-dom, or various ideas of freedom. I do not think that we should be inter-ested in definitions. I leave aside the very general philosophical point that if we mean, seriously, definitions, there are no very interesting definitions of anything. There is a more particular reason. In the case of ethical and political ideas, what puzzles and concerns us is the understanding of those ideas—in the present case, freedom—as a value for us in our world. I do not mean that we are interested in it only as it figures in precisely our set of values—meaning by that, those of a liberal democratic society. Mani-festly it is equally part of our world that such ideas are also used by those who do not share our values or only partly share them—those with whom we are in confrontation, discussion, negotiation, or competition, with whom in general we share the world. Indeed, we will disagree among ourselves about freedom within our own society. We experience conflicts between freedom and other values, and—a point I shall emphasize—we understand some desirable measures as involving a cost in freedom.

Whatever our various relations may be with others in our world who do or do not share our conception of freedom, we will not understand our own specific relations to that value unless we understand what we want that value to do for us—what we, now, need it to be in shaping our own institutions and practices, in disagreeing with those who want to shape them differently, and in understanding and trying to co-exist with those who live under other institutions.

In all their occurrences, these various conceptions or understandings of freedom, including the ones we immediately need for ourselves, involve a complex historical deposit, and we will not understand them unless we grasp something of that deposit, of what the idea of freedom, in these various connections, has become. This contingent historical deposit,

An earlier version of this paper was given as the Dewey Lecture at the University of Chi-cago Law School, April 2001.

which makes freedom what it now is, cannot be contained in or antici-
pated by anything that could be called a definition. It is the same here as
it is with other values: philosophy, or as we might say a priori anthropology, can construct a core or skeleton or basic structure for the value, but
both what it has variously become, and what we now need it to be, must
be a function of actual history. In the light of this, we can say that our
aim is not to define but to construct a conception of freedom.

I shall not attempt a general account of what might count as constructing one or another conception of freedom. One might say that the
notion of construction applies at different levels. We need to construct a
value of freedom specifically for us; and we need a more generic construction or plan of freedom which helps us to place other conceptions of it in
a philosophical and historical space—which shows us, one might say, how
other specific conceptions might be constructed in their own right. Some
of the questions raised by these requirements would simply be a matter
of terminology, of how we might use the term 'construction.' But there is
a more significant consideration which links these two levels. The conception of freedom we need for ourselves is both historically self-conscious
and suitable to a modern society—and those two features are of course
related to one another. Because of this, our own specific and active conception of freedom, the one we need for our practical purposes, will contain
implicitly the materials for a reflective understanding of the more general
possibilities of construction.

However, it is just as important that the disputes that have circled
around the various definitions and concepts of liberty do not just represent a set of verbal misunderstandings. They have been disagreements
about *something*. There is even a sense in which they have been disagreements about some one thing. There must be a core, or a primitive conception, perhaps some universal or widely spread human experience, to
which these various conceptions relate. This does not provide, as it were,
the ultimate definition. Indeed, this core or primitive item, I am going to
suggest, is certainly not a political value, and perhaps not a value at all.
But it can, and must, explain how these various accounts of the value of
freedom are elaborations of the same thing, that these various interpretations are not just talking past each other.

There is another consideration which the familiar philosophical disputes and attempts at definition indeed take for granted, but they do not
give the right weight to it. In the sense that concerns these discussions,
freedom is a *political* value. (They are not addressing, for instance, metaphysical questions about the freedom of the will.) I am going to suggest
that this point itself, when it is properly understood, has a very significant
effect on the kind of construction we should be trying to achieve. In particular, we must take seriously the point that because it is a political value,

the most important disagreements that surround it are political disagreements. What kinds or registers of politics are involved, what the relevant understanding of politics will be, will depend on which disagreements are at issue—those within our own society, for instance, or those with other societies. But our overall construction of freedom as a political value must allow the fact that it *is* a political value to be central and intelligible.

I am certainly not going to offer a definition or any general characterization of the political. That would once again be impossible. But it may be helpful to mention now four things I believe to be true about the political, which will shape the discussion and affect my overall construction of freedom as a political value.

a. First, a point about philosophy: political philosophy is not just applied moral philosophy, which is what in our culture it is often taken to be.[1] Nor is it just a branch of legal philosophy, a point that will concern us later. In particular, political philosophy must use distinctively political concepts, such as power, and its normative relative, legitimation.

b. The idea of the political is to an important degree focused in the idea of political disagreement; and political disagreement is significantly different from moral disagreement. Moral disagreement is characterized by a class of considerations, by the kinds of reasons that are brought to bear on a decision. Political disagreement is identified by a field of application—eventually, about what should be done under political authority, in particular through the deployment of state power. The reasons that go into political decisions and arguments that bear on them may be of very various kinds. Because of this, political disagreement is not merely moral disagreement, and it need not necessarily involve it, though it may do so; equally, it need not necessarily be a disagreement simply of interests, though of course it may be.

c. Possible political disagreements include disagreements about the interpretation of political values, such as freedom, equality, or justice. These disagreements may involve many different kinds of understanding and political traditions; they can tap into various areas of what I called the historical deposit. It follows that the relation of these values to each other cannot be established on the model of interpreting a constitution, where questions typically take the form of determining *what counts as*, say, lim-

---

[1] John Rawls has said in *Political Liberalism* (New York: Columbia University Press, 1993), p. xvi, "In *[A] Theory [of Justice]* a moral conception of justice general in scope is not distinguished from a strictly political theory of justice," and the aim of the later book is to give such a political theory. But the later account still represents the political conception as itself a moral conception, although one directed to a special subject matter (p. 11). It is significant how far moral conceptions still structure the theory: the solution to the central problem of the stability of a just society, for instance, is worked out in terms of the moral powers of its citizens.

iting the freedom of speech. Of course, there is such an activity, and it plays an important part in some cultures, such as that of the United States. But even in those cases, it would be a mistake to equate political thought about questions of principle with thought about actual or ideal constitutional interpretation.[2] We and our political opponents—even our opponents in one polity, let alone those in others—are not just trying to read one text. This will be an important point in what follows.

d. The last of these preliminary signals is provided by that word "opponents." Carl Schmitt famously said that the fundamental political relation was that of friend and enemy.[3] This is an ambiguous remark, and it can take on a rather sinister tone granted the history of Schmitt's own relations to the Weimar Republic and eventually to the Third Reich. But it is basically true in at least this sense, that political difference is of the essence of politics, and political difference is a relation of political opposition, rather than, in itself, a relation of intellectual or interpretative disagreement. Many things can be covered by the idea of "opposition" itself. But they all bring with them the question of how we understand our opponents, how far our opposition is a matter of interests, how far a matter of principle, what sentiments are engaged, why we and they feel so strongly about it if we do, and in what ways we each differently tap into the historical deposit. We may for various reasons think that our opponents are, among other things, in intellectual error, but the relations of political opposition cannot simply be understood in terms of intellectual error. Our construction of freedom as a political value must make sense of the fact that disagreements involving that value are typically matters of political opposition, and that this carries substantial implications about the ways in which we should regard the disagreement, and regard our opponents themselves.

II. Primitive Freedom

Some of the arguments I shall consider are, inevitably, very familiar. My excuse for putting on parade some of the usual suspects from Political Philosophy 101 is rather like that which Descartes offered when he excused himself for "warming up the stale cabbage" of ancient skeptical

---

[2] The somewhat Manichean distinction between "principle" and "policy," where the latter is understood in consequentialist terms, is sometimes understood as roughly parallel to that in the United States between the Supreme Court and the Congress. To the extremely limited extent that this is true, it can be regarded as a special product of history as well as something of a misfortune.

[3] Carl Schmitt, *Das Begriff des Politischen* translated as *The Concept of the Political* (Chicago: University of Chicago Press, 1996).

arguments.[4] He admitted that the materials were very familiar, but he thought that it made all the difference what you wanted to do with them. They had to serve a particular method, and he wanted to illustrate that method. More modestly, my aim is the same: the usual suspects have to be put to work, but on a rather different task.

Mill, in Chapter 5 of *On Liberty*, says, informally enough: "liberty consists in doing what one desires." He cannot quite mean this: he must at any rate mean the capacity to do what one desires (you are not unfree if you simply choose not to do something you desire). Amended in this way, Mill agrees with Locke: "Liberty, 'tis plain, consists in a power to do or not to do; to do or forbear doing as we will. This cannot be denied."[5]

This is an idea of liberty as ability or capacity. It has an obvious disadvantage: we already have a concept of ability or capacity, and on this showing 'liberty' or 'freedom' turns out boringly just to be other names for it. More importantly, it misses the point of why we want these terms in the first place. That point is registered for the first time when we add to this kind of account a further condition, which concerns the kind of obstacle that is stopping us from doing something we want to do. We say, more narrowly, that we are unfree if our inability is the product, specifically, of coercion, where that is taken, at least in the central cases, to mean—using the term 'coercion' in a broad sense—the intentional obstructive activities of other people. This is incorporated in Isaiah Berlin's famous account of "negative" liberty, and of course, as he noted, it goes back a long way.[6] Berlin quotes, for one, Helvétius: "The free man is the man who is not in irons, nor imprisoned in a gaol, nor terrorized like a slave by the fear of punishment . . . it is not lack of freedom, not to fly like an eagle or swim like a whale." Though I shall be concerned with what Berlin called "negative freedom," I shall not use that term nor discuss the distinction between "negative" and "positive" freedom itself. (It is misleading in several respects, particularly if it is identified, as it is sometimes by Berlin, with a distinction between "freedom from" and "freedom to".)[7] The simple idea of being unobstructed in doing what you want by some form of humanly imposed coercion, I shall call "primitive freedom."

[4] Reply to the Second Set of Objections to the *Meditations: The Philosophical Writings of Descartes*, vol. 2, translated by John Cottingham (Cambridge: Cambridge University Press, 1984), p. 94.

[5] John Locke, *Essay on Human Understanding*, ii.1.56.

[6] Isaiah Berlin, "Two Concepts of Liberty" (1958), reprinted in *Four Essays on Liberty* (Oxford: Oxford University Press, 1969).

[7] On the distinction between negative and positive freedom, see Gerald C. MacCallum, Jr., "Negative and Positive Freedom," *Philosophical Review* 76 (1967); John Rawls, *A Theory of Justice* (Oxford: Clarendon Press, 1972), sec. 32.

The range of obstacles, those identified with "coercion," can itself be interpreted more or less broadly. Some candidates, ordered roughly from the obvious and agreed to the more disputable, are:

(a) Prevention by force (Helvétius's irons and gaol);
(b) Threats of force, penalties, social rejection, and so forth (Helvétius's fear of punishment);[8]
(c) Competition in (something like) a zero-sum game, where one competitor sets out to stop another reaching his goal;
(d) By-products of another enterprise, not aimed at the agent;
(e) By-products of an arrangement which structurally disadvantages (those in the position of) the agent.

Some of these variations will concern us later. There is an obvious division in the list, between cases in which an agent's activities are deliberately directed against another agent's capacity to do something, and those in which they merely bring about that the agent loses that capacity. There is a further extension beyond this, where what is in question is someone's omission or failure to remove an obstacle to the other agent's capacity. However, this requires more background, in particular the political framework at which we shall eventually arrive, to make it reasonable to say that the person in question *has* "failed" or "omitted" to do something about this obstacle—that is to say, that this person should do something about it. The more it can be said that there is a person or agency in this position, the wider the range of complaints in freedom may be. However, we should not conclude from this that we should drop the reference to coercive or limiting action altogether and revert to the conception of freedom as simply power or capacity.[9] We shall come back shortly to the basic question of why this restriction to obstacles that are intended by other agents, or created by them, or at the very least not removed by them, should be so significant.

III. Freedom as a Ratio Concept

First, however, there is a different point to be made about primitive freedom. Primitive freedom is a ratio concept: it is a matter of the ratio between

---

[8] Hobbes famously argued that such things do not reduce freedom, but merely raise the cost of a particular course of action. Although it suited Hobbes's purpose to treat this as a consideration relevant to the theory of political freedom, it is better understood in the context of an account of voluntary action: the fact that an action is coerced in this sense does not mean, standardly, that it fails to be a fully intentional action.

[9] As is argued by Raymond Geuss in *History and Illusion in Politics* (Cambridge: Cambridge University Press, 2001), pp. 96–98.

what people desire to do and what they are prevented by others from doing. This implies that there are two ways to increase people's freedom. I may remove the forces or obstacles that prevent them from satisfying their desires. But equally I may bring it about that they do not have desires that cannot be satisfied. This leads to a paradox. Suppose, implausibly and for the sake of argument, that there were a body of entirely contented slaves. They are not physically abused, and they do not want to do any of the things their slavery prevents them from doing. Under this concept of freedom, they are free. If reformers appear and tell them what they are missing and make them for the first time discontented, it might even be said that it is the reformers who have taken away their freedom. A concept of freedom that leads to this cannot be adequate.

One reaction to this is to say that freedom should be measured not in terms of what people actually desire, but in terms of what they should reasonably, properly, or appropriately desire. This idea can take various forms. It can also be applied not just to a deficit of appropriate desire, as in the case of the slaves, but to an excess of inappropriate desire, as indeed it has been by moralists in the Stoic tradition. The construction of freedom as a political value should certainly leave room for arguments of this form: besides the familiar answer to a complaint in freedom, that the constraint on desire is necessary (for instance in the interests of others), there is a possible answer in some cases that the desire is unreasonable and the agent would be better off without it. In particular, he would be more free. But as a general principle of argument, this runs the risk of heading in the direction of what Berlin called "positive freedom": at the limit, the argument will be heard that coercive force can be justified to prevent the formation of inappropriate desires or to encourage the formation of appropriate ones, so that people, as Rousseau put it, can be forced to be free. That notorious phrase has rightly been seen as paradoxical.[10] What is true, though, is that this kind of idea is not simply an arbitrary appropriation of the word "freedom"—it is rooted in certain features of the concept, although it develops them in an irresponsible way.[11]

There is another way of dealing with the ratio paradox, which appeals not to a normatively approved list of desires, but rather to some special explanations of why people do not have certain desires they might be expected to have. So in the slave case, the absence of a desire for freedom

[10] Quentin Skinner ("The Paradoxes of Political Liberty," in S. M. McMurrin, ed., *Tanner Lectures on Human Values* VII [Salt Lake City: University of Utah Press, 1986]) points out that this is not a paradox in the context of positive liberty theory. Indeed. But since it is a paradox, that is a problem for the theory.

[11] More irresponsibly than the tradition of republican liberty, which, as Skinner has shown ("The Paradoxes of Political Liberty"), is something different. It is not surprising, however, that it should be suspect for some of the same reasons: see note 18.

may be diagnosed as itself a product of coercion: it is precisely because of the way in which they are treated, prevented from hearing of other options and so on, that the state of their desires is as it is. The idea of this is the same as that employed in the Critical Theory test for beliefs which supposedly legitimate some prima facie oppressive institution: whether the belief is the product of the coercion which it supposedly helps to legitimate. The principle of these tests seems entirely sound and to flow naturally from the structure of the idea of coercion; the problem with them is of course going to lie in the prospects of making good an interpretation in these terms in any given case. We shall come back to the happy slaves later, and try to fix rather more definitely where the Critical Theory test fits into the construction of liberty.

IV. WHY COERCION?

Why should we pick on, specifically, primitive freedom, with its concentration on human sources of constraint, as the starting point? The answer is that primitive freedom is, as we might put it, a "proto-political" concept. This does not merely mean that if we are interested in freedom as a political value (as we are), this is the place to start. It means something stronger: that this is the place to start because it involves a quite basic human phenomenon, and that phenomenon already points in the direction of politics.

In a frequently quoted remark, Heracleitus said, "They would not have known the name of justice, if it had not been for these things," and it is virtually certain that "these things" are disputes, quarrels, and conflict.[12] Justice, hence an authoritative source of justice, hence an empowered enforcer of justice, is needed to impose solutions on what would otherwise be unbounded conflicts of interest. Similarly, the restriction of our activities by the intentional activities of others, as contrasted with the ubiquitous limitations we face in nature, can give rise to a quite specific reaction, resentment; and if resentment is not to express itself in more conflict, noncooperation, and dissolution of social relations, an authoritative determination is needed of whose activities should have priority (needless to say, that determination itself may well use concepts of justice). In an appropriate context, resentment can be directed to inaction, to a refusal to remove some obstacle if it can be claimed that it is the other party's business to remove it. But it cannot extend to what are recognized as blankly the obstacles of nature. Rousseau's distinction between being confined in

---

[12] Fragment B23, in Herman Diels and Walther Kranz, *Die Fragmente der Vorsokratiker*, 6th ed. (Berlin: Weidmann, 1951–52).

one's house by a snowstorm and being locked in it by someone else remains in place.[13]

But now there is a further development peculiarly connected with freedom. As soon as the authoritative source is indeed empowered and deploys coercion to enforce its rulings, that coercion itself can give rise to resentment. Questions arise of how that power is being used, questions that demand legitimating accounts. Those questions are likely to become more pressing, the closer the situation comes to that in which the authority uniquely commands the means of some kinds of coercion (such as (A) above, and to some extent (B))—that is to say, the closer it comes to the ideal type of there being a state. To various degrees in different societies, these questions will be the subject of discussion. The political, in some of its many forms, now exists.

V. Towards Liberty

We do not yet have freedom as a political value: a political value which from now on, making a distinction I have not used up to now, I shall call liberty.

Primitive freedom is not itself that political value.[14] We can see this by considering an idea which arises as soon as we have the conditions of the political, that is to say, an authority, together with appeals to that authority. This is the idea of a *claim in liberty.* The following points are obvious:

(a) No one can intelligibly make a claim against others simply on the ground that the activities of those others restrict his primitive freedom, or that the extension of his primitive freedom requires action by them. At best, that is the start of a quarrel, not a claim to its solution.

(b) Similarly, no sane person can expect that his primitive freedom merely as such should be protected.

(c) Equally, suppose that someone uses the notion of a right: no sane person can think that he has a right against others to what is demanded by his primitive freedom as such (i.e., to anything he happens to want).

(d) A similar point can be made in terms of the good: no one can intelligibly think that it is good (period, as opposed to good for him) that his primitive freedom should be unlimited.

[13] Geuss (*History and Illusion in Politics*) refers to this remark, pp. 104, 108–9, but he does not discuss it in relation to the argument mentioned above at note 9.

[14] The following arguments suggest that it is not a value of any kind, but I shall not take up that question here.

The effect of these points is that the resolution of questions of how far a person's freedom should be protected or extended, how far it is good that it should be, how far he has a right that it should be, requires some degree of impartiality (a general point of view, in Hume's phrase) which is not contained in the idea of an individual's primitive freedom as such.

The importance of these points has been emphasized by Ronald Dworkin.[15] However, he assumes that a claim in liberty must be a claim to a specific kind of right to do the thing in question, such as a right of free speech. He concludes from this that there can be no conflicts between liberty, properly understood, and any rightful claim. For suppose some other value, such as equality or more generally justice, when properly interpreted, requires that I not do a certain thing. Then I have no right to do that thing. So I cannot correctly make a claim in liberty to do it, and so, if I am prevented from doing it, this cannot be a restriction on my liberty (though it is of course a restriction of primitive freedom).

It cannot be necessary that this conclusion should follow from the understanding of liberty. Indeed, in my view, it is necessary that it should not follow. We are constructing liberty as a political value, which means among other things that we can make sense of its role in political argument and political conflict, and generally of the experience of life under a political order. It is one datum of that experience that people can even recognize a restriction as rightful under some political value such as equality or justice, and nevertheless regard it as a restriction on liberty. The notion of a cost in liberty is at least as well entrenched in historical and contemporary experience as that of a rightful claim in liberty.

This notion of a cost in liberty can apply, I just suggested, even to people who agree with some restrictive measure, introduced for instance in the interests of equality—they can still regard it as a restriction on liberty, though a justified one. Dworkin's view cannot make sense of the attitude of such people: on his view, they are merely confused. But the point about a cost in liberty applies even more significantly to those who do not agree that the cost is necessary. The state enacts, by quite proper process, some measure in the name of equality, say, which restricts the activities of some people. Those people oppose it, and let us suppose that they oppose it on principle: they do not accept the ideal of equality, or this application of it, or this way of going about it. They certainly regard the measure as a

---

[15] Ronald Dworkin, *Sovereign Virtue* (Cambridge, Mass.: Harvard University Press, 2000), ch. 3. It is fair to say that Dworkin's disinclination to accept conflicts between liberty and equality depends as much on his account of equality as on his account of liberty. I am grateful to Dworkin for many discussions of this subject, which have done much to shape the present discussion.

restriction on their liberty. Dworkin's view can in its own terms give a coherent account of this reaction (they do not think the measure is rightful), but it now raises a different question: suppose we are supporters of the measure, what attitude should we take towards the people who have this reaction, our political opponents? Since we think that they are wrong in opposing the measure, specifically in denying that the measure is justified in the name of equality, we must suppose, on Dworkin's view, that they are wrong in thinking that their liberty is being restricted. They are coerced by the state, they resent it, they vividly think that their liberty is curtailed. Dworkin patiently explains to them that they are simply wrong in thinking this; they may think that there is a cost in liberty, their liberty, but there is not. This is exactly the attitude that Rousseau thought appropriate, and it seems to me just as objectionable now as it was with him.

We should take seriously the idea that if, under certain conditions, people think that there is a cost in liberty, then there is. Taking that idea seriously, I suggest, is a condition not only of taking seriously the idea of political opposition, but of taking our political opponents themselves seriously.

There is one class of complainants about costs in liberty whom, I think, we need not take seriously: those who complain that their liberty, or indeed their primitive freedom, is curtailed by the mere existence of a state. Certainly not their liberty: since liberty is freedom as a political value, no complaint is a complaint in liberty if it would apply to any political system or any state whatsoever, so the existence of the state is not itself an offense against or limitation on liberty (though some particular forms of the state may of course readily be so). Moreover, this is not simply a verbal point about the understanding of "liberty"; we need not agree, either, that the fact that a person is subject to a state is, in itself, a limitation on his primitive freedom. The reason for this is that the amount of freedom that a person would have without the state is entirely indeterminate or, at any rate, very small. Two conclusions follow about anarchism: from the point about liberty it follows that it is not a political position, and from the point about primitive freedom, that it is not interesting, and I happily accept both these conclusions.

VI. Beyond Claims in Liberty

The Rousseau outlook (as we might call it) fails to make sense of an entirely familiar reaction that is basic to politics and to the understanding of political opposition. For that reason, it does not encourage a helpful—one might say, healthy—relation to one's opponents. What we should take seriously are their reactions, or at least their deeper reactions, rather than the extent to which we are disposed to share or morally approve of their reactions, and this applies in different forms whether they are opponents outside our polity or opponents within it. There is a potentially instructional, potentially patronizing, element in the Rousseau outlook which, to take just the case of local opponents, is hostile to the relations of fellow citizenship which we must hope can co-exist with political opposition—so long at least as we believe that there should be one polity and political opposition has not irreparably divided it. Indeed, this moralized outlook in some of its more spectacular historical expressions, such as the Terror, has shown that it can destroy not just citizenship but citizens.

The philosophical fault at the heart of this outlook might be said to be this, that it bases the idea of liberty on that of a rightful claim in liberty. The notion of a claim in liberty, I have said, is useful in distinguishing liberty from primitive freedom in the first place. It can do this because any adequate idea of liberty must at any rate accommodate the idea of a claim in liberty, and the idea of primitive freedom, in itself, cannot do so at all. But the idea of a rightful claim in liberty implies a juridical conception, of an agreed authority which can rightfully grant or refuse such a claim, and political opponents do not necessarily understand their situation in these terms. As I put it earlier, they are not all interpreting the same text.

In the case of opponents in different political systems, they may not agree on terms in which such an authority, if they imagined it to exist, might legitimate its decisions to them. Between opponents who share a polity and neither of whom wants to destroy it, they will agree on an authority or process which decides *what will happen*, but this is not at all equivalent to the authority's deciding that one or another claim in liberty is rightful. The reason for this lies in a characteristic of the political that I mentioned before, that political disagreements are not identified through the kinds of reasons that are deployed in them. The reasons for which an agreed political authority decides what will happen are various, and the decision in various ways may affect people's liberty, but the decision is not itself an announcement of what is a rightful claim in liberty.

In the very special case of a polity that has an institution of judicial review, executive and legislative decisions can be checked against claims in liberty. In such a state, some political decisions, in the widest sense, are judicial ones: i.e., the decision which decides what will happen is made for judicial reasons. (This is not the same as the familiar charge, in criticism of such an institution or of its operation, that some of these judicial decisions are, in a narrower sense, political ones.) But even here the sense that one's liberty is restricted by a decision cannot be identified with the thought that the court, if it acted rightly, would grant or would have granted or indeed should have granted one's claim in liberty. One may agree that the court, if it was doing its job properly, would not have granted such a claim, but one can still feel that the decision restricts or even violates one's liberty. First, the court itself may accept that its decision, though rightful, involves a cost in liberty.[16] A more general reason, however, is that judicial reasons, the kinds of reason that a constitutional court, however inventive, must attend to, are only one kind of reason. (Even those such as Dworkin who think that judicial review should include explicit and wide-ranging moral reasons accept that since these are decisions within a given legal system, they are bound by other constraints, such as *stare decisis*.) So the person who feels his liberty injured may feel this in virtue of other reasons, indeed other reasons of principle, which he does not suppose would vindicate a claim of right in the judicial forum. If he is angry at the outcome, then the focus of his anger might be this, that things are such that the final court of appeal must rightfully decide against him, and this thought might survive the understanding that given the legal history and the court's situation there was no realistic alternative to things being this way.

The thought that an action, say a political decision, involves a cost in one's liberty does not necessarily involve the thought that one would have a rightful claim in liberty before some specified or indeed unspecified authority. So what does go into the idea of a cost in liberty? We should recall that we are trying to construct this idea as part of constructing an idea of liberty itself which will serve our needs. The construction started from certain experiences associated with perceived limitations on primitive freedom. We should turn back to that again, and approach the construction of the idea of a cost in liberty by considering what it is to feel that something involves a cost in one's liberty.

VII. Resentment and Other Such Reactions

When I considered in the first place the transition from primitive freedom to liberty, I said that the reaction to coercion in the most elementary case was resentment. But the experience of feeling that one's liberty is being restricted need not necessarily take the form of resentment. How far it can be expected to do so is not an easy question to pursue, because resentment so readily merges into other negative feelings, such as anger and dislike, not just for conceptual but also for various familiar psychological reasons. In relation to freedom, the primitive and purest case of resent-

---

[16] The U.S. Supreme Court itself implicitly accepts this when it engages in "balancing." An illustration is the "undue burden" test for the constitutionality of regulations on abortion: *Planned Parenthood v. Casey*, 505 US 833 (1992). (I am indebted here and elsewhere to Robert Post.)

ment is perhaps that in which another person acts manifestly and effectively in a way that prevents me from doing what I want, and does so with that intention, and I think, moreover, that there is nothing to be said at all in favor of his doing so from any point of view except his. There are of course many cases of resentment in which this strongest condition is not satisfied. I may think, for instance, that the action was in my long-term interests, even that it was done with that intention, and still I may resent it. (Of course there may be a problem in such a case of sorting out what exactly it is that I resent—I may just resent, for instance, the fact that he took for granted his own ideas about my interests.)

It is usually said that the particular reaction of resentment is tied to the idea of the other person's action being not rightful. If we accept this idea, and also identify as (necessarily) resentment the feelings that go with a sense of a restriction on one's liberty, we shall be back on the road to Rousseau's outlook. But I think that we should loosen both these connections. Resentment is not so closely tied to the idea of right,[17] and a sense of coercion or restricted liberty can be connected to reactions that range more widely than resentment in the strictest sense. A helpful consideration here is the extent to which the person whose liberty is in question is *identified* with the actions that might be felt to restrict or violate that liberty. This idea helps us to explain the case of the citizen who thinks that a certain political decision is both procedurally correct and right in principle, but nevertheless experiences its consequences for himself as a cost in liberty. The reason that this is possible is that his sense of himself is not entirely that of a person identified with the state's decisions, however rightful. Rousseau of course wanted each person in a virtuous republic to be identified totally with himself or herself as citizen, but it is inevitable and appropriate and an entirely good thing that on any conception of a modern society—and I suspect also, on a realistic conception of any society whatsoever—this is not going to be so.[18]

Someone who disapproves of a measure in principle but not on procedural grounds is less identified with it than someone who approves of it

---

[17] The idea that resentment is grounded in thoughts about right is encouraged by the familiar phenomenon of back-formation, in which someone who is merely disadvantaged by an action projects on it the idea that it is not rightful. But then the idea of right must be salient in those particular cases, precisely because the reaction is identified as a moralistic rationalization. We can recognize resentment in less moralized circumstances: for instance, where A *bears a grudge* against B because B beat him (fairly) in a contest.

[18] Here Rousseau's outlook coincides with the tradition of republican virtue (see note 11 above). The idea that in a virtuous ancient republic the constraint to engage in public service did not involve a cost in liberty, if it implies anything about citizens' actual reactions, should surely be treated with some skepticism. If it says, rather, that because an ideally rational

in both these respects. Someone who finds it both procedurally and in principle objectionable is even less identified with it, and one who thinks that all the procedures are a sham is less identified still. At the end of this line, when the action that constrains someone is experienced as nothing but coercion, sheer force in the interests of others, the lack of identification is total, and this certainly is resentment. But right from the beginning of this progression there is room for the idea that the action, whatever there is to be said for it, is a limitation of someone's liberty, to the extent that he identifies with the desires and projects which this action will frustrate.

It is not a necessary condition of there being a cost in someone's liberty or a restriction of it that he has such experiences of resentment, frustration, or whatever. This takes us back to a point we noticed earlier in this construction, in the example of the happy slaves. We deplore their lack of liberty; they—we are fancifully supposing—do not. But if they do not, is there anything, on the present line, on which we can build our complaint? I suggested earlier that there is, in what I called the Critical Theory principle. The slaves are subject to a regime which (simply as a matter of fact) would pursue much the same objectives whatever they desired. We are supposing that they do not experience any frustration, although they are not allowed to satisfy some desires that human beings in general might be expected to have (e.g., they cannot marry or travel or stop work). In actual fact, of course, it is very unlikely that they will not feel frustrated in these respects, which is what makes this a rather objectionable fantasy, but suppose it to be so. In addition, they do not have certain other desires or aspirations which others have *in those historical circumstances*, such as a desire for political representation. In both respects, the state of their desires is identifiably a product of that regime, a regime, moreover, which would not be responsive even if they had the desires in question. In those circumstances, the absence of the desires does not refute the complaint in liberty, once it is made; if anything, it gives it extra force. It is the Critical Theory principle that explains, I think, why a complaint in liberty is not turned away in such a situation, and hence why the presence of frustrated desire is not a necessary condition of a cost in liberty.[19]

---

citizen would not react in that way, those reactions do not count, republican liberty will certainly court many of the same dangers as "positive liberty."

[19] It is not suggested that this is a sufficient account of a Critical Theory test. Obviously, beliefs and states of desire can be quite properly the causal product of regimes to which people have been exposed or even subjected: educational regimes, for instance. Further questions are involved: partly, about the kinds of belief in question, and what they, or the presence or absence of certain desires, are supposed to justify; partly, about the attitude that the people would have to the beliefs or desires if they knew how they came about. I discuss

VIII. Liberty Now

Let us try to assemble some conditions on liberty. We may recall

(i) A practice is not a violation of liberty if it is necessarily involved in there being a state at all.

However,

(ii) The principle of (i) cannot be relativized to a particular state or polity, since particular states or polities can obviously be criticized for violations or undue restrictions of liberty. At the same time, there is limited interest in comparing all existing states to some ideal model of a state. In particular, what desires or frustrations people might have under increasingly counterfactual conditions is increasingly indeterminate. Utopian political discourse is of course possible and may have its uses, but it is at best obliquely related to arguments about the liberty we can hope to find in our world. This is not to say that Utopian discourses about liberty are analytically or definitionally incoherent. In terms of the broadest construction of liberty, we can find a place for some of them, if they are not otherwise too incoherent. But they, and the comparisons they invite with the actual, do not do much for the more specific construction of liberty as a value for us.

In pursuing that construction, it seems to me that we should restrict the Utopia factor by accepting in particular that

(iii) Modernity is a basic category of social and hence of political understanding, and so a politically useful construction of liberty for us should take the most general conditions of modernity as given. This was the lesson of Benjamin Constant's marvelous speech, given in 1819, *The Liberty of the Ancients compared with that of the Moderns*,[20] in which he pointed out that whatever the merits for an ancient republic of a concept of liberty linked to republican virtue, they were essentially limited to the conditions of an ancient republic, and only disaster could follow, as indeed it had followed in France, from trying to apply such an ideal to a modern commercial society.

---

some of the problems involved in *Truth and Truthfulness* (Princeton: Princeton University Press, 2002).

[20] See Benjamin Constant, *Political Writings*, ed. Biancamaria Fontana (Cambridge: Cambridge University Press, 1988), pp. 309 ff. Cf. in these connections "St Just's Illusion," in my *Making Sense of Humanity* (Cambridge: Cambridge University Press, 1995).

Of course there is room for much argument about what the conditions of modernity are, what forms a modern society can intelligibly take, and so on: but that is as it should be, for that is the substance of much significant political argument. But granted in a general sense the conditions of modernity as shaping the construction of our idea of liberty, there will be a variety of consequences. For instance, I mentioned earlier a range of things that can count as coercive restrictions on an agent's doing what he wants, intentional activities of others that can count as limiting freedom. In the context of modernity, it will be clear why in general factor (C) above, the effects of competition in something like a zero-sum game, will not count, because competition is integral to the social system.

This is not to deny that there can be political arguments to the effect that certain kinds of competition are so damaging to the general interest, and perhaps to the interests of losers, that they need to be controlled: it is merely that these are not per se arguments based on the losers' liberty. Rather similarly, factor (D) above—by-products of another enterprise not aimed at the person in question—do not presumptively count as limiting that person's liberty, though there are many special cases in which they do so. This is because they are a ubiquitous phenomenon essentially connected with the society's central activities. Factor (E), on the other hand, arrangements which structurally limit the opportunities of some class of citizens, are more likely to count, and complaints about power structures which have such effects are readily understood as complaints in liberty. This is because we have a better and typically modern understanding of such power structures, and, we hope, some achievable means of changing the situation.

Granted that a person's complaint that he has sustained a cost of liberty lies within such limits implicit in the conditions of modernity, however exactly we understand them; granted the wider condition (i), that the restriction is not one that would be necessary under any state; and granted of course that it is factually correct, that is to say that his desires really are frustrated or limited by the activities about which he is complaining; then we should accept the idea that emerged from the earlier arguments, that if someone feels that some action or arrangement imposes on him a cost in liberty, then it does indeed do so. This does not mean, of course, that the action or arrangement should not be allowed: the cost in his liberty is very often outweighed by the values served by the action or arrangement. Moreover, it need not justify or call for any compensation. He need not have a claim in liberty in any court. But a cost in liberty is still what it is, even if he quite properly has to carry the cost himself.

A construction of liberty on these lines might be thought to spread the idea of a cost in liberty too wide. It means that, within certain limits, anyone with a grievance or who is frustrated by others' actions can appropriately complain about restrictions on his liberty. If "appropriately" means that it is semantically, conceptually, indeed psychologically, intelligible that he should do so, that is right. If it means that it is necessarily useful, helpful, to be taken seriously as a contribution to political debate, and not a waste of everyone's time, it is not right. The point is that these latter considerations are in the broadest sense political considerations, and that is the point of the construction.

The conditions I have suggested for complaints of the loss of liberty might be expressed in terms of "realism." A form of liberty that could not be offered by any state is an entirely unrealistic basis of objection, and the limitation to the conditions of modernity implies a further step towards a realistic political position or claim, which can be taken seriously. It may be said that there are two different questions here, which this approach runs together: whether it is true that someone has sustained a cost in liberty and whether it is sensible, useful, reasonable, or sane to complain about it. These ideas are indeed not the same. It is not a reason for supposing that there has been no loss of liberty, that it is not politically prudent to say that there has been: the loss of liberty lies in the good sense attached to the resentment, not in the good sense or otherwise of expressing it. However, what it is reasonable to count as something that it is sensible for someone to resent is a matter of one's overall view of the political world, and so, while the two ideas are certainly distinct, there is an extensive area in which they overlap, and a properly political conception of liberty acknowledges this. Resentment about the loss of liberty, like resentment about anything else, implies the thought of an alternative world in which that loss does not occur, and just because liberty is a political value, the distance of that possible world from the actual world must be measured in terms of political considerations of relevance and practical intelligibility. The world of the anarchists is too far away—too far away from anything—to ground complaints in liberty at all. Many complaints that fly in the face of modernity equally do not even cross the threshold of offering a serious political consideration. It is also true, of course, that even if "Utopian politics" is a contradiction in terms, "Utopian political thought" is not, and someone may make a case for taking seriously complaints in liberty that would not get a hearing in everyday political activity. He may show that some dimension of resentment is more sensible than conventional opinion supposes; or he may, just as effectively or more so, claim that whether it is what people call "sensible" is not the point. The aim, he may rightly say, is to change the world, and his elevation of his or others' resentment into a complaint about liberty may indeed succeed in making it into a complaint about liberty.

What we should be arguing about with such a complainant, if it is worth arguing with him at all, is whether it is in the least sensible for him to expect that a desire of that kind should not be frustrated; whether his conception of a social world in which it would not be frustrated is not a fantasy, either in general or in relation to historical circumstances in which he necessarily finds himself; whether, on reflection, he does not identify more deeply with the considerations that justify the coercion than with his original desire. These are the materials of political persuasion, in the broadest sense, and this is what we should be engaged in. A major aim of constructing liberty in the way I have suggested is that it should leave space in which these arguments can take place.

There is a further and benevolent consequence. He may indeed persuade us our sense of what is "realistic" will change, and with it, the dimensions of liberty. But if, on the other hand, our persuasions succeed, he will cease to feel the frustration. His resentment will go away. He may come to identify fully with the grounds of coercion in such a case; he may cease to desire what he originally desired; in any case he will not care any more that he cannot have what he desires. If this happens, then, on the construction I am offering, there will be no frustrated desire (and not for reasons that fail the Critical Theory test); so his liberty will no longer be restricted, and there will no longer be a cost in liberty.

IX. THE VALUE OF LIBERTY

Someone may ask why liberty is a value at all. This might mean, why is liberty in any of the various constructions that have been given of it in different historical circumstances a value at all? Why should human beings in general be concerned with some value of that form? I do not know that I can answer that question, beyond suggesting a set of questions to put in its place: What view would one have to take of one's desires and projects and other values if there were never even a question of its being something to be resented and resisted if others aimed to frustrate them? What view would one have to take of those others, in particular of a political authority, for that question never to arise?

A better question might be: why is liberty the special value it is for us? Why does it play the particular role that it does in our political thought and aspirations? In particular, why is it so important? That question must be directed to liberty under the kind of construction that is appropriate to our circumstances, and one answer to it, an "internal" answer, will lie in inviting the questioner to think about liberty in terms of those circumstances and in relation to other political values and beliefs that belong to our world. We invite him to acknowledge who and where he is, and ask him what alternative he has to this structure of ideas and at what Utopian distance the alternative, and the political arrangements that might go with it, lie from the world in which we and he all live. We can argue about the merits of those other arrangements, and this will be, once more, a political argument, one that works with the materials which, in this condition, he and we can use.

This is fine, so far as it goes. Yet there is something unsatisfactory about saying just this much. On the one hand, we are insisting that if we are to think realistically about political values, we must do so, so to speak, from here. At the same time, indeed in making this very statement, we seem to acknowledge that "here" is just one place among others: that we can consider the modern condition, our condition, to some extent from the outside and compare it with others. If we can do that, then we should be able to say rather more than we have said about this modern construction of liberty, and its value, as compared with others. This touches on a familiar point which I mentioned very briefly before. One of the most prominent characteristics of modernity is its historical self-consciousness, and that carries with it certain demands on how we understand ourselves. What we have said to this questioner so far does not seem to do enough to meet those demands. Can we do any more?

Perhaps we can. In conclusion, I shall try to sketch in the barest outline some more that we might say. To do so, I must go back for a last time to primitive freedom and its being, as I put it, a "proto-political" concept. I argued that primitive freedom is not itself a political value (and perhaps not a value of any kind). This is because the notion of a political value implies an impartial standpoint to determine the priority of different agents' desires, a standpoint which is not given simply by the idea of each person's desires. That standpoint must be that of an authority with a power to enforce. Once we have such an authority, I said, the question of freedom and coercion arises again, now in relation to the coercion which the authority exerts. If this is not to be merely another contribution to conflict, the authority must *have* authority; and this means that in some terms or other, it must be acknowledged as legitimate. Let us now say there is need for legitimate government (where this means that it is counted or recognized as legitimate in a given society, not that we would necessarily accept it by our standards of legitimacy).

I take it that the following is a universal truth: legitimate government is not just coercive power. It is true, moreover, in the sense of "legitimacy" I am using, in which the idea is relativized to local understandings: everyone everywhere where there is such a thing as government recognizes some distinction between legitimate government and a mere conspiracy of effective coercion, even if many people have lived and do live under such a conspiracy or in a state which is not much more. For there to be legitimate government, there must be a legitimation story, which explains why state power can be used to coerce some people rather than others and to allow people to restrict other people's freedom in some ways rather than others. Moreover, this story is supposed to legitimate the arrangements to *each* citizen, that is to say, to each person from whom the state expects allegiance; though there may be other people within the state, slaves or captives, who are nakedly the objects of coercion and for whom there is no such legitimation story.[21]

The fact that everywhere there is a legitimation story to be told to each citizen does not imply, of course, that in terms of the story there is some presumption that citizens should be treated equally. Most such stories in the past have delivered various forms of inequality and hierarchy, with corresponding constraints on the activities of some citizens in relation to other citizens and to the state itself. The fact that there is a legitimation story to be told is indeed enough to distinguish these societies as examples of legitimate government, in contrast to mere successful examples of banditry. The significant point for us, however, and for our construction of liberty and the value we attach to it, is that we do not believe these stories, and it is a notable feature of modernity that we do not. I do not mean merely that we do not accept the stories as legitimating stories for us. I mean that to a considerable degree we regard the content of these stories, in particular those that involve religious or other transcendental justifications, as simply untrue. It follows—or would follow with much further argument—that in telling our own legitimation story we start, in a sense, with less. In interpreting and distributing liberty we allow each citizen a stronger presumption in favor of what he or she certainly wants, to carry out his or her own desires.

Of course the presumptions in favor of equal and extensive liberty in modern societies are intimately connected with the central activities of those societies, in particular their forms of economic organization. This is an historical platitude, but by itself it will not help our questioner who wanted to hear more of why we value liberty as we do. Something on the lines of the absurdly rough sketch I just outlined can perhaps give him more. The sketch indeed connects our construction of liberty, and the value we give it under that construction, with the condition of modernity, but it offers more than the consideration (which is in itself a perfectly sound consideration) that this is our condition. It connects our ideas of

---

[21] I have claimed in *Shame and Necessity* (Berkeley: University of California Press, 1993), ch. 5, that this was the situation with slavery in the ancient world, which was typically regarded as necessary rather than just: the Helots in Sparta were indeed explicitly understood to be enemies in captivity. The racist justifications of modern slavery were presumably meant in some sense to legitimate the institution; I am less clear how far they were meant to legitimate it to the slaves.

liberty with a universal truth, that everywhere legitimacy requires more than mere coercion, and it adds to this the conviction that under the conditions of modernity, whatever else may be worse, we at any rate have a better grasp on the truth. I do not mean on the truth about liberty—in relation to this questioner, that would be marching on the spot. Rather, we have a grasp on truths that destroy those fantasies that once provided the fabric of pre-modern legitimation stories.

If that account could be made good, it would yield the conclusion that modern societies, or some of them, are rightly more concerned with liberty and aim to deliver more of it than did earlier societies. Of course, the liberty they aim to deliver is understood or constructed in terms appropriate to modernity, but that does not make their promise merely circular or empty. It is backed by the idea that whatever else they may have taken away or made impossible, modern societies can offer and perhaps sustain a construction of liberty in which the constraints on it are fewer and, above all, more truthfully motivated than in most societies of the past.

EIGHT

The Idea of Equality

THE IDEA OF EQUALITY is used in political discussion both in statements of fact, or what purport to be statements of fact—that people *are* equal— and in statements of political principles or aims: that people *should be* equal, as at present they are not. The two can be, and often are, combined: the aim is then described as that of securing a state of affairs in which people are treated as the equal beings which they in fact already are, but are not already treated as being. In both these uses, the idea of equality notoriously encounters the same difficulty: that on one kind of interpretation the statements in which it figures are much too strong, and on another kind much too weak, and it is hard to find a satisfactory interpretation that lies between the two.[1]

To take first the supposed statement of fact: it has only too often been pointed out that to say that all people are equal in all those characteristics in respect of which it makes sense to say that people are equal or unequal, is a patent falsehood; and even if some more restricted selection is made of these characteristics, the statement does not look much better. Faced with this obvious objection, the defender of the claim is likely to offer a weaker interpretation. It is not, he may say, in their skill, intelligence, strength, or virtue that people are equal, but merely in their being people: it is their common humanity that constitutes their equality. On this interpretation, we should not seek for some special characteristics in respect of which all beings are equal, but merely remind ourselves that they are all human beings. But that if all that the statement does is to remind us that human beings are human beings, it does not do very much and in particular does less than its proponents in political argument have wanted it to do. What looked like paradox has turned into a platitude.

I shall suggest in a moment that even in this weak form the statement is not as vacuous as this objection makes it seem; but it must be admitted that when the statement of equality ceases to claim more than is warranted, it can rather rapidly reach the point where it claims less than is interesting. A similar discomfiture tends to overcome the practical maxim

---

[1] For an illuminating discussion of this and related questions, see Richard Wollheim and Isaiah Berlin, "Equality," *Proceedings of the Aristotelian Society* 56 (1956): 281–326 (reprinted in *Justice and Social Policy*, ed. Frederick A. Olafson [Englewood Cliffs, N.J.: Prentice-Hall, 1961]).

of equality. It cannot be the aim of this maxim that everyone should be treated alike in all circumstances, or even that they should be treated alike as much as possible. Granted that, however, there is no obvious stopping point before the interpretation which makes the maxim claim only that they should be treated alike in similar circumstances; and since "circumstances" here must clearly include reference to what people are, as well as to their purely external situations, this comes very much to saying that for every difference in the way people are treated, some general reason or principle of differentiation must be given. This may well be an important principle; some indeed have seen in it, or in something very like it, an essential element of morality itself.[2] But it can hardly be enough to constitute the principle that was advanced in the name of *equality*. It would be in accordance with this principle, for example, to treat blacks differently from others just because they were black, or women differently just because they were women, and this cannot accord with anyone's idea of equality.

In what follows I shall try to advance a number of considerations that can help to save the political notion of equality from these extremes of absurdity and of triviality. These considerations are in fact often employed in political argument, but are usually bundled together into an unanalyzed notion of equality in a manner confusing to the advocates, and encouraging to the enemies, of that ideal. These considerations will not enable us to define a distinct third interpretation of the statements which use the notion of equality; it is rather that they enable us, starting with the weak interpretations, to build up a position that in practice can have something of the solidity aspired to by the strong interpretations. In this discussion, it will not be necessary all the time to treat separately the supposedly factual application of the notion of equality, and its application in the maxim of action. Though it is sometimes important to distinguish them, and there are clear grounds for doing so, similar considerations often apply to both. The two go significantly together: on the one hand, the point of the supposedly factual assertion is to back up social ideals and programmes of political action; on the other hand—a rather less obvious point, perhaps—those political proposals have their force because they are regarded not as gratuitously egalitarian, aiming at equal treatment for reasons, for instance, of simplicity or tidiness, but as affirming an equality which is believed in some sense already to exist, and to be obscured or neglected by actual social arrangements.

---

[2] For instance, R. M. Hare: see his *The Language of Morals* (Oxford: Clarendon Press, 1952).

1. COMMON HUMANITY

The factual statement of men's equality was seen, when pressed, to retreat in the direction of merely asserting the equality of human beings as human beings, and this was thought to be trivial. It is certainly insufficient, but not, after all, trivial. The tautology is a useful one, serving as a reminder that those who belong anatomically to the species *homo sapiens*, and can speak a language, use tools, live in societies, can interbreed despite racial differences, and so forth, are also alike in certain other respects more likely to be forgotten. These respects are notably the capacity to feel pain, both from immediate physical causes and from various situations represented in perception and in thought; and the capacity to feel affection for others, and the consequences of this, connected with the frustration of this affection, loss of its objects, and the like. The assertion that people are alike in the possession of these characteristics is, while indisputable and (it may be) even necessarily true, not trivial. For it is certain that there are political and social arrangements that systematically neglect these characteristics in the case of some groups of people being fully aware of them in the case of others; that is to say, they treat certain people as though they did not possess these characteristics, and neglect moral claims that arise from these characteristics and which would be admitted to arise from them.

Here it may be objected that the mere fact that ruling groups in certain societies treat other groups in this way does not mean that they neglect or overlook the characteristics in question. They may recognize the presence of these characteristics in the worse-treated group but insist that in the case of that group, the characteristics do not give rise to any moral claim; the group being distinguished from other members of society in virtue of some further characteristic (for instance, by being black), this may be cited as the ground of treating them differently, whether they feel pain, affection, and so forth, or not.

This objection rests on the assumption, common to much moral philosophy that makes a sharp distinction between fact and value, that the question whether a certain consideration is relevant to a moral issue is an evaluative question: to state that a consideration is relevant or irrelevant to a certain moral question is, on this view, itself to commit oneself to a certain kind of moral principle or outlook. Thus, in the case under discussion, to say (as one would naturally say) that the fact that people are black is, by itself, quite irrelevant to the issue of how they should be treated in respect of, say, welfare, would, on this view, be to commit to oneself to a certain sort of moral principle. This view, taken generally, seems to me quite certainly false. The principle that people should be differentially treated in respect of welfare merely on grounds of their colour is not a special sort of moral principle, but (if anything) a purely arbitrary assertion of will, like that of some Caligulan ruler who decided to execute everyone whose name contained three *R*s.

This point is in fact conceded by those who practice such things as colour discrimination. Few can be found who will explain their practice merely by saying, "But they're black: and it is my moral principle to treat blacks differently from others." If any reasons are given at all, they will be reasons that seek to correlate the fact of blackness with certain other considerations which are at least candidates for relevance to the question of how a person should be treated: such as insensitivity, brute stupidity, and ineducable irresponsibility. Now these reasons are very often rationalizations, and the correlations claimed are either not really believed or quite irrationally believed by those who claim them. But this is a different point; the argument concerns what counts as a moral reason, and the rationalizer broadly agrees with others about what counts as such—the trouble with him is that his reasons are dictated by his policies, and not conversely. The Nazis' "anthropologists" who tried to construct theories of Aryanism were paying, in very poor coin, the homage of irrationality to reason.

The question of relevance in moral reasons will arise again, in a different connection, in this paper. For the moment its importance is that it gives a force to saying that those who neglect the moral claims of certain people that arise from their human capacity to feel pain, and so forth, are *overlooking* or *disregarding* those capacities; and are not just operating with a special moral principle, conceding the capacities to these people but denying the moral claim. Very often, indeed, they have just persuaded themselves that the people in question have those capacities in a lesser degree. Here it is certainly to the point to assert the apparent platitude that these human beings are also human.

I have discussed this point in connection with very obvious human characteristics of feeling pain and desiring affection. There are, however, other and less easily definable characteristics universal to humanity, which may all the more be neglected in political and social arrangements. For instance, there seems to be a characteristic which might be called "a desire for self-respect"; this phrase is perhaps not too happy, in suggesting a particular culturally limited, bourgeois value, but I mean by it a certain human desire to be identified with what one is doing, to be able to realize purposes of one's own, and not to be the instrument of another's will unless one has voluntarily accepted such a role. This is a very inadequate and in some ways rather empty specification of a human desire; to a better specification, both philosophical reflection and the evidences of psychology and anthropology would be relevant. Such investigations enable us to understand more deeply, in respect of the desire I have gestured toward and of similar characteristics, what it is to be human.

2. MORAL CAPACITIES

So far we have considered respects in which people can be counted as all alike, which respects are, in a sense, negative: they concern the capacity to suffer, and certain needs that people have, which involve them in moral relations as the recipients of certain kinds of treatment. It has certainly been a part, however, of the thought that people were equal, that there were more positive respects in which they were alike: that they were equal in certain things that they could do or achieve, as well as in things that they needed and could suffer. In respect of a whole range of abilities, from weight lifting to the calculus, the assertion is, as was noted at the beginning, not plausible, and has not often been supposed to be. It has been held, however, that there are certain other abilities, both less open to empirical test and more essential in moral connections, for which it is true that people are equal. These are certain sorts of moral ability or capacity, the capacity for virtue or achievement of the highest kind of moral worth.

The difficulty with this notion is that of identifying any purely moral capacities. Some human capacities are more relevant to the achievement of a virtuous life than others: intelligence, a capacity for sympathetic understanding, and a measure of resoluteness would generally be agreed to be so. But these capacities can all be displayed in non-moral connections as well, and in such connections would naturally be thought to differ from one person to another like other natural capacities. That this is the fact of the matter has been accepted by many thinkers, notably, for instance, by Aristotle. But against this acceptance, there is a powerful strain of thought that centres on a feeling of ultimate and outrageous absurdity in the idea that the achievement of the highest kind of moral worth should depend on natural capacities, unequally and fortuitously distributed as they are, and this feeling is backed up by the idea that these natural capacities cannot themselves be the bearers of the moral worth, since those who have them are as gifted for vice as for virtue.

This strain of thought has found many types of religious expression; but in philosophy it is to be found in its purest form in Kant. Kant's view not only carries to the limit the notion that moral worth cannot depend on contingencies, but also emphasizes, in its picture of the Kingdom of Ends, the idea of *respect* which is owed to each person as a rational moral agent—and, since people are equally such agents, is owed equally to all, unlike admiration and similar attitudes, which are commanded unequally by people in proportion to their unequal possession of different kinds of natural excellence. These ideas are intimately connected in Kant, and it is not possible to understand his moral theory unless as much weight is given to what he says about the Kingdom of Ends as is always given to what he says about duty.

The very considerable consistency of Kant's view is bought at what would generally be agreed to be a very high price. The detachment of moral worth from all contingencies is achieved only by making a person's characteristic as a moral or rational agent a transcendental characteristic; the capacity to will freely as a rational agent is not dependent on any empirical capacities and, in particular, is not dependent on empirical capacities which people may possess unequally, because, in the Kantian view, the capacity to be a rational agent is not itself an empirical capacity at all. Accordingly, the respect owed equally to each person as a member of the Kingdom of Ends is not owed to that person in respect of any empirical characteristics, but solely in respect of the transcendental characteristic of being a free and rational will. The ground of the respect owed to each person thus emerges in the Kantian theory as a kind of secular analogue of the Christian conception of the respect owed to everybody as equally children of God. Though secular, it is equally metaphysical: in neither case is it anything empirical *about* people that constitutes the ground of equal respect.

This transcendental, Kantian conception cannot provide any solid foundation for the notions of equality among people, or of equality of respect owed to them. Apart from the general difficulties of such transcendental conceptions, there is the obstinate fact that the concept of "moral agent," and the concepts allied to it such as that of responsibility, do and must have an empirical basis. It seems empty to say that all people are equal as moral agents, when the question, for instance, of people's responsibility for their actions is one to which empirical considerations are clearly relevant, and one which moreover receives answers in terms of different degrees of responsibility and different degrees of rational control over action. To hold people responsible for their actions is presumably the central case of treating them as moral agents, and if people are not treated equally as responsible, there is not much left to their equality as moral agents.

If, without its transcendental basis, there is not much left to people's equality as moral agents, is there anything left to the notion of the *respect* owed to everyone? This notion of "respect" is both complex and unclear, and I think it needs, and would repay, a good deal of investigation. Some content can, however, be attached to it, even if it is some way away from the ideas of moral agency. There certainly is a distinction, for instance, between regarding a person's life, actions, or character from an aesthetic or technical point of view, and regarding them from a point of view which is concerned primarily with what it is *for that person* to live that life and do those actions in that character. Thus from the technological point of view, a man who has spent his life in trying to make a certain machine which could not possibly work is merely a failed inventor, and in compiling a catalogue of those whose efforts have contributed to the sum of technical achievement, one must "write him off": the fact that he devoted himself to this useless task with constant effort, and so on, is merely irrelevant. But from a human point of view, it is clearly not irrelevant: we are concerned with him, not merely as "a failed inventor," but as a man who wanted to be a successful inventor. Again, in professional relations and the world of work, people operate, and their activities come up for criticism, under a variety of professional or technical titles, such as "plumber" or "junior executive." The technical or professional attitude is that which regards the person solely under that title, the human approach that which regards the person as *someone who has* that title (among others), willingly, unwillingly, through lack of alternatives, with pride, and so forth.

That people should be regarded from the human point of view, and not merely under these sorts of titles, is part of the content that might be attached to Kant's celebrated injunction "treat each person as an end in himself or herself, and never as a means only." But I do not think that this is all that should be seen in this injunction, or all that is concerned in the notion of "respect." What is involved in the examples just given could be explained by saying that each person is owed an effort at identification and should not be regarded as the surface to which a certain label can be applied; rather, one should try to see the world (including the label) from that person's point of view. This injunction will be based on the notion that people are conscious beings who necessarily have intentions and purposes and see what they are doing in a certain light. But there seem to be further injunctions connected with the Kantian maxim, and with the notion of "respect," that go beyond these considerations. There are forms of exploiting people or degrading them which are excluded by these notions, but which cannot be excluded merely by considering how the exploited or degraded people see the situation. For it is precisely a mark of extreme exploitation or degradation that those who suffer it do not see themselves differently from the way they are seen by the exploiters; either they do not see themselves as anything at all, or they acquiesce passively in the role for which they have been cast. Here we evidently need something more than the precept that one should respect and try to understand other people's consciousness of their own activities; it is also that one may not suppress or destroy that consciousness.

These are vague and inconclusive considerations, but we are dealing with a vague notion: one, however, that we possess and attach value to.

To try to put these matters properly in order would be itself to try to reach conclusions about several fundamental questions of moral philosophy. What we must ask here is what these ideas have to do with equality. We started with the equality of people as moral agents. This notion appeared unsatisfactory, for different reasons, in both an empirical and a transcendental interpretation. We then moved, via the idea of "respect," to the different notion of regarding people not merely under professional, social, or technical titles, but with consideration of their own views and purposes. This notion has at least this much to do with equality: that the titles which it urges us to look behind are the conspicuous bearers of social, political, and technical *inequality*, whether they refer to achievement (as in the example of the inventor), or to social roles (as in the example of work titles). It enjoins us not to let our fundamental attitudes to people be dictated by the criteria of technical success or social position, and not to take them at the value carried by these titles and by the structures in which these titles place them. This does not mean, of course, that the more fundamental view that should be taken is in the case of everyone the same: on the contrary. But it does mean that everyone is owed the effort of understanding, and that in achieving it, people should be abstracted from certain conspicuous structures of inequality in which we find them.

These injunctions are based on the proposition that people are beings who are necessarily to some extent conscious of themselves and of the world they live in. (I omit here, as throughout the discussion, the clinical cases of people who are mad or mentally defective, who always constitute special exceptions.) This proposition does not assert that people are equally conscious of themselves or their situation. It was precisely one element in the notion of exploitation considered above that such consciousness can be decreased by social action and the environment; we may add that it can similarly be increased. But people are at least potentially conscious, to an indeterminate degree, of their situation and of what I have called their "titles," are capable of reflectively standing back from the roles and positions in which they are cast; and this reflective consciousness may be enhanced or diminished by their social condition.

It is this last point that gives these considerations a particular relevance to the political aims of egalitarianism. The mere idea of regarding people from "the human point of view," while it has a good deal to do with politics, and a certain amount to do with equality, has nothing specially to do with political equality. One could, I think, accept this as an ideal, and yet favour, for instance, some kind of hierarchical society, so long as the hierarchy maintained itself without compulsion, and there was human understanding between the orders. In such a society, everyone would indeed have a very conspicuous title which related him or her to the social structure; but it might be that most people were aware of the human beings behind the titles and found each other for the most part content, or even proud, to have the titles that they had. I do not know whether anything like this has been true of historical hierarchical societies, but I can see no inconsistency in someone's espousing it as an ideal, as some (influenced in many cases by a sentimental picture of the Middle Ages) have done. Such a person would be one who accepted the notion of "the human view," the view of people as something more than their titles, as a valuable ideal, but rejected the ideals of political equality.

Once, however, one accepts the further notion that a person's consciousness of such things as his or her role in society is itself in some part the product of social arrangements, and that it can be increased, this ideal of a stable hierarchy must, I think, disappear. What keeps stable hierarchies together is the idea of necessity, that it is somehow foreordained or inevitable that there should be these orders, and this idea of necessity must be eventually undermined by the growth of people's reflective consciousness about their roles, still more when this is combined with the thought that what they and the others have always thought about their roles in the social system was the product of the social system itself.

Someone who admitted that people's consciousness of their roles was conditioned in this way might nevertheless believe in the hierarchical ideal and think that in order to preserve the society, the idea of the conditioning of consciousness should not get around to too many people, and that their consciousness about their roles should not increase too much. Such a view is really a very different thing from its naive predecessor. Someone who thinks this, no longer "immersed" in the system, is beginning to think in terms of compulsion, the deliberate *prevention* of the growth of consciousness, which is a poisonous element absent from the original ideal. Moreover this attitude toward the other people in the society must now contain an element of condescension or contempt, since their acceptance of what they suppose to be a necessity turns out to be delusion. This is alien to the spirit of human understanding on which the original ideal was based. The hierarchical idealist cannot escape the fact that certain things which can be done decently without self-consciousness can, with self-consciousness, be done only hypocritically. This is why even the rather hazy and very general notions that I have tried to bring together in this section contain some of the grounds of the ideal of political equality.

3. Equality in Unequal Circumstances

The notion of equality is invoked not only in connections where people are claimed in some sense all to be equal, but in connections where they are agreed to be unequal, and the question arises of the distribution of, or access to, certain goods to which their inequalities are relevant. It may be objected that the notion of equality is in fact misapplied in these connections, and that the appropriate ideas are those of fairness or justice, in the sense of what Aristotle called "distributive justice," where (as Aristotle argued) there is no question of regarding or treating everyone as equal, but solely a question of distributing certain goods in proportion to recognized inequalities. But there is some foothold for the notion of equality even in these cases. It is useful here to make a rough distinction between two different types of inequality, inequality of *need* and inequality of *merit*, with a corresponding distinction between goods—on the one hand, goods demanded by the need, and on the other, goods that can be earned by the merit. In the case of needs, such as the need for medical treatment of illness, it can be presumed for practical purposes that those who have the need actually desire the goods in question, and so the question can indeed be regarded as one of distribution in a simple sense, the satisfaction of an existing desire. In the case of merit, such as for instance the possession of abilities to profit from a university education, there is not the same presumption that everyone who has the merit has the desire for the goods in question, though it may, of course, be the case. Moreover, the good of a university education may be legitimately, even if hopelessly, desired by those who do not possess the merit; while medical treatment or unemployment benefits are either not desired or not legitimately desired by those who are not ill or unemployed—that is, do not have the appropriate need. Hence the distribution of goods in accordance with merit has a competitive aspect lacking in the case of distribution according to need. For these reasons, it is appropriate to speak in the case of merit not only of the distribution of the good, but of the distribution of the opportunity of achieving the good. But this, unlike the good itself, can be said to be distributed equally to everybody, and so one does encounter a notion of *general* equality, notion of equality of opportunity.

Before considering this notion further, we do well to notice certain resemblances and differences between the cases of need and of merit. In both cases, we encounter the matter of the relevance of reasons. Leaving aside preventive medicine, the proper ground of distribution of medical care is ill health: this is a necessary truth. Now in very many societies, while ill health may work as a necessary condition of receiving treatment, it does not work as a sufficient condition, since such treatment costs money, and not all who are ill have the money; hence the possession of sufficient money becomes in fact an additional necessary condition of actually receiving treatment. (Yet more extravagantly, money may work as a sufficient condition by itself, without any medical need, in which case the reasons that actually operate for the receipt of this good are just totally irrelevant to its nature; however, since only a few hypochondriacs desire treatment when they do not need it, this is, in this case, a marginal phenomenon.) When we have the situation in which, for instance, wealth is a further necessary condition of the receipt of medical treatment, we can once more apply the notions of equality and inequality: not now in connection with the inequality between the well and the ill, but in connection with the inequality between the rich ill and the poor ill, since we have straightforwardly the situation of those whose needs are the same not receiving the same treatment, though the needs are the ground of the treatment. This is an irrational state of affairs.

It may be objected that I have neglected an important distinction here. It may be said that I have treated the ill health and the possession of money as though they were regarded on the same level, as "reasons for receiving medical treatment," and that this is a muddle. The ill health is, at most, a ground of the *right* to receive medical treatment; whereas the money is, in certain circumstances, the causally necessary condition of securing the right, which is a different thing. There is something in the distinction that this objection suggests: there is a distinction between people's rights, the reasons why they should be treated in a certain way, and their power to secure those rights, the reasons why they can in fact get what they deserve. But this objection does not make it inappropriate to call the situation of inequality an "irrational" situation: it just makes it clearer what is meant by so calling it. What is meant is that it is a situation in which reasons are insufficiently *operative*; it is a situation insufficiently controlled by reasons—and hence by reason itself. The same point arises with another form of equality and equal rights, equality before the law. It may be said that in a certain society, citizens have equal rights to a fair trial, to seek redress from the law for wrongs committed against them, and so forth. But if a fair trial or redress from the law can be secured in that society only by moneyed and educated people, to insist that everyone *has* this right, though only these particular people can *secure* it, rings hollow to the point of cynicism: we are concerned not with the abstract existence of rights, but with the extent to which those rights govern what actually happens.

Thus when we combine the notions of the *relevance* of reasons, and the *operativeness* of reasons, we have a genuine moral weapon, which can be applied in cases of what is appropriately called unequal treatment, even where one is not concerned with the equality of people as a whole. This represents a strengthening of the very weak principle mentioned at the beginning of this paper, that for every difference in the way people are treated, a reason should be given: when one requires further that the reasons should be relevant, and that they should be socially operative, this really says something.

Similar considerations will apply to cases of merit. There is, however, an important difference between the cases of need and merit, in respect of the relevance of reasons. It is a matter of logic that particular sorts of needs constitute a reason for receiving particular sorts of good. It is, however, in general a much more disputable question whether certain sorts of merit constitute a reason for receiving certain sorts of good. For instance, let it be agreed, for the sake of argument, that the public school system[3] provides a superior type of education, which it is a good thing to receive. It is then objected that access to this type of education is unequally distributed, because of its cost: among children of equal promise or intelligence, only those from wealthy homes will receive it, and, indeed, those of little promise or intelligence will receive it, if from wealthy homes; and this, the objection continues, is irrational.

The defender of the public school system might give two quite different sorts of answer to this objection (besides, that is, the obvious type of answer which merely disputes the facts alleged by the objector). One is the sort of answer already discussed in the case of need: that we may agree, perhaps, that children of promise and intelligence have a right to a superior education, but in actual economic circumstances, this right cannot always be secured, and so forth. The other is more radical: this would dispute the premise of the objection that intelligence and promise are, at least by themselves, the grounds for receiving this superior type of education. While perhaps not asserting that wealth itself constitutes the ground, the defender of the system may claim that other characteristics significantly correlated with wealth are such grounds; or, again, that it is the purpose of this sort of school to maintain a tradition of leadership, and the best sort of people to maintain this will be people whose parents were at such schools. We need not try to pursue such arguments here. The important point is that, while there can indeed be genuine disagreements about what constitutes the relevant sort of merit in such cases, such disagreements must also be disagreements about the nature of the good to be distributed. As such, the disagreements do not occur in a vacuum, nor are they logically free from restrictions. There is only a limited number of reasons for which education could be regarded as a good, and a limited number of purposes which education could rationally be said to serve; and to the limitations on this question, there correspond limitations on the sorts of merit or personal characteristic which could be rationally cited as grounds of access to this good. Here again we encounter a genuine strengthening of the very weak principle that, for differences in the way that people are treated, reasons should be given.

---

[3] In Great Britain, the phrase "public school" stands for what are in fact *private* or independent schools, and this is the kind of institution that Williams has in mind here.

We may return now to the notion of equality of opportunity, understanding this in the normal political sense of equality of opportunity for *everyone in society* to secure certain goods. This notion is introduced into political discussion when there is question of the access to certain goods which, first, even if they are not desired by everyone in society, are desired by large numbers of people in all sections of society (either for themselves, or, as in the case of education, for their children), or would be desired by people in all sections of society if they knew about the goods in question and thought it possible for them to attain them; second, are goods which people may be said to earn or achieve; and third, are goods which not all the people who desire them can have. This third condition covers at least three different cases, however, which it is worth distinguishing. Some desired goods, like positions of prestige, management, and the like, are *by their very nature* limited: whenever there are some people who are in command or prestigious positions, there are necessarily others who are not. Other goods are *contingently* limited, in the sense that there are certain conditions of access to them which in fact not everyone satisfies, but there is no intrinsic limit to the numbers who might gain access to them by satisfying the conditions: university education is usually regarded in this light nowadays, as something which requires certain conditions of admission to it which in fact not everyone satisfies, but which an indefinite proportion of people might satisfy. Third, there are goods which are *fortuitously* limited, in the sense that although everyone or large numbers of people satisfy the conditions of access to them, there is just not enough of them to go around; so a rationing system has to be imposed, to govern access in an imperfect situation. A good can, of course, be both contingently and fortuitously limited at once: owing to shortage of supply, not even the people who are qualified to have it, limited in numbers though they are, can in every case have it. It is particularly worth distinguishing those kinds of limitation, as there can be significant differences of view about the way in which a certain good is limited. While most would now agree that higher education is contingently limited, a Platonic view would regard it as necessarily limited.

Now the notion of equality of opportunity might be said to be the notion that a limited good shall in fact be allocated on grounds which do not a priori exclude any section of those that desire it. But this formulation is not really very clear. For suppose grammar school education (a good perhaps contingently, and certainly fortuitously, limited) is allocated on grounds of ability as tested at the age of eleven; this would normally be advanced as an example of equality of opportunity, as opposed to a system of allocation on grounds of parents' wealth. But does not the criterion of ability exclude a priori a certain section of people—viz. those that are not able—just as the other excludes a priori those who are not wealthy?

Here it will obviously be said that this was not what was meant by a priori exclusion: the present argument just equates this with exclusion of anybody—that is, with the mere existence of some condition that has to be satisfied. What then is a priori exclusion? It must mean exclusion on grounds other than those appropriate or rational for the good in question. But this still will not do as it stands. For it would follow from this that so long as those allocating grammar school education on grounds of wealth thought that such grounds were appropriate or rational (as they might in one of the ways discussed above in connection with public schools), they could sincerely describe their system as one of equality of opportunity—which is absurd.

Hence it seems that the notion of equality of opportunity is more complex than it first appeared. It requires not merely that there should be no exclusion from access on grounds other than those appropriate or rational for the good in question, but that the grounds considered appropriate for the good should themselves be such that people from all sections of society have an equal chance of satisfying them. What now is a "section of society"? Clearly we cannot include under this term sections of the populace identified just by the characteristics which figure in the grounds for allocating the good—since, once more, any grounds at all must exclude some section of the populace. But what about sections identified by characteristics which are *correlated* with the grounds of exclusion? There are important difficulties here: to illustrate this, an imaginary example may be helpful.

Suppose that in a certain society great prestige is attached to membership of a warrior class, the duties of which require great physical strength. This class has in the past been recruited from certain wealthy families only, but egalitarian reformers achieve a change in the rules, by which warriors are recruited from all sections of the society on the results of a suitable competition. The effect of this, however, is that the wealthy families still provide virtually all the warriors, because the rest of the populace are so under-nourished by reason of poverty that their physical strength is inferior to that of the wealthy and well nourished. The reformers protest that equality of opportunity has not really been achieved; the wealthy reply that in fact it has, and that the poor now have the opportunity of becoming warriors—it is just bad luck that their characteristics are such that they do not pass the test. "We are not," they might say, "excluding anyone *for* being poor; we exclude people for being weak, and it is unfortunate that those who are poor are also weak."

This answer would seem to most people feeble, and even cynical. This is for reasons similar to those discussed before in connection with equality before the law; that the supposed equality of opportunity is quite empty—indeed, one may say that it does not really exist—unless it is made more effective than this. For one knows that it could be made more effective; one knows that there is a causal connection between being poor and being undernourished, and between being undernourished and being physically weak. One supposes further that something could be done—subject to whatever economic conditions obtain in the imagined society—to alter the distribution of wealth. All this being so, the appeal by the wealthy to the "bad luck" of the poor must appear disingenuous.

It seems then that a system of allocation will fall short of equality of opportunity if the allocation of the good in question in fact works out unequally or disproportionately between different sections of society, if the unsuccessful sections are under a disadvantage which could be removed by further reform or social action. This was very clear in the imaginary example that was given, because the causal connections involved are simple and well known. In actual fact, however, the situations of this type that arise are more complicated, and it is easier to overlook the causal connections involved. This is particularly so in the case of educational selection, where such slippery concepts as "intellectual ability" are involved. It is a known fact that the system of selection for grammar schools by the "eleven-plus" examination favours children in direct proportion to their social class, the children of professional homes having proportionately greater success than those from working-class homes. We have every reason to suppose that these results are the product, in good part, of environmental factors; and we further know that imaginative social reform, both of the primary educational system and of living conditions, would favourably effect those environmental factors. In these circumstances, this system of educational selection falls short of equality of opportunity.[4]

This line of thought points to a connection between the idea of equality of opportunity, and the idea of equality of persons, which is stronger than might at first be suspected. We have seen that one is not really offering equality of opportunity to Smith and Jones if one contents oneself with applying the same criteria to Smith and Jones at, say, the age of eleven; what one is doing there is to apply the same criteria to Smith as affected by favourable conditions and to Jones as affected by unfavourable but curable conditions. Here there is a necessary pressure to equalize the conditions: to give *Smith* and *Jones* equality of opportunity involves regarding their conditions, where curable, as themselves part of what is done to Smith and Jones, and not part of Smith and Jones themselves. Their identity, for these purposes, does not include their curable environment, which is itself unequal and a contributor of inequality. This abstraction of persons in themselves from unequal environments is a way, if not of regarding

---

[4] See on this C.A.R. Crosland, "Public Schools and English Education," *Encounter*, July 1961.

them as equal, at least of moving recognizably in that direction; and is itself involved in equality of opportunity.

One might speculate about how far this movement of thought might go. The most conservative user of the notion of equality of opportunity is, if sincere, prepared to abstract the individual from some effects of the environment. We have seen that there is good reason to press this further, and to allow that the individuals whose opportunities are to be equal should be abstracted from more features of social and family background. Where should this stop? Should it even stop at the boundaries of heredity? Suppose it were discovered that when all curable environmental disadvantages had been dealt with, there was a residual genetic difference in brain constitution, for instance, which was correlated with differences in desired types of ability; but that the brain constitution could in fact be changed by an operation.[5] Suppose further that the wealthier classes could afford such an operation for their children, so that they always came out at the top of the educational system; would we then think that poorer children did not have equality of opportunity, because they had no opportunity to get rid of their genetic disadvantages?

Here we might think that our notion of personal identity itself was beginning to give way; we might well wonder *who were* the people whose advantages and disadvantages were being discussed in this way. But it would be wrong, I think, to try to solve this problem simply by saying that in the supposed circumstances our notion of personal identity would have collapsed in such a way that we could no longer speak of the individuals involved—in the end, we could still pick out the individuals by spatio-temporal criteria, if no more. Our objections against the system suggested in this fantasy must, I think, be moral rather than metaphysical. They need not concern us here. What is interesting about the fantasy, perhaps, is that if one reached this state of affairs, the individuals would be regarded as in all respects equal in themselves—for in themselves they would be, as it were, pure subjects or bearers of predicates, everything else about them, including their genetic inheritance, being regarded as a fortuitous and changeable characteristic. In these circumstances, where everything about a person is controllable, equality of opportunity and absolute equality seem to coincide; and this itself illustrates something about the notion of equality of opportunity.

I said that we need not discuss here the moral objections to the kind of world suggested in this fantasy. There is, however, one such point that is relevant to the different aspects of equality that have been discussed in

[5] A yet more radical situation—but one more likely to come about—would be that in which an individual's characteristics could be *pre-arranged* by interference with the genetic material. The dizzying consequences of this I shall not try to explore.

this paper as a whole. One objection that we should instinctively feel about the fantasy world is that far too much emphasis was being placed on achieving high ability; that the children were just being regarded as locations of abilities. I think we should still feel this even if everybody (with results hard to imagine) was treated in this way; when not everybody was so treated, the able would also be more successful than others, and those very concerned with producing the ability would probably also be over-concerned with success. The moral objections to the excessive concern with such aims are, interestingly, not unconnected with the ideal of equality itself; they are connected with equality in the sense discussed in the earlier sections of this paper, the equality of human beings despite their differences, and in particular with the complex of notions considered in the second section under the heading of "respect."

This conflict within the ideals of equality arises even without resort to the fantasy world. It exists today in the feeling that a thoroughgoing emphasis on equality of opportunity must destroy a certain sense of common humanity which is itself an ideal of equality.[6] The ideals that are felt to be in conflict with equality of opportunity are not necessarily other ideals of equality—there may be an independent appeal to the values of community life, or to the moral worth of a more integrated and less competitive society. Nevertheless, the idea of equality itself is often invoked in this connection, and not, I think, inappropriately.

If the idea of equality ranges as widely as I have suggested, this type of conflict is bound to arise with it. It is an idea which, on the one hand, is invoked in connection with the distribution of certain goods, some at least of which are bound to confer on their possessors some preferred status or prestige. On the other hand, the idea of equality of respect urges us to give less consideration to those structures in which people enjoy status or prestige, and to consider people independently of those goods, on the distribution of which equality of opportunity precisely focusses our, and their, attention. There is perhaps nothing formally incompatible in these two applications of the idea of equality: one might hope for a society in which there existed both a fair, rational, and appropriate distribution of these goods, and no contempt, condescension, or lack of human communication between people who were more and less successful recipients of the distribution. Yet in actual fact, there are deep psychological and social obstacles to the realization of this hope. As things are, the competitiveness and considerations of prestige that surround the first application of equality certainly militate against the second. How far this situation is inevitable, and how far in an economically developed and dynamic society, in

[6] See, for example, Michael Young, *The Rise of the Meritocracy* (London: Thames and Hudson, 1958).

which certain skills and talents are necessarily at a premium, the obstacles to a wider realization of equality might be overcome, I do not think that we know. These are in good part questions of psychology and sociology, to which we do not have the answers.

When one is faced with the spectacle of the various elements of the idea of equality pulling in these different directions, there is a strong temptation, if one does not abandon the idea altogether, to abandon some of its elements: to claim, for instance, that equality of opportunity is the only ideal that is at all practicable, and equality of respect a vague and perhaps nostalgic illusion; or, alternatively, that equality of respect is genuine equality, and equality of opportunity an inegalitarian betrayal of the ideal—all the more so if it were thoroughly pursued, as now it is not. To succumb to either of these simplifying formulae would, I think, be a mistake. Certainly, a highly rational and efficient application of the ideas of equal opportunity, unmitigated by the other considerations, could lead to a quite inhuman society (if it worked—which, granted a well-known desire of parents to secure a position for their children at least as good as their own, is unlikely). On the other hand, an ideal of equality of respect that made no contact with such things as the economic needs of society for certain skills, and human desire for some sorts of prestige, would be condemned to a futile Utopianism, and to having no rational effect on the distribution of goods, position, and power that would inevitably proceed. If, moreover, as I have suggested, it is not really known how far, by new forms of social structure and of education, these conflicting claims might be reconciled, it is all the more obvious that we should not throw one set of claims out the window but should rather seek, in each situation, the best way of eating and having as much cake as possible. It is an uncomfortable situation, but the discomfort is just that of genuine political thought. It is no greater with equality than it is with liberty, or any other noble and substantial political ideal.

NINE

Conflicts of Liberty and Equality

1. INTRODUCTION

The aim of this paper is to show how there can be conflicts between liberty and equality as political values. It might be thought that this undertaking was either unnecessary or impossible. On one account of liberty (or, to use the word more usual at this point of the argument, freedom) there are quite obviously conflicts between freedom and equality: this is the account by which (very roughly indeed) I am free to do X if I am able to do X (if I have the "capability" to do it). Any form of co-existence restricts freedom in this sense; so, in further ways, does co-existence under government; in yet further ways, so does co-existence under government dedicated to policies of equality.

However, it is not clear that freedom in this sense is yet any form of political value. It is unclear, for instance, what of value has been lost by a restriction of capability as such. Something has been lost by the agent whose activities have been restricted, but that fact in itself does not give him any claim on society's concern: "It stops me doing something I want (or might want) to do" is not yet, in itself, a political argument. It has the shape of an argument, it might be thought, only if it means "It stops me doing something I have a right to do." But if this is the necessary form of a complaint in liberty, then conflicts between liberty and equality (where equality, also, is understood as implying rights) appear to be impossible; in aiming at coherent interpretations of liberty and equality as implying rights, we must look for accounts under which they do not imply conflicting rights. There has been a long tradition of argument in this direction. Rousseau supported one version of it, and Ronald Dworkin has recently offered another.[1] On these accounts, the aim of this paper is impossible.

I shall try to find a path—or rather, perhaps, a set of connected spaces—between these two positions which will enable us to accept that there are genuine conflicts between liberty and equality, while giving an account of liberty as a political value which does not make this consequence trivial. This might be thought to agree with Dworkin in his premiss, that liberty

---

[1] "What Is Equality? Part 3: The Place of Liberty," *Iowa Law Review* 73 (1987). Henceforth "PL."

should be understood as "a distinct and compelling political ideal" (PL 6), but not in his conclusion from it, that the favoured interpretations of liberty and equality should be such that these values cannot conflict.[2] However, this does not locate our disagreement exactly, because I do not agree with Dworkin on what counts as understanding liberty as a *political* ideal or value. Indeed, part of my case will be that his approach does not adequately acknowledge the political character of this value.

2. FLAT FREEDOM AND CAPABILITY

I introduced the minimum sense of freedom, under which freedom inevitably conflicts with equality (and with many other things) in terms of capability, or what has sometimes been called "power." However, this is not how Dworkin draws his contrast between a sense of "liberty" in which it does not yet represent a value, and the sense in which it does. "We use 'liberty' in its flat sense," he says (PL 5), "simply to indicate the absence of constraint." He says, further, that this is a descriptive sense (cf. PL 12), whereas the other sense is normative: in the normative sense, liberty is something like "rightful freedom."

I agree with Dworkin in identifying the flat or minimum sense of freedom in terms of the absence of constraint, but not with the claim that such an account is not normative. It seems that it must be to some extent normative because what counts as "constraint" is, beyond a certain point, a normative matter. (Some questions about constraint will be of concern later.) I do not think that it matters that flat freedom is a partly normative concept. Indeed, both Dworkin and I want flat freedom not yet to be a political value, and my own strategy will be to build up an account of liberty as a political value by starting from flat freedom; but neither this strategy nor Dworkin's depends on supposing that flat freedom is in no way normative.

The notion of freedom as mere capability does seem untouched by that source of normativity, at any rate, since it does not import the notion of constraint. However, I do not think that it is free from normativity. Any useful notion of capability is surely going to have to construe the idea of "things I cannot do" in such a way as to include (at least) things that I cannot do except at some quite unacceptable cost, and this involves a normative notion.

---

[2] Dworkin holds in fact that the consequence may break down under various extreme or primitive circumstances; he has room for what Rawls calls "imperfect compliance theory." I shall ignore the exceptional cases here.

In fact, I do not believe that capability is a plausible candidate for a notion of *freedom* at all, unless it is understood in a way that has quite elaborate normative implications. This is not the place to develop the point, but very roughly the idea is that a notion of freedom is useful only if we can deploy "more" and "less," particularly in the context of extending or restricting someone's freedom.[3] A main reason why freedom as capability has seemed attractive to political theory is that it allows us to say that extensive formal freedoms can co-exist with very restricted capability freedoms: an increase in resources to poor people can, under this interpretation, itself be understood as offering increased freedom. However, we can say this only if we can assess greater, less, increased, and so forth, capabilities, and without heavy normative help there is no way of doing this, because there is no non-arbitrary way of identifying a capability or an increase in capabilities.[4] It is only in terms of what counts as a significant or worthwhile human capability that we can make these kinds of arguments.

It may be that there is a helpful sense of freedom to be expressed in these terms, but if there is, it is already a richly conceived ethical and political value. It is certainly no candidate for flat or minimum freedom. The only candidate for that, I think, is the traditional one that Dworkin selects, absence of constraint.

3. The Primitive Situation and Its Extensions

The most elementary model of not having freedom (losing it, having it restricted, etc.) seems to be *being in someone else's power*. The most elementary form of this, again, is that of being in a situation in which someone else (call him "A") has the intention that I should act in certain ways and forces me to do so "against my will"—that is (in the simplest case), where I would want not to act like that if not forced. If we want to extend and better understand this *primitive situation* (PS), we have to consider

---

[3] The so-called freedom of the will would presumably be an exception: one that proves the rule.

[4] If I introduce a new commodity, do I increase your capabilities by making it possible for the first time for you to choose this one? Or decrease them, by making it impossible for you to make an informed choice without assessing this one? Or both? Again, theorists might think of a capability as the possibility of one's making a sentence true. Then if you can make it true that Q, and I now for the first time make it true that P, then I have given you a new capability, that of making Q true in conjunction with P. And so on. I have argued that there are related difficulties for Amartya Sen's construction of equality on a space of capabilities, in a review of his *Inequality Re-examined*, *London Review of Books*, November 18, 1993.

four elements of it: (a) the intentionality of A; (b) the identity of A; (c) what counts as "forces"; (d) (relatedly) what counts as "against my will."

(a) immediately raises the prospect of two ways in which the PS may be extended. In the PS, A wants precisely a certain thing to happen and adopts means to extract it from, specifically, me. But, first, A may want some general result and may apply pressure to me only to the extent that this is necessary or advantageous to his getting that result. Alternatively, he may have no intention directed toward forcing me to do anything. A restriction on my power may follow only as a side effect of his pursuing something else. In terms of the PS, this is a restriction on my power and not on my freedom. But it might come to be understood as a restriction on my freedom if certain other conditions were met.

One is that, although A has no relevant intentionality, and his professed purposes are such that the disadvantage imposed on me and others is simply a side effect, there might be an account of the situation in which those "side effects" were understood as functional. In such a case it might be said that while it was not an aim of A's, it was an aim of the system, that my powers should be restricted. Such accounts are notoriously hard to make good, and I shall not pursue the issue here. The point is simply to locate this kind of problem on the map of liberty. If an account in some such terms were made good, it is fairly clear how the PS account of freedom would be extended naturally to cover such a situation.

Another possibility, of much wider significance, is that it may depend on certain normative conditions on my and A's activities, whether what he is doing to me counts as a limitation of my freedom or not. In one direction, a restriction on my activities which is a side effect of A's activities may be more readily identified as an affront to freedom if I for some special reason have a right to do that thing. Conversely, interference that would unqualifiedly be an offence to freedom if it had no special reason may not count as such if it has certain kinds of legitimation. In order to mark such points, we require *normative supplements* to the PS account. We shall have to consider at more than one point various normative supplements, and to ask about their usefulness in building up notions of freedom more complex (and more political) than the basic one displayed in the PS. I shall mark various points as ones in which the question of such a supplement will come up. This is the first: QNS 1 (activity).

(b) The agency may become more collective or, again, abstract: Dick Turpin, Don Corleone, the Mafia, the king, the monarchy, the party in power, the government, the law. This variation itself may be taken to have normative implications for ascriptions of freedom. To live under the rule of law rather than that of men is often said to be a paradigm of political freedom.[5] This is QNS 2 (agency).

---

[5] General Galtieri to a political prisoner in jail: "Your name is Rosaria? It is my daughter's name. You may live."

(c) What counts as forcing? This is a famously difficult, and in general terms perhaps insoluble, question (cf. Nozick on coercion). One point is particularly relevant here. When an agency is allowed to try to bring about results by forcing, a question will arise whether a given method of forcing is allowable: at all, or in relation to particular objectives. It is a further question whether an objection to particular means could naturally take the form of saying that these means, though not some others, make the attempt to force into a violation of freedom. It seems that it sometimes may: if so, this is QNS 3 (means).

(d) Does "against my will" mean against my actual desires? My actual and operative desires? Against the desires I would have if better informed? Against those I would have if some yet more elaborate condition were satisfied? It seems to me that both intellectual and political history suggest that only bad news follows from trying to do much of the normative work at this point of the construction. I suggest that "against the balance of my actual desires" is a sufficient condition of "against my will."[6] This is so even if my actual desires are dependent on, for example, gross and easily corrigible ignorance. Such a case might justify peremptory, even violent, paternalistic action in my interests, and it does seem a paradox to deny that that is a temporary incursion into my freedom, though it is one that may be easily justified.

If "against my will" roughly means "against the balance of my actual desires," then there can be offences against my freedom which are not "against my will," because there are, manifestly, ways of offending against freedom by manipulating people's desires.[7] There is a further normative question here, about what people might naturally be expected to want, but I shall not pursue it.

4. Normative Supplements

It may be said that it is misleading to use the phrase "normative *supplement*" to what was offered in the PS, since even in the PS there are normative assumptions, at least to the effect that A and I are not in legitimate competition, or that my activities do not constitute a deliberate and sus-

---

[6] In considering this proposal, one must bear in mind that "against my will" may not be a sufficient condition of a limitation, violation, or the like, of freedom in some more complex or political sense: cf. QNS 1 and 2. Rousseau, of course, thought that it was always a sufficient condition; hence he concluded legitimate political authority could never go against my will (really).

[7] This is related to a well-known paradox in J. S. Mill's view that the measure of freedom is the ratio between one's actual desires and one's ability to satisfy them: the reformer who gives the apathetic slaves for the first time a desire for freedom makes them less free.

tained threat to A. I think we can avoid controversy here. Take "supplement" to mean whatever it is thought appropriate to add to whatever are the minimal normative assumptions appropriate to the identification of a limitation of freedom in the PS.

The question now is, how the normative supplements should be set to yield, from the concept of freedom illustrated by the PS, a concept which may be said to express freedom as a political value. This, political, concept—whatever exactly it will turn out to be—we can mark with the original political expression, "liberty." Just as we saw at the beginning that if we took minimum freedom as capability, it would not yet in itself constitute a political value, so equally the freedom displayed in the PS is not in itself such a value. The mere fact that I am being required to do something against my will by a government is a limitation of freedom at the level of the PS account, but this cannot, in itself, count as a violation of liberty, if there is to be a concept of liberty at all. At the very least, liberty, a political value, has to be able to co-exist with the political.

To mark this point, let us say that a certain claim of a loss of liberty is (minimally) *socially presentable*, if it can be urged consistently with accepting a legitimate political order for the general regulation of the society.[8] (It follows that the anarchist objection is not a socially presentable claim to loss of liberty.) An objection merely to the fact that I am prevented by the police from removing my neighbour's property is not a socially presentable claim. An objection to the operations of Franco or James II was a socially presentable claim: one could, and most objectors did, accept that these rulers should be replaced by some other rulers, and more generally they accepted a state system.

Being socially presentable of course does not entail that the claim is correct, in the sense that the activity complained of should be stopped or discouraged in the name of liberty. Nor does it follow, necessarily, that it is correctly claimed that there is a loss of liberty. It is merely that these claims can be coherently discussed within the assumption that there can be legitimate regulation of the society by a political order. We still have to consider how much has to be added, besides social presentability, to yield a concept of freedom which is liberty.

5. ROUSSEAU AND DWORKIN

Rousseau believed that there were no socially presentable claims against the state in a just society. This was because, for him, the only legitimate

---

[8] "The" rather than "a" society: a degree of relativization to historical circumstances is acceptable.

political order was just. To get these results, he operated with some strong assumptions in the areas of the various normative supplements of activity, agent, and means:

(1) anything a just state stopped me doing I had no right to do anyway;
(2) a legitimate state is simply an expression of the General Will, which is my own, and this means that its coercive activities are not even against my will;[9]
(3) the question of means (more or less) falls away, since they are being applied *ex hypothesi* to traitors or outlaws.

Dworkin does not agree with Rousseau that the only legitimate order is just, and hence is not committed by Rousseau's reasons to thinking that there are no socially presentable claims in a just society. He does, however, more or less, accept that there are no correct claims in liberty against the state in a just society. This is because a just society is one that is properly equal, and liberty and equality are defined in an interrelated way.

Dworkin's view, too, relies on some strong normative supplements. In the matter of (3) (means), he holds of course, contrary to Rousseau, that the matter of what means the state employs even toward defaulters is itself important both for liberty and for equality. His views about area (2), the identity of the state as agent, equally embody liberal assumptions, about the need for impersonal agencies, the rule of law, and the like, if interventions are not to count as violations of liberty. Like liberal opinion in general, he will also think, unlike Rousseau, that it is possible to be on the losing side in a just society without being alienated from the body politic.

So much is common ground among liberals. Dworkin's distinctive conclusion that there can be no correct claims in liberty in a just society follows from an assumption in the area of (1), the supplement concerning the normative status of the complainant's activity. This denies that it is, other things being equal, a loss of liberty if I am stopped from doing something that I would not be allowed to do if certain ideal arrangements obtained. On Dworkin's view, a person who claims that his liberty has been violated, or that he has suffered a loss of liberty, may make this claim entirely sincerely and while thinking, not merely that some political order could be legitimate, but that this very political order is legitimate; and yet this claim may not be correct, because the claimant's activity does not satisfy the normative demands in area (1). His activity is not rightful, for instance, under the preferred interpretation of equality.

---

[9] I ignore the point, important in Rousseau, of the distinction between executive and legislative activities.

This is likely, in fact, to be a fairly common phenomenon. Let E(I) be the favoured Dworkin interpretation of equality. In political fact, if there is a properly elected government engaged in applying E(I) in social reform, there will be many who reject the interpretation E(I), while there may be others who are, for instance, suspicious of the political mandate for some particular proposals (though not doubtful that they have duly become law). All this is consistent, of course, with its being, and their thinking that it is, a legitimate political order. Indeed, they may well share a lot more than this with those who, against these people's wishes, are enacting E(I).

6. Reasonable Resentment

This very familiar type of situation should encourage us to look again at how we should set the normative supplement in area (1). Let us say that a claim to the effect that one's liberty is being infringed is *responsible* if the claim-maker makes it sincerely, is convinced that the political order is legitimate, and moreover remains persuaded of his claim despite attending to serious argument, and so forth. The maker of a responsible claim will typically feel resentful at his activities' being curtailed. The suggestion I want to make is essentially that we should understand the normative supplement in area (1) in such a way that a responsible claim to a loss of liberty means that there is a loss of liberty.

Even if a person in this situation will feel resentful, it may be asked whether he rightly feels resentful. The force of this question reveals why Dworkin's stronger normative supplement in this area (if the government's activity is in fact rightful, there is no complaint in liberty) looks tempting. One way of setting out the temptation is by way of the suggestion that the following are (roughly) equivalent:

(i)   A ought to be allowed to do X (e.g., retain certain resources which the government proposes to take from him);
(ii) A ought not to be prevented from doing X;
(iii) it is an affront to A's liberty to prevent his doing X.

Moreover, (iii) may be thought to imply

(iv) A would be rightly resentful about being prevented from doing X.

Suppose policies directed to increasing equality under the interpretation E(I) imply that A shall not do X (e.g., retain the resources). Grant that we accept E(I). Then, by these supposed equivalences, we get denials of (i) and (ii); denying (ii), it seems plausible to deny (iv); if we deny (iv), we deny (iii). This is enough to motivate Dworkin's strong normative supplement.

In terms of this structure, I think that we should resist the middle step, to the effect that if we deny (ii), we must deny (iv); or alternatively, if we wish to reserve "rightly resentful" for this purpose, then we must admit that you can be reasonably resentful when you are not rightly so (and not through the ignorance of any facts). You may be reasonably resentful about a move against your activities even if you think it ought to be accepted, not stopped, and so forth: in particular, you may think this if you accept the system that generated the result, but think that the system ought not to have generated it. (Cf. the so-called Paradox of Democracy.)

I suggest that it is sensible to connect the account of liberty, and of what counts as a violation of it, with what people may reasonably resent in this sense. People's sense of freedom is given to them through experiences such as those described in the PS, and it is through them that its value, too, is grasped. It is a requirement on them that they should move beyond the limits of the PS, and not complain of arrangements without which the society of which they are members could not exist or would not provide a legitimate order. Normative supplements related to that are entirely appropriate to a conception of liberty. They might, for various reasons, be taken further; a sense of shared citizenship might support a conception of liberty that was more heavily normative still. But it is still true that there will be people who do not subscribe to particular political and ethical programmes, such as the extension of equality interpreted in terms of E(I), and if they do not, they may be reasonably resentful of the effects of such policies on them.

It is offensive to these people, in a way rather reminiscent of Rousseau, to suggest that they are as much in error in resenting and complaining, in the name of liberty, about the restrictions on their activities that are imposed in the name of equality, as people are certainly in error who complain, in the name of liberty, of restrictions simply because they are made by the state. It is better to restrain the demands of the normative supplements in area (1) and accept that if a restriction on activities is reasonably resented in the kind of circumstances described, then it *is* a restriction on liberty. This is a conclusion that can be accepted by everyone, including those who favour the interpretation E(I) and who favoured its being enacted. They will see the loss of liberty of these people as a price that has to be paid for the extension of equality. They will have accepted, that is to say, that liberty and equality can conflict.

The relevant conditions can helpfully be put in terms of "reasonable resentment," under the explanations I have sketched, though the fact of resentment is not itself the ground of the political judgement in such cases: it is, rather, a helpful reminder or indicator of what values are involved. But resentment can occur with regard to both liberty and equality. Equally, someone may be resentful who feels that his claims in equality are improperly being neglected. If we examine this more closely, we shall see why the interpretation of liberty that is being suggested, and an interpretation of equality such as Dworkin's, stand in different relations to politics.

7. LIBERTY, EQUALITY, AND POLITICS

Consider two copybook cases. A has more than B

(i) because he has stolen it from him;
(ii) because he drew the lucky straw in a randomized allocation to which they both uncoercedly agreed.

Presumably everyone thinks that B may have reasonable resentment in (i) but not (ii); and that A would not have reasonable resentment in (i) if there were an intervention to change the situation, but that his resentment in (ii) would be reasonable. Resentment from a disadvantaged party is more reasonable in circumstances that approximate to (i), circumstances that call for rectification.

How do the hypothetical scenarios that Dworkin uses in giving his interpretation of equality, E(I), stand in relation to this? In their light, the actual social situation lies between (i) and (ii): nearer (i), since it demands rectification, but not so near that an item or sum that belongs to a given A should be uniquely reallocated to a given B. So what rights does B have under such an interpretation? As has just been said, he does not have

(a) a right to what A distinctly has.

This comes out also in the consideration that a jacquerie to secure it would (except in unusual circumstances) be criticized for more than, so to speak, impatience. Even in (i), B would be open to criticism, if there is effective legal redress, for taking the law into his own hands; in this case, it is not even the law he would be taking. B certainly does have, on the other hand,

(b) a right to whatever redistributed resources he will get when redistribution is enacted;

but this is uncontroversial. He has this right under E(I), so it looks as though B has

(c) a right to what he would get under the application of E(I).

So is it then true that he has

(d) a right that (the application of) E(I) be enacted?

(d) is quite hard to defend. Certainly it is not like (b), which appeals to what everyone would concede of a well-ordered and legitimate state, and would be accepted both by those who accept and those who reject E(I). But (c), and hence (if at all) (d), are accepted only by those who accept E(I); and (d) commits them to thinking not only that there is good reason for others to agree with them, but that the disadvantaged have the right to demand that they agree with them. This is very strong; it is in fact another Rousseau-like tack, to suppose that all the urgency and dignity of justice applies to one's own political interpretation of justice.

Faced with this, there are two opposite temptations, both well-known from history. One is to weaken (c) and (d) into something like

(e) a right to a political system in which E(I) and its rivals are fairly discussed, and so forth.

This (it might be called, Popperian) line is politically conservative, and it also leaves a mystery about what is said about E(I) and its rivals in the course of the discussions it recommends: can a holder of E(I) not express him/herself by talking in terms such as (c)? The alternative (Saint-Just) line is to accept (c) and (d) and suspend the courtesies of the liberal democratic state. This is objectionable and, for Dworkin, incoherent, since among the things people have a right to under E(I) are the courtesies of the democratic state. So the supporter of E(I) has to accept, it seems, a state of mind which rejects (d) while accepting democracy and (c). This is not necessarily confused or inconsistent; rather, it is double-minded in a way that is perhaps necessary in pluralistic free societies.

Even if we accept (d), we need some double-mindedness in seeing E(I) in relation to other interpretations. For the holder of E(I), what is wrong with the situation of the disadvantaged is what is set out by E(I); it does not depend on the political outlook of those who reject E(I). But our attitude to E(I)'s not being enacted, and hence the use we make of (d), do depend on what those outlooks are. It makes some difference, for instance, whether those who vote against the policies flowing from E(I) do so because they have some other responsible interpretation of equality.

This kind of consideration helps to motivate constructing liberty in the way I am suggesting. The resentment of B with regard to the substance of (c), if E(I) is not enacted, co-exists with a sense (if not in B himself, in his political advocates) that others need to be persuaded, have other views, and so forth; just as the resentment of the person who does not accept E(I) but is being required to pay co-exists, if E(I) is enacted, with the acceptance that it has been enacted. There is no incoherence in this— merely the containment within the law of, and a shared political system of, conflicting interests, passions, and interpretations. But it is not merely that for each interpretation of equality there will be a corresponding interpretation of liberty, such that each interpretation adjusts its liberty and its equality to each other without loss. Rather, *the proposed interpretation of liberty is what we need in order to live in society with others who have different interpretations of equality.*

Even though you and I share a certain conception of equality, and are happy to see its policies being enacted, we can and should use a political concept of liberty in terms of which we can not only sympathize but agree with our fellow citizen who does not share this conception of equality, resents what is being done to him in its name, and says that he has lost some of his liberty. He is reasonably resentful of what is happening to him, because he is being coerced against his will; and these are the complaints of someone who accepts, not only some political order, but this one.[10] Can we really tell him that if he only understood liberty better, he would see that he was deluded in thinking that he had lost some?

This is a thoroughly political concept of liberty, because it acknowledges in its construction the on-going existence of political conflict. Dworkin's picture, on the other hand, assimilates these questions to the interpretation of terms in a constitutional text. But governments, parties, political actors, and complainants are not justices or advocates contributing their various inputs to the unfolding interpretation of what they all agree to be a unitary text. If a given conception of equality is politically dominant at a given time, this is because of a certain conjunction of political forces, aspirations, and opportunities; other conceptions continue to move around society in their variously resentful or hopeful ways.

For these various forces and passions to co-exist in some semblance of a stable political order under democratic forms requires a good deal of what I called "double-mindedness." We need it, in part, because the on-going political framework that contains all this conflict is not given to us, as, for instance, the institutional protocols of the Supreme Court supply an on-going framework for its decisions. We have constantly to reinvent the political framework—in part, through our attitudes to our fellow citizens. It is a contribution to this process that we bear in mind that when their activities are restricted in the name of objectives which they seriously do not accept, they are indeed being coerced against their will, and that when they describe that as a loss of liberty, we should not simply tell them that they are wrong. Our relation to them is not that of offering them instruction in reading a document which we believe we can read better than they can. It is that of sharing a society with them under some degree

---

[10] The case of someone who satisfies all these conditions is offered as a sufficient condition of a claim to loss of liberty that we should accept while agreeing that what is being done to him is rightly done. It represents a high setting of the normative supplement about activity. I think that settings lower than this might well be appropriate—basically because I doubt that the question whether we can identify with someone's reasonable resentment depends very directly on what we see as the virtue of his opinions. But the sufficient condition is enough for now.

of liberty, and an expression of that is our sharing with them a concept of liberty which allows us to say that there has been a cost when (at the least) what we believe is right has to be imposed against the will of people who do not think it is right and who are adversely affected by it. We should agree that liberty is normatively richer than primitive freedom, but at the same time not forget that there are many cases in which the fact that people are coerced against their will represents a loss, even though the coercion is done in the name of right.

TEN

Toleration, a Political or Moral Question?

THERE IS SOMETHING OBSCURE about the nature of toleration, at least when it is regarded as an attitude or a personal principle. Indeed, the problem about the nature of toleration is severe enough for us to raise the question whether, in a strict sense, it is possible at all. Perhaps, rather, it contains some contradiction or paradox which means that practices of toleration, when they exist, must rest on something other than the attitude of toleration as that has been classically described by liberal theory.[1]

There are undoubtedly *practices* of toleration. Holland in the seventeenth century pursued different, more tolerant, policies towards religious minorities than Spain in the seventeenth century, and there are many other examples. However, the mere existence of such examples does not tell one all that much about the underlying attitudes. Practices of toleration may, for instance, merely reflect skepticism or indifference. Such attitudes were certainly important for the growth of toleration as a practice at the end of the wars on religion. Some people became skeptical about the distinctive claims of any church, and began to think that there was no truth, or at least no truth discoverable by human beings, about the validity of one church's creed as opposed to another's. Other people began to think that the struggle had helped them to understand God's purposes better: that he did not mind how people worshiped so long as they did so in good faith within certain broad Christian limits. These two lines of thought, though in a certain sense they run in opposite directions, do end up in the same position, with the idea that precise questions of Christian belief did not matter as much as people had supposed. This leads to toleration as a matter of political practice, but, as an attitude, it is less than toleration as that has been strictly understood. Toleration "requires us to accept people and permit their practices even when we strongly disapprove of them;"[2] but skepticism and indifference mean that people no longer strongly disapprove of the beliefs in question, and their attitude is not, in a strict sense, that of toleration.

---

[1] For an analysis of these problems see D. Heyd (ed.), *Toleration: An Elusive Virtue*, Princeton: Princeton University Press, 1996, and the particular contributions by B. Williams ("Toleration: An Impossible Virtue?"); G. P. Fletcher ("The Instability of Tolerance"); T. M. Scanlon ("The Difficulty of Tolerance").

[2] T. M. Scanlon, "The Difficulty of Tolerance," in: ibid., p. 226.

It is true that for even a practice to be called "tolerant" there has to be some history or background of intolerance, or at least a comparison to be drawn with practices elsewhere. If there never has been anything except indifference on a certain matter, then there is no room for the concept of toleration. Indeed, when the norm begins to be indifference or absence of disapproval, references to toleration may seem inappropriate and even offensive: the homosexual couple living in an apartment block would probably be insulted to be told that the other inhabitants of the block "tolerated" their ménage. It is a feature of "toleration," as that term is standardly used, that it represents an asymmetrical relation: the notion is typically invoked when a more powerful group tolerates a less powerful group. This point in itself relates to toleration as a practice rather than to toleration as an attitude. Indeed, it relates to a particularly important instance of toleration as a practice, namely the refusal to use the law as an instrument for discouraging a group and its beliefs. The very fact that the question to be considered is the use of the law implies that the decision is being made by a more powerful group, that is to say the group which has the opportunity of so using the law. As we have already seen, this practice in itself can express more than one attitude, only one or a few of which earn the title of "toleration" in a strict sense. All those attitudes, however, whether those of indifference or of genuine toleration, can hold just as well between groups who have roughly equal power, where neither of them would be in a position to enforce a law against the other, even if it wanted to. It is the practice of toleration or intolerance as a *political undertaking* that introduces the asymmetry associated with the concept, and not the underlying attitudes, whatever they may be. A tolerant attitude, and equally a tolerant disposition born of indifference, can obtain just as much between groups who are equal in power.

So what is an attitude of genuine tolerance, as opposed, for instance, to mere indifference? As Scanlon has pointed out,[3] it has to find a place between two opposed possibilities. On the one hand, there are behaviors and attitudes that ought not to be tolerated, to which toleration is inappropriate. Towards murder and child abuse, one is not supposed to hold back one's disapproval, or one's disposition to deploy the law, in the name of toleration. For the liberal these intolerable attitudes will of course include attitudes of tolerance: no liberal feels called upon to tolerate racism or bigotry, and overt expressions of racisms and bigotry are things that he may well think are properly restrained by the law (even though, above all in the United States, liberals have a problem in determining the point at which the proper restraint of racist or bigoted expressions becomes a restraint on free speech, and itself offensive to toleration). The first area,

[3] Ibid.

then, in which toleration does not apply is that in which the agent's negative attitude towards other views is not appropriately restrained by an accompanying attitude of toleration. The second kind of case in which toleration is not appropriate is that in which the agent feels that his negative attitude towards other views should not itself exist, and that what he has to learn is not to sustain that attitude, nor to restrain it through toleration, but to cease to have that attitude altogether. This will be so, for instance, in the case of an attitude towards homosexual relations, of the kind that has already been mentioned.

So the sphere of toleration has to be one in which the agent has some very strong view on a certain matter; thinks that people with conflicting views are wrong; and thinks at the same time that, in some sense, those others should be allowed to have and express those views. This formulation certainly captures an outlook which is enough to sustain a practice of toleration; however, it is still not enough to capture the attitude of toleration in a strict sense. An agent might, for instance, feel that others should be allowed to express their views, because he regards the balance of power between his own group and that other group as too sensitive and unstable to be challenged by an attempt to impose what he regards as the correct view. This is not toleration. Toleration implies, rather, that one believes that the other has a right not to be constrained in the matter of the views that he holds and expresses.

What is the nature of this right? At this point, I believe, there are two ways that we may go, and they lead to two different conceptions of toleration. Under one of these conceptions, the right in question can (very roughly) be labeled as moral right, while on the other it may be labeled (equally roughly) a political right. The distinction can be seen if we consider a formulation that Thomas Nagel has written of the relations between toleration and liberalism. Nagel writes, "[L]iberalism purports to be a view that justifies religious toleration not only to religious skeptics but to the devout, and sexual toleration not only to libertines but to those who believe extra-marital sex is sinful. It distinguishes between the values a person can appeal to in conducting his own life and those he can appeal to in justifying the exercise of political power."[4] It is this outlook that is supposed to save liberalism from being, in Rawls's memorable formulation, "just a sectarian doctrine." The idea is that the principles of toleration associated with liberalism will occupy a higher ground relative to particular moral outlooks, enabling them to co-exist in a framework of mutual toleration and respect forming a stable pluralistic society of the kind that Rawls has described.[5]

[4] T. Nagel, *Equality and Partiality*, Oxford: Oxford University Press, 1991, p. 156.
[5] J. Rawls, *Political Liberalism*, New York: Oxford University Press, 1993.

In Nagel's formulation, the tension characteristic of the attitude of toleration is expressed by saying that the tolerant agent will, on the one hand, think that a certain conduct or a certain way of life is sinful, but at the same time think that the power of the state should not be used to suppress that conduct. But there are at least two ways of understanding this contrast. On one reading, the agent's thought is this: "This other agent has a sinful and disgusting way of life and engages in sinful and disgusting practices. However, it is nobody's business to make him, force him, induce him, or (perhaps) even persuade him to take another course. It is up to him—his morality is in his own hands." It is as a particular consequence of all this that political power should not be used to constrain him. The contrast in this form expresses what I take to be a moral doctrine, one that has, incidentally, a political conclusion. This moral doctrine expresses an ideal of moral autonomy.

On the second reading of the contrast expressed in Nagel's formulation, the agent's thought is, rather, this: "This person's way of life is sinful and disgusting. Indeed we should do everything we decently can to persuade him to change his ways and to discourage other people from living like him. We may appropriately warn our children not to consort with his children, not to share his social life, and discourage as many people as we can from thinking well of him so long as he lives in this way. However, it is not appropriate that the power of the state be used in this way." This I take to express a political doctrine, a doctrine expressive of the liberal concept of the state. It may be that the tolerant agent's contrast in this second, political, form itself rests on some moral ideas in particular about the nature of the state; but, in this form, the political conclusion does not follow as a special case from a moral doctrine which is more generally and also intrinsically related to toleration even outside politics—a doctrine such as what might emerge from the first reading of Nagel's formulation as expressing the value of autonomy.

If toleration as a moral attitude is grounded in the value of autonomy, as just suggested, then there are strong arguments for thinking that liberalism's defense of toleration as a practice should not essentially rest on its belief in the value of that attitude. There are several reasons for this. First, it is very difficult both to claim that the value of autonomy is the foundation of the liberal belief in toleration, and at the same time to hold, as Nagel and Rawls and other liberals hold, that liberalism is not just another sectarian doctrine. A belief in autonomy is quite certainly a distinctive moral belief, and one that carries elaborate philosophical considerations along with it.

A second difficulty is that the moral attitude that focuses on autonomy presents, in a peculiarly severe form, the difficulties which, as has already been suggested, are associated with the attitude of toleration. On this account, the agent who disapproves of the other's values should refrain from any untoward pressure on the other to change his outlook. There is, of course, the question of what "untoward" will mean, but it is essential that the account of the liberal outlook, that the idea of such untoward pressure, goes wider than merely the matter of direct political interference. No doubt, on the usual account of autonomy, rational argument will be regarded as appropriate as a means of influencing the other's opinion. But if one takes the ideals of autonomy seriously, there will be a real question about, for instance, the kind of expressions of disapproval that apply social or psychological pressure upon the other. The concept of autonomy is supposed to leave the other free from external, causal, "heteronomous" influences which may cause him to change his opinion for non-moral reasons, such as those of desire for social conformity. But if the agent who disapproves of the other's values and is committed to the attitude of toleration is cut off from all such expressions, it becomes increasingly unclear what room is left for the agent genuinely and strongly to disapprove the other's values. The idea of a strong, moral disapproval which can be expressed only in (something like) a rational argument, and is otherwise required by the demands of toleration to remain private, seems too thin and feeble to satisfy what has been agreed to be the requirement of a tolerant attitude, namely that the agent does in fact strongly disapprove of the practices about which he is being tolerant.

Of course, it is in fact impossible to draw any clear, or perhaps reasonable, line between kinds of influence and persuasion that are supposedly compatible with the ideal of autonomy, and those that are not. This is an inherent weakness in the concept of autonomy, grounded as the ideal is in a Kantian conception of what is and what is not within the province of the rational will. However, the aim of the present argument is not to dismiss the ideal of autonomy altogether, but to ask how far, if it is accepted in some form, it can provide the grounding of a tolerant attitude which in turn can be taken to underlie liberal tolerant practice. The immediate point can be put like this: there is one question of what kinds of influence or social pressure would count as trespassing on the other's autonomy, and there is another question about the forms of expression that will have to be available to agents if they are to count as seriously disapproving of the other's conduct and values to the degree that calls upon the supposed attitude of toleration; and there is simply no reason to believe that the answers to those two questions will necessarily coincide. We could guarantee that they would coincide only if we drew the boundaries round the other's autonomy in the light of what the disapproving agents need to do in order effectively to express their disapproval; but this manifestly is not available under the present construction of the tolerant attitude, since it is precisely the value of the other's autonomy which is supposed to be drawing the limits to what the tolerant but disapproving agent is permitted to do. It is for this reason that the construction of the tolerant attitude in terms of autonomy presents a particularly extreme version of the conflict always inherent in toleration, between disapproval and restraint.

A version of this problem can arise with defenses of liberal toleration, even if they are not based on such demanding notions of autonomy. Critics who deny that the liberal state can avoid being just another sectarian doctrine often claim that liberal states indeed enforce one set of attitudes rather than another—attitudes roughly in favor of individual choice (or at least consumer choice), social cooperation, secularism, and business efficiency. The methods by which these values are forced on a liberal society are more subtle than those condemned by liberalism, but the outcome is much the same. Thomas Nagel gives a liberal answer to this criticism by distinguishing sharply between *enforcing* something like individualism, on the one hand, and the practice of liberal toleration, on the other, though he does not in the least deny that liberal educational practices and other social forces in liberal society are not "equal in their effects." It may well be in fact that liberal society tends to erode religious and other traditional values, even though liberal practice is tolerant of them.

I have criticized this distinction of Nagel's[6] on the ground that the use that he makes of it is not neutral in its inspiration, but rather begs the question in a liberal direction. I put this by saying, "[The use of this distinction] makes a lot out of a difference of procedure, whereas what matters to a non-liberal believer is the difference of outcome." What I mean by this is that the non-liberal believer is not going to be persuaded that this distinction makes all the difference. However, it is perfectly compatible with this that the liberal state could decently use Nagel's distinction to defend, at a political level, what it is doing. What the liberal state cannot do—and this is the immediate point—is to rely on the distinction *and also to ground its tolerant practice in the value of autonomy*, in the way that is presently being considered. For there is surely no substantive sense of autonomy—except one that has been designed precisely to coincide with liberal practice—in which a group of believers could be said to enjoy autonomy in deciding on preserving their religious beliefs when they are overwhelmingly affected by social influences which tend to erode those beliefs.

It may be that the project of grounding liberal toleration in a moral value of autonomy has been particularly encouraged by the historical and ideological importance of religious toleration. One very important argument in favor of religious toleration has traditionally been found in the

[6] T. Nagel, *Equality*, p. 24.

idea that the attempt to coerce religious belief is essentially fruitless, because the forces of the state cannot reach a person's center of conviction. The most that the states could secure would be conforming behavior, but for many, at least, the aim of religious persecution was to secure more than this. This argument can be seen as appealing to a certain conception of autonomy, a free exercise of the individual's capacities to arrive at religious conviction. However, the appeal to autonomy in this connection is really quite special. The argument between those who supported religious toleration and those who were against it revolved around ideas of salvation, and correspondingly the ideas of autonomy that may be invoked here appeal to the relations between individuals and God, together with some conception of what God might expect of his creatures with regard to their dispositions to worship him—a conception which, in the hands of those favoring religious toleration, is likely to suggest that God is not particularly interested in conforming behavior delivered by the power of the state. When the question of toleration is generalized beyond the issue of religious toleration, the structure of ideas is not available. In the religious case, the tolerant party could, at the limit, claim that, so far as we can understand God's purposes, the idea of coerced religious belief makes no sense, and that coerced religious practice without belief can make no sense in the eyes of God. But there is no comparable set of considerations that can be used if we are trying to resolve the question, for instance, of tolerating the sale or display of pornographic materials, and an appeal to the value of autonomy is not going to do much to resolve that question.

For all these reasons, it seems to me that the attempt to ground the practice of toleration in a moral attitude directed to the value of autonomy is bound to fail. At this point it will be helpful to turn our attention to the second interpretation of Nagel's formulation that was distinguished above, the one that leads to a distinctively political conception. Here the idea that the political power is withheld from enforcing certain outcomes, not because the people affected have a right under the good of autonomy to choose their way of life without undue external influence, but because state power should not be used in that kind of purpose. As I have already said, the political idea itself may well have one or another kind of moral root, but under the interpretation we are now considering it does not have its root in furthering or expressing an ideal of autonomy. Prohibition, rather, is simply and solely on the use of state power to affect the behavior in question. If such a view is taken about the restriction of state power, then toleration as a practice will indeed follow. This leaves open the question whether any distinctive *attitude* of toleration at all will underlie the tolerant practice. All that has been argued so far is that tolerant practice is not plausibly grounded in a moral attitude affirming the value of autonomy. Autonomy has in fact played a particularly prominent role in moral conceptualizations of toleration, and this may encourage the idea that the search for a directly moral defense of the attitude of toleration may be a mistake. However that may be, instead of trying to reach the politics of liberalism from a moral assumption that concerns toleration, we should rather consider first the politics of liberalism, including its practices of toleration, and then ask what, if any, kinds of moral assumption are related to that.

There is an essential difference between legitimate government and unmediated power: one of the few necessary truths about political right is that it is not merely might. Those who claim political authority over a group must have *something to say* about the basis of that authority, and about the question of why the authority is being used to constrain in some ways and not others. Moreover, there is a sense in which, at least ideally, they must have something to say *to each person* whom they constrain. If not, there will be people whom they are treating merely as enemies in the midst of their citizens, as the ancient Spartiates, consistently, treated the helots whom they had subjugated. This requirement on a political authority we may well call the *Basic Legitimation Demand*.

There are many substantial questions about the Basic Legitimation Demand and its consequences, which cannot be considered here.[7] There are two very general principles which seem reasonable, and which are relevant to the present discussion. First, the idea that the Basic Legitimation Demand has been met by a certain state is not the same as the idea that it has been met in a way that would satisfy us. The distinction between the use of power which can reasonably claim authority, and the arbitrary use of power, tyranny or mere terror, applies for instance to historical formations, such as medieval kingdoms, whose claims and practices could not be acceptable to us. When those other states exist now, in our world, of course other questions arise, of our moral and political relations to illiberal regimes. It may possibly be true that, in the modern world, only a liberal order can adequately meet the Basic Legitimation Demand, but, if so, this is because of distinctive features of the modern world, not because legitimate government, necessarily and everywhere, means liberal government.

The second general point is this: when it is said that government must have "something to say" to each person or group over whom it claims authority—and this means, of course, that it has something to say which purports to legitimate its use of power in relation to them—it cannot be implied that this is something that this person or group will necessarily

---

[7] See chapters 1, 5 and 7 in this collection.

accept.[8] This cannot be so: they may be anarchists, or utterly unreasonable, or bandits, or merely enemies. *Who* has to be satisfied that the Basic Legitimation Demand has been met by a given formation at one given time is a good question, and it depends on the circumstances. Moreover, it is a political question, which depends on the political circumstances. Obviously, the people to be satisfied should include a substantial number of the people; beyond that, they may include other powers, groups, elsewhere sympathetic to the minority, young people who need to understand what is happening, influential critics who need to be persuaded, and so forth. (If this position seems alarmingly relativist, it is important, indeed essential to these questions, to reflect that in the end no theorist has any way of advancing beyond it. He or she may invoke absolute or universal conditions of legitimacy, which any "reasonable" person should accept; but in doing this, he or she speaks to an audience in a given situation, who share these conceptions of reasonableness, or whom the theorist hopes to persuade—by this very text, among other things—to accept them.)

In these terms, the problem of liberal toleration can be understood as follows. With regard to a contested issue of religious or moral belief, the liberal state addresses a number of different groups. They include (1) minorities who would like, if they had the power, to impose their own belief. If they take the liberal state to be legitimate, and to have some claim of authority over them, then they must recognize that there are some legitimate demands of government other than those inspired by their own creed. They will also recognize, if they have any sense, that in their actual situation these demands will be shaped by other citizens. If they do see all this, then, if their beliefs and practices do not offend too grossly against the core beliefs of liberalism (a point we shall return to), it will be sensible for the liberal state to meet their acceptance by tolerating them, and so sustaining a situation, so far as possible, in which this group can accept that the liberal state makes a claim on them.

Alternatively, such a group may think (or, if the liberal state acts ineptly, come to think) that there is no legitimate government outside their own creed, and that the liberal state makes no legitimate demand on them. If they do think this, then they are potential secessionists or rebels, who must make their own political decisions about the extent to which they are prepared to carry their secession. The liberal state must meet this as any prudent state which wants to avoid violence meets the possibilities of secession, or, on the way to that, of disruption. Their methods may sensibly include, as long as things go moderately well, the continuation of

---

[8] This is one of the reasons for which the idea of satisfying the Basic Legitimation Demand does not coincide with this insatiable ideal of many a political theoretician: universal consent.

toleration. But if the point comes at which toleration has to cease, the liberal state has an entirely reasonable account of why it has ceased, and the minority group, whatever they say for political reasons, cannot be surprised at what is happening.

Among the groups that the liberal state addresses, there may be (2) a majority with the belief which they could impose. If this majority is powerful and convinced enough, and if this belief is not itself part of the core liberal outlook, it is perhaps unlikely that there will be a liberal state: if there is, this will be because the majority, or enough of it, has reason to think that it should not be imposed. One kind of reason may be that they think that it is not the kind of belief that is worthwhile trying to impose: this is the kind of outlook that has already been recognized in the case of religious toleration. This outlook will be the product of a certain kind of reflection on certain kinds of beliefs. Another, different, reason may be that the people in the majority recognize that the minorities who disagree with them—who may or may not be of the type (1)—will feel coerced if this belief is imposed, and they do not think that in this matter the price is worth paying in terms of the loyalty, cooperation and amicable relations of those peoples.

It is in this area, of course, that the outlooks of minority groups (or of their co-believers elsewhere) are very often misrepresented. In particular, such groups may be depicted as consisting entirely of intransigent fanatics or disloyal secessionists. (This is a standard move, at the present time, in the demonization of Islam.) The attitudes needed here by liberals are, above all, realistic social understanding, a desire for cooperation if possible, and political intelligence.

Last among these examples (but not last among all the political possibilities), the liberal state may be addressing (3) a group, the members of whom may have no desire to impose their beliefs, but whose practices and outlook offend against core liberal beliefs. This may be so, for instance, if the group structurally offends against what the liberal majority sees as a gender equality. But at this point liberal toleration falls away in any case, and we are at a level of substantive disagreement (about gender roles and the nature of sexuality, for instance) where liberalism simply cannot avoid presenting "another sectarian doctrine." At this point, there is no hope of liberalism's gaining indisputably higher ground. The only higher-order considerations it can deploy in thinking about what to do are the resources of political good sense: to consider how things look to the minority (not something, in fact, that liberals have excelled in doing); weighing the cost, already mentioned, of coercion; and reflecting on the precedent effects of coercion in disputed matters of morality, as part of liberalism's generally healthy respect for the unintended effects of coercive power. There is no reason why these considerations in a given case should prevail.

If they do prevail, however, so that the minority's practices are tolerated rather than seen as intolerable, the attitudes that will have brought this about will be the kind of political attitude and understanding that have been mentioned.

These rough and superficial sketches of various possibilities that may comfort the liberal state support, I believe, the conclusion that if we approach toleration as a political rather than in the first place a moral issue, we shall find hard to discover *any* one attitude that underlies liberal practice. What the sketches suggest is that, given a liberal state and its typical patterns of legitimation, in the cases where toleration is thought appropriate (and we have seen that there are many cases in which it is not), toleration will be supported by a variety of attitudes, and none of them is very specifically directed to a value of toleration as such—still less to the moral belief in toleration based on the value of autonomy which was identified earlier in the discussion. The attitudes which are needed include such social virtues as the desire to co-operate and to get on peaceably with one's fellow citizens and a capacity for seeing how things look to them. They also include understandings that belong to a more specifically political good sense, of the costs and limitations of using coercive power. Behind these, again, will certainly be needed some of the skepticism, the lack of fanatical conviction on religious issues, in particular, which earlier we saw made an important contribution to the practice of toleration, even though they are inconsistent with toleration strictly understood as a moral attitude.

The case of toleration is, unsurprisingly, a central one for distinguishing between a strongly moralized conception of liberalism as based on ideals of individual autonomy, and a more skeptical, historically alert, politically direct conception of it as the best hope for humanly acceptable legitimate government under modern conditions. The first of these conceptions has been dominant in American political philosophy in the last twenty-five years. The present arguments, such as they are, favor the second conception, one nearer to what the late Judith Shklar called "the liberalism of fear."[9] But, as Judith Shklar herself would have been the first to point out, it must itself always be a political and historical question, how far conditions will allow that form of liberalism, or indeed any other, to exist or to achieve anything.

[9] J. Shklar, "The Liberalism of Fear," in: N. Rosenblaum (ed.), *Liberalism and the Moral Life*, Cambridge, MA: Harvard University Press, 1989. See also the collection of essays on Judith Shklar's work in: B. Yack (ed.), *Liberalism without Illusions*, Chicago: University of Chicago Press, 1996, and Chapter 5 in this collection.

ELEVEN

Censorship

IN ITS BROADEST SENSE, the term "censorship" is applied to any kind of suppression or regulation, by government or other authority, of a writing or other means of expression, based on its content. The authority need not apply to a whole judicature, and the effects of its censorship may be local. The term is sometimes used polemically by critics of a practice which would not be described as "censorship" by those who approve of it: in the United States the term has often been applied in this way to the activities of school or library boards in preventing the use or purchase of books which contain sexual scenes or teach Darwinism. It does seem that an activity has at least to be publicly recognized in order to count as censorship; interference with the mails by the secret police, or covert intimidation of editors, would be examples of something else. Accordingly, any censorship implies a public claim of legitimacy for the type of control in question.

The most drastic methods of control involve *prior restraint*: a work is inspected before it is published, and publication may be forbidden, or permitted only after changes have been made. Traditional absolutist regimes sought to control book publication by these means, and the Inquisition similarly regulated publication by Catholic writers. Legal procedures to the same effect still exist in many states for the control of material affecting national security, and in illiberal states for the control of political content and social criticism. Until 1968, theatrical performances in England were controlled in this way by a court official, the lord chamberlain, whose staff monitored the script before production, demanded changes on a variety of grounds (including disrespect to the monarchy), and visited performances to see that their instructions were being carried out. In many jurisdictions, cinema films are inspected by some official agency before release, and its powers may include that of suppressing some or all of a film. However, the emphasis of these inspections has increasingly moved from suppression to labelling, the agency not so much censoring films as classifying them by their suitability for young people (in Britain the relevant body changed its name to express this).

Prior restraint is essential when censorship is motivated by official secrecy: once the information is out, the point of the censorship is lost (the British government attracted ridicule in the 1980s by trying to ban a book on security grounds which had already been published elsewhere). There are other aims of censorship, however, that do not necessarily demand prior restraint. If a work is thought objectionable on grounds of indecency, evil moral character, or its possible social effects, its suppression after publication may still be thought to have a point, in limiting people's exposure to it. The word "censorship" is sometimes used to apply only to methods of prior restraint, but legal provisions aimed at suppression after publication can reasonably be seen as having similar purposes and effects, and the term will be taken here to cover these procedures as well. Except in relation to media such as broadcasting, questions of principle are now normally discussed in terms of censorship after publication. It is important that censorship even in this wider sense still aims at suppression. Schemes of restriction or zoning applied to pornographic materials, which require them to be sold only in certain shops and only to adults, are analogous to film classification and should be distinguished from censorship.

In 1774 Lord Mansfield said, "Whatever is *contra bonos mores et decorum* the principles of our laws prohibit, and the King's Court as the general censor and guardian of the public morals is bound to restrain and punish." Although this dictum was approvingly mentioned by another English Law Lord as recently as 1962, few now would offer quite such a broad justification for censorship. In part, this is because of doubts about what "the public morals" are, and by whom they are to be interpreted: pluralism, scepticism, sexual toleration, and doubts about the social and psychological insight of judges have played their part in weakening confidence in the notion. A more basic point is that even where there is a high degree of moral consensus on a given matter, it remains a question what that may mean for the law, and what, if anything, can count as a good reason for using the law in an attempt to suppress deviant opinions or offensive utterances.

Liberal theories claim that freedom of expression is both an individual right and a political good, which can be curtailed only to prevent serious and identifiable harms. They can agree on this even though they may disagree to some extent about the main basis of these values, some emphasizing the danger of political and other power which is not transparent, some the importance of artistic and other expression, and some the idea, influentially urged by John Stuart Mill, that it is only through an open "market place of ideas" that truth can be discovered. Liberals will agree, obviously, that the presumption against censorship is always very strong. They will differ to some extent, depending on their other views, about the kinds and the severity of harm that may in certain cases justify it. All will want to defend serious political speech; those who emphasize self-expression may be particularly concerned to protect potentially offensive artistic activity.

Those who stress the idea that free speech is a *right* (as Mill usually did not) insist that the reasons for suppression must take the particular form of a threatened violation of someone's rights.

A very strong version of such principles is embodied in U.S. law, which has interpreted the First Amendment to the Constitution ("Congress shall make no law . . . abridging the freedom of speech or of the press") in such a way as to make censorship on any grounds very difficult. Mr. Justice Holmes in 1919 produced an influential formula: "The question in every case is whether the words used are used in such circumstances and are of such a nature as to create a clear and present danger that they will bring about the substantive evils that Congress has a right to prevent"; and restrictions in such terms have been taken to protect even overtly racist demonstrations, let alone publications. The "clear and present danger" test is not used with regard to pornography, but the effect of Supreme Court decisions in that area has been that, at most, hard-core pornography can be suppressed. In many parts of the United States, all that the law enforces are zoning restrictions.

English law allows greater powers of suppression than does that of the United States: publications designed to arouse racial hatred, for instance, may be illegal, and the same is true in other jurisdictions. (In Germany and elsewhere, it is illegal to deny the Holocaust.) In the case of pornography, the main concept used in English law is *obscenity*; in a formula inherited from a judgement of Chief Justice Cockburn in 1868, the principal statute defines a publication as obscene if it has a "tendency to deprave or corrupt" those exposed to it. This professedly causal concept of obscenity implies that the rationale of the law is to be found in the harmful consequences of permitting a particular publication. However, as the House of Lords has itself observed, the courts could not apply this formula in a literal sense and do not really try to do so. No expert evidence is allowed on the matter of causation, and in practice the question is whether a jury or a magistrate finds the material sufficiently offensive. As critics have pointed out, this not only makes the law's application arbitrary but re-opens the question of its justification. In contrast to the principle that rights to free speech may be curtailed only through an appeal to harms or the violation of rights in the particular case—the principle which Holmes's "clear and present danger" test expresses in a very strict form—only those who think that it is the business of the law to express any correct, or at least shared, moral attitude are likely to justify a work's suppression simply on the ground that it is found deeply offensive.

There has been a great deal of controversy about the effects of pornographic and violent publications, and a variety of anecdotal, statistical, and experimental evidence has been deployed in attempts to find out whether there is a causal link between such publications and some identifiable class of social harms, such as sexual crime. It is perhaps not surprising that such studies are inconclusive, and more recent advocates of censorship, such as some radical feminists, have moved away from thinking of censorship in this area on the model of a public health measure, and concentrate on the idea that certain publications unacceptably express a culture of sexual oppression. This approach tends to treat legal provisions against pornography as like those against publications that encourage racial discrimination. In some systems, of course, this would still not make such censorship constitutional, even if the problem can be solved of making the provisions determinate enough for them not to be void for uncertainty.

A legal provision drafted by Catharine MacKinnon (which has not been accepted in any U.S. state, though it has influenced Canadian law) would offer a ground of civil action against publishers or manufacturers of pornography by someone who can show she has been damaged by it. This procedure might be said not to be an example of censorship as that is normally understood, but it is relevant to see it in terms of censorship, to the extent that the legal action is based on the content of the material. If a woman is assaulted or raped in the course of a pornographic film's production, there is already a ground of legal action; the proposals against pornography will differ from this in being essentially connected with the existence and content of the pornographic material itself.

A radical feminist outlook reinterprets the relation of pornography to other phenomena and, with that, the rationale of trying to control it. Traditional views, whether liberal or conservative, are disposed to regard pornography as a particular and restricted phenomenon, ministering to fantasy, and extreme sadistic pornography as even more so. The radical feminist thesis is that not just the fantasy but the reality of male domination is central to pornography, and that sadistic pornography involving women is only the most overt and unmediated expression of male social power. The objectifying male gaze to which pornography offers itself is thought to be implicit not only throughout the commercial media, but in much high art. It follows from this that there is a contrast of principle between pornography involving women, and other pornography or sadistic material. At the same time, there is a less important contrast, not based on principle, between pornography and other material involving women. Sadistic material involving women will be seen as merely a less reticent version of what is more respectably expressed elsewhere, and if it is specially picked out for censorship, this will be for reasons of policy, somewhat as gross racial insults, rather than trivial ones, may attract legal attention. In practice, the claim is often made by feminists (in uneasy alliance with conservative forces) that sadistic pornography has worse social effects than does other material; this returns the argument to the traditional "public health" approach and its diagnostic problems.

It is censorship directed against pornography that typically encounters problems about artistic merit. With other kinds of censorship, in support of church or state, it is obvious that works to be censored may have artistic merit, and even more obvious that this will be of no particular concern to the censors, who may well see a good work as more dangerous than a bad one. In the case of pornography, there has been a question, first, whether there can be a pornographic work of art at all. It is not disputed that most pornography is of no aesthetic or artistic interest, but there is disagreement whether this is so merely because it is not worth anyone's while to make it more interesting, or because it is inherent in the content and intention of pornography. It has been argued in favour of the second view that the defining aim of pornography, to arouse its audience sexually, necessarily excludes the more complex intentions and expressive features necessary to aesthetic interest. Against this, there are in fact some visual and literary works which it is hard to deny are pornographic in terms of their content and (it is reasonable to suppose) their intention, but which have been widely thought to have merit.

There is strong pressure to use "pornographic" in an unequivocally negative way, to imply condemnation on moral, social, or aesthetic grounds. If the term is used in this way, there is a danger that different issues may be run together, and some important questions begged: it may be harder to separate, intellectually and politically, the question whether some objectionable work has merit, from the question whether it should be censored whatever its merit.

The English law is not alone in allowing a "public good defence," which permits acquittal of a work that possesses serious aesthetic, scientific, or other such merits. It is significant that in English law a jury who acquit in a case where this defence has been made are not required to say whether they found the work not obscene or found it meritorious although it was obscene. The public good defence has secured the publication of serious works, such as *Lady Chatterley's Lover*, which were previously banned, but there are difficulties of principle, which are clearly illustrated in the practice of allowing expert testimony on the merits of the works under prosecution. Besides the inherent obscurity of weighing artistic merit against obscenity, and the fact that evidence bearing on this has to be offered under the conditions of legal examination, the process makes the deeply scholastic assumption that the merit of a given work must be recognizable to experts at the time of its publication. Moreover, the works that can be defended under such a provision must presumably be meritorious, which implies that they are to some considerable degree successful; but if a law is to protect creative activity from censorship, it needs to protect the right to make experiments, some of which will be unsuccessful.

The idea of making *exceptions* to a censorship law for works with artistic merit seems, in fact, essentially confused. Granted that there is a particular value attaching to significant works of art, or, again, that people have an important right to try to express themselves artistically (whether successfully or not), these concerns will not be best met by a system that provides a special exemption just for artistic merit which at a given time can be proved by experts in a court of law. If one believes that censorship on certain grounds is legitimate, then if a work of artistic merit does fall under the terms of the law, it is open to censorship: this point is acknowledged in the practice of traditional political and religious censors. If one believes in freedom for artistic merit, then one believes in freedom and accepts censorship only on the narrowest of grounds.

TWELVE

Humanitarianism and the Right to Intervene

MY TITLE needs one or two explanations. I hope that these will not be too fiddly and tedious.

As some publications of the Oxford Refugee Studies Programme have very helpfully pointed out, many discussions of these areas, and indeed no doubt many interventions themselves, have not been clear about what sort of situation is in question. I confess that I am not altogether clear about what kind of situation is in question in my discussion either, but let me start with saying a little about that. It will not be a precise demarcation, but it will lay down, I hope, some markers.

The reference to humanitarianism is meant to signal that on a significant scale in some area people are suffering what by more or less universal consent would be regarded as a disaster from their point of view, something basically to be feared: they are starving, under-nourished, terrorized, murdered, under attack, forcibly moved, and so forth. I take these to be the materials of what may be called Hobbesian fear. They are related to the first question of politics, to the claim that the first aim of a political order is to reduce the probability of such things, if possible. This is connected with further Hobbesian aims of a political order, the securing of trust, and so of co-operation, the division of labour, and so on.

I assume, further, at least at the beginning of the discussion, that we are concerned with cases in which these conditions of Hobbesian fear actually obtain. Prevention is something else; I will touch on it later.

The title refers to a *right* to intervene. I shall also be considering, however, for some of the time, a different idea, related no doubt, but different, which is the *duty* to intervene. It is easier, in some ways, to start with that, if we are going to consider the resemblances between international intervention and the everyday morality of rescue, which is what I shall be considering.

For the question to arise, of the *right* to intervene, some conditions have to be satisfied. First, someone wants to or has reason to intervene. If people want to do this, and want to do it for humanitarian reasons, because of the suffering, then they may think that they have a duty to do so: the *duty* question will already have been answered. But as we shall see, they can have reasons that are not in that way *simply* humanitarian. Second, they must be able to make some sort of relevant intervention. If they can't, there's no very interesting question about their right to do so. Third, there's a question of right only if there's some sort of objection, or appears to be, to their intervening. What that may be critically depends on the kind of disaster in question, and what sort of intervention is proposed, which of course depends on what sort of intervention could be effective.

If there is a question of a *right* to intervene, and there is, therefore, some potential objection, there will be a question whether someone's rights will be violated if there is an intervention. Who is this going to be? In the international case, the significant answer is that the state's rights are going to be violated.

Here we have to remember that the circumstances of Hobbesian fear don't merely represent the *absence* of government, or even the breakdown or partial breakdown of government. They may be caused by the activities of government. In a discussion of these subjects, Michael Walzer has mentioned, among possible disasters which merit intervention, civil war, political tyranny, and ethnic or religious persecution. Now it is obvious that the idea that these invite intervention can be highly ideological. I shall come back to this. Even disasters which can up to a point be identified as the product of natural causes can raise such issues, both in the identification of the causes (Amartya Sen, for example, on famines) and if a government resists actually acknowledging the disaster or receiving aid for it (as in the case of famine in North Korea in the 1990s). As I say, I shall come back to some issues in this area. But I do want to make clear some restrictions on the discussion. To repeat: I am concentrating, as the word "humanitarian" implies, on cases in which everyone would agree that what is happening to the group in question is bad news for that group. So it does not include cases of the subordinate position of women in some societies—not that this isn't a subject, or one that could raise questions of intervention; it's simply not today's. As suggested by the references to states' rights, obstacles to intervention, warfare, and the like, I am principally concerned with cases in which the intervening party needs, or may need, to use force. Of course, many forms of intervention, and many of those of interest to those who study refugees, do not involve this, and that is a good thing. However, the interest of cases that may involve the use of force is not, I believe, confined to these cases themselves. In some ways, they can illustrate, more dramatically, issues that arise in other cases as well.

Let us now turn to an everyday moral idea, the principle of rescue.

I take it that the moral principle of rescue in everyday life goes something like this:

(1) If X is in peril and
(2) Y is saliently related to X's peril and

(3) Y can hope to offer effective aid to X

(4) at a cost to Y, which is not unreasonably high, Y ought to help X.

There are some well-known questions about this principle and its applications. What counts as salience? For obvious reasons—which interact with the question of Y's being able to offer effective aid—in standard everyday cases, Y's being salient implies that Y is near at hand. Importantly, one thing that may contribute to salience is the very fact that Y can hope to give effective aid: the person who should help may be the person who has best hope of saving. The source of salience may be institutional: thus Y may be the lifeguard. In such cases there is more than a moral obligation on Y to try to help; it is part of his job. But there is also a moral obligation, and he will receive moral condemnation if he fails to rescue, both because he is seen as under a moral obligation to do his job (particularly so, when it is a job like this), and also because of other considerations: for instance, the person who is the lifeguard may well be anyway the person around most able to help.

There are additional considerations when, further,

(1A) X is in peril at the hands of Z.

I shall call this *the hostility case*. In this case, it may be difficult to satisfy the conditions that Y should be able to help, and at not too great a cost. Moreover, this point is, once more, connected with a difficulty about salience. A single person Y is unlikely as an individual to be able to help at reasonable cost to himself; or, at any rate, he is unlikely to think that he is. A collection of people may be able to help at reasonable cost. But then there is a difficulty with salience, which takes the form of a co-ordination problem: who dares, or will take the responsibility, to take the lead? This seems to be the most general explanation of the notorious failure of rescue in modern urban circumstances; and when the situation does favour a spontaneous solution to the co-ordination problem (in particular, when there is appropriate common knowledge), rescue may emerge.

However, there is the further fact that in a modern functioning state there are usually agents who are institutionally salient, in the form of the police, and private citizens predictably think that the police must be at hand, someone else must have called them, and so forth. The motives for these thoughts include fear and reasonable expectation, but in addition there is a problem of authorization. In the hostility case, there is someone to object to the rescue, and questions may arise of X's entitlement, as well as his capacity, to confront Z. It may be thought that there are issues of trespass. (A well-known Catholic philosopher in Oxford once delivered an attack—which I heard—on the National Society for the Protection and Care of Children, as it was then called, for interfering with her spouse's

God-given right to chastise their children.) Such considerations strengthen the motives for waiting for the police.

The question I want to take as framing my discussion is how far decisions to engage in international rescue can be helpfully modelled on private decisions under the moral principle of rescue. I consider in the first place decisions made by governments or at best by agencies, which are fairly directly answerable to governments. This is connected with the point I made at the beginning, that I am primarily concerned with cases that involve the use of force. My answer is: not very far. I think that when we seriously consider the asymmetries between the international and the private cases, we should conclude that we obtain the right slant on these questions by seeing such decisions as political decisions. This is not to deny that moral considerations are involved. Since the reasons for any international intervention directed toward humanitarian rescue must include the consideration that people are suffering, and this consideration in itself is a moral consideration, to this extent the matter is a moral one. But the basic point is that the decision to intervene must be political. Political decisions can be made, in part, for reasons that involve moral considerations, and they regularly are so made, when legislation is introduced to control cruelty, abuse, and so forth. To say that the decision is a political decision is to say more than that the decision is made by a government. This, as we shall see, does not even have to be true. But even when it is true, the point is that the content of the decision, and the reasons that bear on it, are non-trivially political.

The first point about international intervention is that someone has to decide to do it. It is important to remember, simply, that this is true. Often, in discussing these matters, those who favour intervention express themselves, significantly, in the passive voice: wars should be ended, tyranny should be suppressed, the hungry should be fed. This is the language of aspiration and wish, not of obligation and decision. Someone has to decide to intervene, and as I have said, I shall take this, for the moment, to mean in the international case that some state has to decide to do it. This immediately raises the question related to (2) in the moral schema, of which state is salient, and that question almost unavoidably gets an answer in terms of condition (3) in that schema: the state that is fingered is the state that has the power to intervene. In many cases, this will in fact mean one and the same state, the most powerful state, at present the United States.

There are other options, which have been mentioned by some writers: notably, neighbours. Their intervention, however, may have other reasons and other disadvantages. They are likely to carry tribal or historical baggage with them, which will mean that their intervention is not simply one of rescue; it may rather be a case of joining a war or resolving the neighbouring conflict in their own interest. In fact, they are especially likely to be in this situation. (It is worth remembering that being a neighbour does not carry with it in the international case the salience, which it often has privately, that the neighbour is the first or the only person to know about the need for rescue.) In any case, even when it is not a powerful state which intervenes, an intervention involves a decision by powerful states to encourage or discourage others. In the private case it is natural, if a bit too easy, to say, "Anyone who can take the initiative should do so." This is a bit too easy anyway, because it conceals a co-ordination problem, but, further, in the international case, it conceals the point that the co-ordination problem will be solved only with the connivance, encouragement, and generally the involvement of powerful states. Thus the powerful states themselves, and quite certainly the neighbours or others who have to take their attitudes into account, have to make a political decision.

If the question of salience lies primarily in power, then it may become insoluble in terms of the rescue paradigm. A uniquely powerful state stands at the same distance from all disasters. Consider Michael Walzer's list of possible cases for intervention: civil war, political tyranny, ethnic or religious persecution. We are confronted with a catalogue of constant and recurrent disasters which clearly has parted company with the model of the moral principle of rescue, where the passing citizen finds himself unusually saliently related to an unexpected emergency. Continual disasters are the business of the rescue *services*, and since many of the situations are of the hostility type, it is a matter of a police force as well.

If a power has a responsibility for providing such services, then it is equally responsible for supplying them in the most efficient form. It follows, surely, that it has a responsibility for preventing the disasters in the first place: a fire department is very inefficient if it only puts out fires and does not make regulations and inspect buildings for fire hazards. If a power has this responsibility for prevention, this will be a responsibility to several classes of people: to potential victims, that they should not become victims: to actual victims, that it should not make arbitrary decisions to save some and not others, when it is equally saliently related to all; and to its own citizens and perhaps to the world, that it should not use its resources inefficiently, in selective interventions after the event rather than in an efficient system of prevention. So if there is a power in a position to give "imperial assistance," that power must have a responsibility for imperial control. This must mean that such a state should use its power to stabilize the political order in the world or in its own region of the world, as the United States and the Soviet Union did before the end of the Cold War. This may be right, but it demands a series of political decisions that reach immeasurably further than what is immediately suggested by the morality of rescue.

These considerations all followed from the point that, when there is to be a rescue, someone has to decide to do it. But, in addition to that, someone has to do it. Here there is another difference from the private case. In the international case, the people who decide to intervene and the people who go on the intervention are not the same people, and this is importantly relevant to condition (4) in the original schema, the condition of reasonable risk. One reason why Y in the private case can decide to intervene is that it is Y who will intervene, and Y has the right to risk death or injury to himself (up to considerations that naturally come into applying this condition, such as his obligations to other parties). When we think of a government deciding to intervene, the first interpretation we are likely to give of "reasonable risk" will concern risks to that government or the country it governs, such as involvement in foreign wars, loss of prestige in case of failure, antagonizing other states who think that their interests are involved, and so forth. These are indeed relevant considerations, and a government would act irresponsibly if it did not weigh them in. That is part of what it is for this to be a political decision. But there is the further point that where there is danger of more than accidents, as with all the hostility cases, someone other than officials or politicians will get killed. The risk of being killed had better be rightfully imposed, and in a democratic state this requires at least that it be justifiable to the public.

I am not claiming that in the cases of rescue it cannot be justified to the public. Nor am I claiming that there is some particular constraint on the reasons that could justify it to the public: for instance, that the reasons have to relate to considerations of national interest. There are reasons that do relate to longer-term national interest, such as those of uncontrolled refugee emigration, political destabilization, the spread of disease, and so on; these are sometimes significant reasons and might reasonably help to convince the public, significant parts of the media, the political class, and so forth. But there is no reason in principle why these people should not be convinced by considerations of the suffering. If the outrages in question are of the kind that, as is often said, "shock the conscience of humankind," then they presumably shock the conscience of that part of humankind that constitutes the electorate, and if they don't, or don't shock them sufficiently for the government to be able to get away with sending troops, that is too bad—too bad, that is to say, for those who would be saved by the intervention, because it will not happen. Indeed, we need an account of why, in these circumstances, it should happen.

I put it no higher than the government "getting away with it," because that is all that is required in most democratic states. There is no need for the electorate specially to authorize the intervention, unless that is what the constitution of the particular country requires. But the government does have to be able to get away with it in the sense, and to the degree, that applies to any other serious political decision. (Nixon was often criticized for the cynicism of this.) The question of how it will play in Peoria, it should be remembered, can involve a consideration of political right, as well as of expediency.

This has all presupposed that an answer has been given to a prior question, about what situations count as cases for rescue at all, which victims qualify. The question is hardest, obviously, in hostility cases, and there are parallels to the question of authorization in the private case. Interventions under the principle of rescue presumably claim to look only to the sufferings of victims, and to be indifferent to the aspects about which it is possible to have different political opinions. But this cannot be achieved in every case; Walzer's catalogue reminds us that not all situations that produce victims produce them incidentally or uncontroversially. The victims of war are part of what makes for success or failure in war. What is seen by the United States as religious persecution may be seen by the state in question as instruction in the true religion, or the suppression of rebellion. There is no a priori reason, so far as I can see, why a powerful state should not intervene in such controversial cases, to rescue victims while at the same time acknowledging that it is likely to be intervening on one side rather than another. It is a traditional aim of enlightened imperialism. (The objectives of such an imperialism may help to meet the last problem, of justifying the intervention to the electorate.) However, it is hopeless to suppose that the world will see these aims as rising above the political level. Any decision to intervene will involve weighing the objectives of an enlightened imperialism alongside other considerations, including the effects, positive and negative, of having such a policy, in order to reach a conclusion about how the state should act if it is to make the world more as it would like the world to be, and that is what it will rightly be seen as doing.

It is standardly thought that this problem, the politically loaded choice of situations for intervention, can be avoided if the agency of intervention is not a state but some incarnation of the UN. This certainly solves the saliency problem, by creating an agent which is salient institutionally, like the rescue services. More exactly, it is like the police, since it has to deal with hostility cases. However, it is not clear how the UN, as it operates, stands in relation to the moral principle of rescue. Presumably the police and other rescue services are empowered by society so that the members of society, except in unusual circumstances, do not need to rescue, since there exists a force—constantly available, indisputably salient, properly equipped and skilled—to do what is needed. However, it is also part of the principled base of this, and not simply a matter of practical convenience, that the particular occasions on which these forces go to work are not decided by a vote of the citizens. Still less are they decided—which is the analogy in the UN—by a vote in which a veto can be exercised by the most powerful citizens (or, perhaps, by representatives of families who were the most powerful citizens fifty years ago). What makes the rescue forces an intelligible substitute for individual actions under the moral principle of rescue, and to some extent an institutional expression of that principle, is in part the fact that while they are ultimately accountable, they are autonomous in deciding when to use their powers of rescue.

This is manifestly not the case with the UN, which is under-resourced to the point of incapacity, and determined in its actions by political decisions about the immediate cases. It is a good question how far it could be anything else. Indeed, it is a plausible guess that it even looks autonomous only to the extent that it is feeble. If it were well-resourced and commanded credible standing forces, it would be of even greater concern to nation-states that they should control, through international politics, how its rescue activities should be applied.

There is a thought experiment that may be worth conducting in this connection. There are of course agencies that to a limited extent carry out rescue operations independent of decisions by major powers: the NGOs such as OXFAM or conflict resolution agencies. Of course, they cannot be completely independent of those powers, and they are dependent on the goodwill of governments or other forces in territories where they operate. Above all, they cannot deal with hostile forces. If they operate to stop conflicts, it is by mediation, advocacy, arranging negotiations, and the like, not by deploying forces. But imagine such an NGO extremely well funded and commanding military forces. The funds would come from charitable billionaires; the forces would consist of idealistic mercenaries; decisions of policy would be made by a guiding committee of respected international figures. Such a body would of course have to negotiate its operations with states, including powerful states whose interests were involved in a given case, but if its prestige were high, and its public relations well managed, and it stuck very firmly to the objectives of rescue, it might be embarrassing for states to impede its activities too frequently or too obviously.

This is not a practical proposal, not altogether serious, but it may help to focus certain questions. Is there an objection in principle to it? The obvious objection is that it is not answerable to anyone. But that, in a sense, is the point. It is, above all, the fact that the governments which intervene, as things are, are politically highly answerable that makes the decision to intervene inescapably and essentially political, in the various ways I have tried to outline. If there were to be a mechanism of intervention that expressed internationally the moral principle of rescue, then perhaps it should be answerable only to the moral consciousness of humankind. The agency I have imagined seems to be at least better designed to do that than any other that has been mentioned.

The question then is, whether those who want the morality of rescue, as such, to be expressed in the world would welcome an agency of this kind. If they would have doubts about it, then they have to consider whether there really is any alternative to the situation we have and which I have described. This is a situation in which the sufferings of victims constitute one consideration among others in political decisions, decisions which have to be justified to people like other political decisions. Because of many features associated with the fact that these are political decisions, the consideration of victims' suffering is likely to determine policy only occasionally. It is hard to imagine a world in which it could be otherwise.

THIRTEEN

Truth, Politics, and Self-Deception

1. THE TRUTH: VIRTUES AND METHODS

There are social practices and virtues which, if we are to characterize them, require us to mention *the truth*. This is not the same as mentioning what other people hold true (their beliefs); or just mentioning what we regard as true (our own beliefs). We may contrast in this respect two different virtues of truth, which may be labelled *sincerity* and *accuracy*. Sincerity (at the most basic level) merely implies that people say what they believe to be true—that is, what they believe. Accuracy implies care, reliability, and so on, in discovering and coming to believe the truth.

Among other questions that involve mentioning *the truth*, there are those concerning the properties of various methods of belief formation. Thus if one is interested in the probable success of some military venture, augury is not a good method of acquiring true belief about it. It seems that there is a genuine property which some methods of inquiry have and others (such as augury) lack, that of being (roughly) truth-acquiring. It is dubious, though, that there is any interesting and non-trivial description of this property *in general*, as opposed to the form that it may take in particular sorts of case.

It may be suggested that we can say at least this much, that no method will have the desirable property if its efficacy in generating the belief that P would extend equally to generating the belief that not-P. In one sense this claim is correct. It is obvious, indeed trivial, that a method of inquiry will be ineffective—indeed, will not be a method for acquiring the truth at all—if its outcome is random with respect to the truth. But in another sense the claim is incorrect. A method of inquiry is a method that can answer a question, and this itself means that it can generate the belief that P (if P), and also can generate the belief that not-P (if not-P). A method which lacks the desired property is, rather, one that will generate the belief that P even if not-P, and conversely. But this simply says that such a method generates belief without regard to its truth, and so is useless, and this is the triviality, which gets us nowhere.

The correct conclusion is that, just as there is no characterization of *the truth* which is both non-trivial and totally general, there is no general and non-trivial account of *finding the truth* or *method which favours finding the truth*.

We need general ideas such as *method of acquiring the truth*, but when we consider ways in which such ideas can be made effective, we are necessarily returned to the platitude that "P" is true if and only if P. Methods of acquiring the truth on the question whether P are methods of establishing whether P, and the question of what they may be is connected with what the particular proposition P is. In particular, it is connected with what the proposition means, though it is not simply determined by that, as various forms of verificationism and operationalism have claimed.

So far we have been concerned with methods of inquiry or truth-discovery: the situation in which no one in the relevant group knows whether P. But similar considerations apply to methods of preserving and transmitting the truth (these include at the basic level the virtue of sincerity). Of course, what is truth-transmission or preservation from one perspective can be truth-discovery from another.

Our present concern is with the transmission of truth over time and transmission between people.[1] Issues raised by this may be related in varying degrees to the medium and to characteristics of the message which are not simply content-related. Besides the straightforward cases of physical preservation, as with nitrate film-stock degeneration and acid paper, there are examples in which some characteristics of the message or the way in which it is expressed affect the outcome, as in famous anecdotes about oral transmission. My interest here will above all be in characteristics of the message and the medium which are relevant to truth-preservation and which are content-related, for instance because they involve interests in propagating, distorting, concealing, or interpreting the message.

The basic point is that (beyond the most elementary and unspecific description) it is a factual question, relative to a given class of information, how far a given method of acquiring or transmitting truth is effective. It is also important, if obvious, that multiple methods which are severally effective, or multiple applications of one effective method, cannot necessarily be combined or superimposed, without loss of effectiveness (e.g., everyone speaking at once). This is a qualification to the encouraging idea that truth is a paradigm of a non-zero-sum good. It is a non-zero-sum good because the mere fact that A comes to possess a given truth does not mean that B has less of it. But, for all that, the joint attempts of A and B to possess, or to express, truth may well mean that both or one has less of it.

The basic point, then, is that effective methods of discovering or transmitting the truth will vary with the kinds of truth in question. Formula-

---

[1] For simplicity, I shall not treat non-personal information storage systems separately.

tions of what makes methods effective are likely to be trivial if they aim to be very general. However, there are some general conditions which are notably less trivial than others; or, even if they are trivial as practical advice, they are significant from a theoretical point of view. One of them is the ubiquitous danger of wishful thinking, which lies in the quite general indifference of the truth to what the inquirer, narrator, recollector, or informant would like it to be.[2] The virtues of accuracy, as I labelled them at the beginning, include, very importantly, dispositions and strategies for combating wishful thinking, and generally sustaining the defences of belief against wish.

In this, there is a consideration relevant to the way in which we should think about self-deception. There is a very well known question, whether what is called "self-deception" can be seriously seen as a species of deception at all. But suppose we jump over that problem and accept for the sake of argument that someone can, more or less literally, deceive himself. We then encounter another, and less discussed, question of where the fault in this transaction is located. The standard picture is that the fault lies with the self as deceiver—that we should concentrate on self-deception as a failure of sincerity. But at the ordinary social, interpersonal, level, when there are deceivers around, it is at least as important to improve the caution of the potentially deceived as it is to censure the motives of the deceivers. The virtue of accuracy in listeners is as important as sincerity in informants. If there is such a thing as self-deception, the same, surely, should apply to it: our failures as self-deceived are to be found more significantly, in fact, in our lack of epistemic prudence as victims than in our insincerity as perpetrators.

My concern in this paper is primarily with applying the considerations about truth, its discovery and transmission, in a political connection, to issues of free speech and public discourse. But the application of those considerations to the question of self-deception is not irrelevant to that purpose. In the political case, there are of course many potential deceivers and many potentially deceived who are straightforwardly separate people, and much of the discussion will necessarily be concerned with questions of how to make life difficult for the former. But there is also the significant phenomenon of collective self-deceit, where (as in the personal case, if we take it a little more seriously) deceiver and deceived conspire with one another, and we shall come back to that.

---

[2] I have discussed this general point, and some relevantly various cases of wanting something to be true, in "Deciding to Believe," reprinted in *Problems of the Self* (Cambridge: Cambridge University Press, 1973).

2. TRUTHFULNESS AND THE POLITICAL

I have not so far used the notion of *truthfulness*. It should be understood as a virtue or desirable property, both of individual people and of collectivities, which combines the qualities that were labelled earlier as sincerity and accuracy. A truthful person both says (with numerous familiar qualifications) what he or she believes, and takes some trouble that his or her beliefs should be true. Because of its connection with accuracy, it is a quality that essentially involves mentioning *the truth*, in the ways discussed earlier, and this will be important to the discussion of truthfulness in politics.

We may start from some questions of why and how truthfulness matters in government, and what follows from its mattering. (The arguments that follow, focussing on government, can be broadened in various ways to apply to political life more generally.) One argument for truthfulness in government is to be found just in arguments for truthfulness. If it is a good thing (other things being equal) for people to be truthful, it is a good thing for people in government to be truthful. But this is rather a modest basis. It follows a general pattern of argument for governmental virtue, against which there stands a moderate version of Machiavelli's thesis: the responsibilities of government are sufficiently different from those of private individuals to make governmental virtue a rather different matter from that of individuals—or rather (and this is very much the point) from that of individuals who are being protected by a government. In particular, any government is charged with the security of its citizens, a responsibility which cannot be discharged without secrecy, and which it will be lucky if it can discharge without force and fraud.

But Machiavelli's axiom itself helps to provide the first argument:

(1) *The anti-tyranny argument*: precisely because of their peculiar powers and opportunities, governments are disposed to commit illegitimate actions which they will wish to conceal, as also to conceal incompetent actions. It is in citizens' interests that these be checked. They cannot be checked without true information.

This yields only the conclusion that someone other than the government should have information, not the populace at large. In some areas, this is a practical point: security secrets, for instance, may be shared in a democracy with non-executive legislators, senior members of opposition parties, and so forth. But the argument may be iterated to suggest that this is not in general enough: either these other groups are sufficiently distinct from government for the government to have interests in deceiving them, or they are close enough to government to form part of the threat of tyranny (that of an elite or political class). This argues for truth's being available, with restrictions, to all the potentially tyrannized.

This, in turn, may be associated with a more a priori argument to the same effect:

> (2) *The argument from democracy*: the people are the source of the government's authority and, under restrictions, of the government's policies. Government is a trust. It is a violation of this conception for secrecy or falsehood to come between trustee and people.

This yields a more comprehensive and less contingent conclusion than does (1). The downside is its high degree of idealization, reflected in such well-known difficulties as this, that either "the people" means everyone, in which case it includes many against whose activities the trust is being exercised, or it is a construct, and—it may be said—an ideological and potentially dangerous construct, of the kind vividly illustrated by the events of 1793/94. This disjunction is not of course exhaustive, but it does make clear that (2) by itself leaves many problems about what should actually happen.

In order to yield more definite and comprehensive results, (1) and (2) can be fortified with a further argument, from yet more distinctive political conceptions:

> (3) *The liberal argument*, which comes in two versions: (3a) the *minimal* version, and (3b) the *self-development* version. (3a) Government should permit maximal freedom (compatible with other political goods); denial of information is an important limitation of freedom in itself and impedes the exercise of freedom in many areas. (3b) Self-development consists of the exercise and development of one's powers in the light of the truth. (3a) might be called the argument from negative freedom, and (3b) the argument from positive freedom, so long as this is not taken to imply that they are, just in themselves, incompatible with one another.
>
> (3b) does lead distinctively to the value of *the truth* in truthfulness, which is much less the case with (3a). On the other hand, it is less clear what (3b) delivers, and the value it calls on is more distinctive and deniable; there is a contrast here with (1), which appeals to what anyone would regard as an evil.

In the light of these very rough categories, we can ask whether—as many would claim—being lied to by the government is worse than being lied to by others. Argument (2) gives a special reason why the answer to this question should be "yes." Argument (1) also yields a positive answer, and of course the word "tyranny" in its normal sense signifies this fact.

However, this is simply because the powers and opportunities that government possesses are what they are: any great concentration of power can generate a great evil in disseminating falsehood. In this sense, the evil of governmental lying is less special under this argument than it is under argument (2). The liberal arguments under (3), and particularly argument (3b), perhaps give us even less reason to regard the lying of government as something special, or as more than contingently so.

A rather different aspect of truthfulness comes out if we turn from deceit to secrecy. It is a truism that in general secrecy may be justified where lying is not: one has a right to be told (if anything) the truth, even where one has no right to be told anything. (This is no doubt related to the values involved in the transmission of truth as contrasted with the acquisition or dissemination of truth.) The two different questions are deliberately run together in the journalists' favourite slogan, "the right to know."[3]

It is in virtue of this ethical truism that governmental secrecy is accepted to a much greater extent than governmental lying. However, there is an old adage, "Who asks no questions gets told no lies," and the question of how many lies have to be told is a direct function of how great the insistence is on being given an answer. This implies the correct conclusion that suspiciousness about government tends to be self-justifying. In fact, the situation is more complicated than this implies. The government's behaviour in information-management depends not just on the degree of curiosity, but also on the public's expectations of government (which themselves can also directly affect the degree of curiosity). The "expectations of government" cover both the matter of whether the public expects the government to behave badly, and also what it counts as "badly." The best results with regard to truth-management are unlikely to follow from the attitude adopted, or more usually feigned, by the media, which is that of unlimited intrusiveness combined with unlimited righteousness on the subject of how government can be expected to behave.

Now this is a conclusion only with regard to *the truth*, based on considerations of what institutions and practices are likely to favour, in political connections, the discovery and transmission of the truth. There may be other arguments in favour of the media's, and other people's, being as intrusive as they like, and taking whatever attitude they like to what they take themselves to have discovered. This will be an argument from freedom, in particular an argument from freedom of speech. The present

---

[3] The casuistical tradition has had much to say about the differences between concealment and deceit, as it has also about what counts as deceit. On one, broad, view what is bad about lying is shared by other forms of deliberately misleading people; on a narrower view, it lies specifically in a misuse of the device of assertion. An approach such as the present one, which starts from our shared interest in the truth, is likely to favour the broader view, but I shall not pursue the issue here.

point is that it must be a substantive question, to what extent given practices based on the value of free speech also serve the values of truth and truthfulness. This is why, as I have already suggested, it cannot be assumed that the liberal argument about negative freedom, (3a), delivers a conclusion that favours, specifically, the values of truth.

The argument (3a) directly implies a strong presumption that anyone can say or ask anything, and the most influential interpretation of this offers a strong presumption against intervention in a marketplace of communication (construed in good part as indeed a marketplace). However, one has to recall at this point the claim made in the first section of this paper, that it is a factual question what systems are favourable to truth-discovery and truth-transmission, with respect to given kinds of truths. It is very doubtful how effective the market system is, with regard to many kinds of truths.

There are two very familiar reasons for doubts about the market system. One is *noise*, the familiar point that messages compete for attention and cancel each other out. This would be a serious problem even if the messages were each true, but in any case the system does not strongly encourage this to be the case, in particular because messages are picked out for reasons that need not have much to do with truth. Further, the system tends not to offer any structured context for understanding messages. Typically, recipients will know that a given message means that P, but not know what that means.

If we take these familiar problems seriously, and if we look at the market system from the point of view of the various arguments in favour of truthfulness in politics, it does not do very well by the arguments other than (3a): this fits the point, already made, that (3a) is not all that interested in truth as such. The market system does not do too badly by a minimum interpretation of (1), since tyrannical outrages have quite a good chance of becoming known.[4] It does not do well for (2), unless democracy is understood in a radically populist sense, particularly because of the point about the absence of a context to make a given piece of information intelligible.

The market system also does badly for (3b), assuming that this is concerned with self-development in the light of some significant or important class of truths, and not just the narcissistic self-construction out of commercially available materials which is sometimes called "autonomy," and which is a well-known target of cultural critics. A position that consists

---

[4] There is of course an interpretation of "tyranny" under which the marker system is precisely its ally and instrument. This was advanced by the Frankfurt School, but it is difficult to detach that interpretation from an immensely ideological construction of (2).

of the conjunction of (3a) and (3b)—idealistic liberalism—runs the risk of being inconsistent, granted the effects of the market system.

The merits of the market system have, perhaps, been exaggerated because liberal historiography tends to treat the history of science as a triumph of the market over restrictive practices. But this is incorrect. The emergence of scientific inquiry from restrictions exercised by the Church involved a change in the legitimation of belief with respect to physical nature, together no doubt with some changes in the notion of "nature," which improved truth-discovery; and it involved free scientific inquiry. But free scientific inquiry is itself a clear example of a managed market, and it must be, since it involves such things as an increasingly high entry fee in terms of training, and, necessarily, a powerful filter against cranks.

The limitations of the market system are acknowledged in modern societies by the presence of compulsory education, which besides its other functions can help under all the arguments. But there is a notable shortfall (at best a compromise between what is necessary and what can reasonably be demanded) between the standard results of such systems, and what would be needed if one took seriously the demands of truthfulness, particularly with regard to arguments (2) and (3b).

Certainly these are not arguments for replacing freedom of speech with a supposedly authoritative source of pronouncements. Apart from the well-rehearsed values of freedom, a mechanism of that kind would certainly do no better by the test of truthfulness itself. What they do remind us, however, is that it is one thing for a system to encourage freedom of expression, and another for it to be a system which is well adjusted to discovering and transmitting the truth in given areas, and it is always a substantive question, how far the first feature helps the second, in itself or by comparison with alternatives—a question which does not always get a positive answer. Consideration of that point should certainly have policy implications, with regard to such things as public education, public broadcasting systems, and control of the ownership of the media.

3. Who Needs Truth?

The argument of section 1 rested on the idea that it is a genuine characteristic of some methods as against others that they favour the discovery or transmission of the truth, in given areas; and section 2 assumed that some such areas are relevant to politics. Some people might doubt both these claims; others might accept the first and doubt the second.

I am not sure how many people really doubt the first, once it has been made clear that it is not a question of some large "positivistic" claim that all questions are to be settled by one general, for instance scientific, method. In any case, this is not the place to try to argue with this scepticism. It is worth pointing out, perhaps, that the most fashionable reasons for such a scepticism in fact rely on its being incorrect. Those reasons rest on claims that various important structures of what is taken to be knowledge, in history, or in the social sciences, or (in the boldest versions) even in the natural sciences, are the product of various kinds of ideological distortion. The objection to this is not that all such claims must be false: some may be true.[5] The objection is that we are given some reason to accept such claims only because *something else* is taken to be discoverably true, such as the findings of a genealogical method which, as Foucault put it, is "gray, meticulous, and patiently documentary."[6] It is in the light of these findings that we can understand how the historical interpretations, or whatever they may be, have come about, and their genesis turns out to have too little to do with truth. The scepticism, then, is not and could not be about the very idea of truth and of methods for discovering it. It is rather about the extent to which certain large-scale stories which are or have been important to our life consist of discoverable truth, and that indeed can be a very real type of question.

But how far does truth matter to politics? It is hard to deny, at least, that some reliable types of inquiry and transmission of truth are necessary for administration. It is hard to resist, too, the force of the anti-tyranny argument, that the fear of abuse is always urgent enough to discourage, from the point of view of mere prudence, institutions of deceit, mystification, and concealment. But beyond those lines—and it is of course a good question, how far and in what directions those lines themselves extend—what follows? If we were deeply participant citizens, then each of us would have an immediate interest in truth in politics. But we cannot all be, and few of us want to be, and in this situation the fact that our institutions of education and communication, in particular the media, are not well designed for the discovery and transmission of politically relevant truths, may seem less to the point.

What they are better designed for, besides selling things, is certain kinds of entertainment. This might be seen, if charitably, as resting simply on a tacit agreement among the consumers, the providers, and those who shape the space in which the market operates, that what is provided is,

---

[5] Nor is it that such a claim will be intelligible only if we have some conception of what an undistorted account, at the same level, would be like: though the issue needs argument, it does not look as though that need be so.

[6] Michel Foucault, "Nietzsche, Genealogy, History," trans. Donald Bouchard and Sherry Simon, in *Language, Counter-Memory, Practice*, ed. Donald Bouchard (Ithaca: Cornell University Press, 1977).

most of the time, concerned neither with truth nor with politics.[7] But apart from the point that this is clearly an exaggeration, it is also too simple, since an important contribution to entertainment in many modern societies is made by what is supposed to be politics. Political leaders and aspirants certainly appear before the public and make claims about the world and each other. However, the way in which these people are presented, particularly if they are prominent, creates to a remarkable degree an impression that they are in fact characters in a soap opera, being played by people of the same name. They are called by their first names or have the same kind of jokey nicknames as soap opera characters, the same broadly sketched personalities, the same dispositions to triumphs and humiliations which are schematically related to the doings of the other characters. When they reappear, they give the same impression of remembering only just in time to carry on from where they left off, and they equally disappear into the script of the past after something else more interesting has come up. It would not be right to say that when one takes the view of these people that is offered in the media, one does not believe in them. One believes in them as one believes in characters in a soap: one accepts the invitation to half believe in them.

The world in which such characters exist is often thought to be a creation of television, and there is certainly a lot here that comes from television, with its disposition to make everything mediatedly immediate. But in itself the basic status of figures of this kind is as old as storytelling. It is the status of myth. With regard to myths, when they are actually alive, questions of true and false are elided: indeed, one might rather say that in the most naive presentations of myth those questions are not even elided, since they had not come up in relation to these stories. It was something of an achievement eventually to raise them, as Thucydides did, when he started to work on the economics of the Trojan War. It is no accident, of course, that many myths have their origins, remotely, in what we would recognize as real events: some battles somewhere underlay the *Iliad* or the *Chanson de Roland*. The tale that is told, though certainly it is not presented by these poems as a piece of positivist historiography, is not presented as merely fictional either.

I mentioned earlier the idea that in self-deception there is a kind of conspiracy between deceiver and deceived, and in those terms there can be such a thing as collective self-deception. This applies to the representation of politics in our societies now. The status of politics as represented in the media is ambiguous between entertainment and the transmission of discoverable truth, and rather as the purveyor of living myth is in league

---

[7] Once again—see n. 4 above—I leave aside the old Critical Theory interpretation that the arrangement functionally works to make the consumers unfree.

with his audience to tell a tale into which they will enter, so politicians, the media, and the audience conspire to pretend that important realities are being seriously considered, that the actual world is being responsibly addressed. However, there is a difference. Those who heard the songs about Troy, when those conveyed living myths, were not at Troy, but when we are confronted with today's politics, we are supposed to be in some real relation to today.

This means that in our case, more than with living myth, the conspiracy comes closer to that of self-deception, the great enemy of truthfulness, because the wish that is expressed in these relations is subverting a real truth, that very little of the world under consideration, our present world, is in fact being responsibly addressed. We cannot after all simply forget the need for our relations to that world to be truthful, or give up asking to what extent our institutions, including the institutions of freedom, help them to be so.

Bernard Williams: Writings of Political Interest

This select bibliography does not include any of the essays in the present volume. A complete bibliography of Williams's philosophical publications appears in his *The Sense of the Past: Essays in the History of Philosophy*, edited by Myles Burnyeat (Princeton: Princeton University Press, 2006), and in his *Philosophy as a Humanistic Discipline*, edited by A. W. Moore (Princeton: Princeton University Press, 2006).

Books

Morality: An Introduction to Ethics. New York: Harper & Row, 1972. Harmondsworth: Penguin, 1973. Cambridge: Cambridge University Press, 1976; Canto edition, with new introduction, 1993.
  German translation: *Der Begriff der Moral*. Leipzig: Reclam, 1978.
  Romanian translation: *Introducere in etica*. Bucharest: Editura Alternative, 1993.
  French translation: see *La fortune morale* (1994).
  Italian translation (of the Canto edition): *La moralità: un'introduzione all'etica*. Rome: Einaudi, 2000.
  Polish translation: *Moralność: Wprowadzenie do etyki*. Warsaw: Fundacia Aletheia, 2000.
A Critique of Utilitarianism. In *Utilitarianism: For and Against*, by J.J.C. Smart and Bernard Williams. Cambridge: Cambridge University Press, 1973.
  German translation: *Kritik des Utilitarismus*. Frankfurt am Main: Klostermann, 1979.
  Spanish translation: *Utilitarismo: pro y contra*. Madrid: Tecnos, 1981.
  Italian translation: *Utilitarismo: un confronto*. Naples: Bibliopolis, 1985.
  French translation: *Utilitarisme: le pour et le contre*. Le Champ Ethique. Geneva: Labor et Fides, 1997.
Ethics and the Limits of Philosophy. London: Fontana Books; Cambridge: Harvard University Press, 1985.
  Italian translation: *L'etica e i limiti della filosofia*. Bari: Laterza, 1987.
  French translation: *L'éthique et les limites de la philosophie*. Paris: Editions Gallimard, 1990.
  Japanese translation: *Ikikata ni tsuite Tetsugaku wa Nani ga Ieru ka*. Tokyo: Sangyoutosho K.K., 1993.
  Spanish translation: *La etica y los limites de la filosofia*. Caracas: Monte Avila Editores, 1997.
  German translation: *Ethik und die Grenzen der Philosophie*. Hamburg: Rotbuch Verlag, 1999.

Shame and Necessity. Sather Classical Lectures, vol. 57. Berkeley and Los Angeles: University of California Press, 1993.
> French translation: *La honte et la nécessité.* Presses Universitaires de France, 1997.
> German translation: *Scham, Schuld und Notwendigkeit.* Polis, vol. 1. Berlin: Akademie Verlag, 2000.

Truth and Truthfulness: An Essay in Genealogy. Princeton: Princeton University Press, 2002.
> German translation: *Wahrheit und Wahrhaftigeit.* Frankfurt am Main: Surhrkamp, 2003.
> Italian translation: *Genealogia della verità: storia e virtù del dire il vero.* Rome: Fazi Editore, 2005.
> French translation: Title still unknown. Paris: Editions Gallimard, 2005.

EDITED BOOK

(With A. K. Sen.) *Utilitarianism and Beyond.* Cambridge: Cambridge University Press, 1982.
> Italian translation: *Utilitarismo e oltre.* Milan: Il Saggiatore, 1984.

ARTICLES

"Democracy and Ideology." *Political Quarterly* 32 (1961).

"Genetics and Moral Responsibility." In *Morals and Medicine.* London: BBC Publications, 1970.

"The Analogy of City and Soul in Plato's *Republic.*" In *Exegesis and Argument: Studies in Greek Philosophy. Essays Presented to Gregory Vlastos,* edited by E. N. Lee, A.P.D. Mourelatos, and R. M. Rorty. The Hague: Martinus Nijhoff, 1973. Reprinted in *The Sense of the Past.*

Remarks in *The Law and Ethics of AIDS and Embryo Transfer.* CIBA Foundation Symposium 17. Amsterdam: Elsevier/North-Holland, 1973.

"The Truth in Relativism." *Proceedings of the Aristotelian Society* 75 (1974–75). Reprinted in Bernard Williams, *Moral Luck: Philosophical Papers 1973–1980.* Cambridge: Cambridge University Press, 1981.

"Rawls and Pascal's Wager." *Cambridge Review,* February 28, 1975. Reprinted in *Moral Luck.*

"The Moral View of Politics." *The Listener,* June 3, 1976.

"Thinking about Abortion." *The Listener,* September 1, 1977.

"Politics and Moral Character." In *Public and Private Morality,* edited by Stuart Hampshire. Cambridge: Cambridge University Press, 1978. Reprinted in *Moral Luck.*

"Conflicts of Values." In *The Idea of Freedom: Essays in Honour of Isaiah Berlin,* edited by A. Ryan. Oxford: Oxford University Press, 1979. Reprinted in *Moral Luck.*

"Internal and External Reasons." In *Rational Action: Studies in Philosophy and Social Science,* edited by T. R. Harrison. Cambridge: Cambridge University Press, 1979. Reprinted in *Moral Luck.*

"Political Philosophy and the Analytical Tradition." In *Political Theory and Political Education*, edited by M. Richter. Princeton: Princeton University Press, 1980. Reprinted in *Philosophy as a Humanistic Discipline*.

"Justice as a Virtue." In *Essays on Aristotle's Ethics*, edited by A. Rorty. Berkeley and Los Angeles: University of California Press, 1981. Reprinted in *Moral Luck* and *The Sense of the Past*.

"Space Talk: The Conversation Continued." (Comment on B. Ackerman's *Social Justice in the Liberal State*.) *Ethics* 93 (1983).

"Professional Morality and Its Dispositions." In *The Good Lawyer: Lawyers' Roles and Lawyers' Ethics*, edited by David Luban. Maryland Studies in Public Philosophy. Totowa, NJ: Rowman and Allenheld, 1983. Reprinted in Bernard Williams, *Making Sense of Humanity and Other Philosophical Papers 1982–1993*. Cambridge: Cambridge University Press, 1995.

"Morality, Scepticism and the Nuclear Arms Race." In *Objections to Nuclear Defence: Philosophers on Deterrence*, edited by N. Blake and K. Pole. London: Routledge, 1984.

"Formal and Substantial Individualism." *Proceedings of the Aristotelian Society* 85 (1984–85). Reprinted in *Making Sense of Humanity*.

"Theories of Social Justice—Where Next?" In *Equality and Discrimination: Essays in Freedom and Justice*, edited by S. Guest and A. Milne. Archiv für Rechts- und Sozialphilosophie, 21. Stuttgart: F. Steiner, 1985.

"What Slopes Are Slippery?" In *Moral Dilemmas in Modern Medicine*, edited by M. Lockwood. Oxford: Oxford University Press, 1985. Reprinted in *Making Sense of Humanity*.

"L'intervista di *Politeia*: Bernard Williams." *Politeia* (Milan) (Winter 1986).

"Types of Moral Argument against Embryo Research." In *Human Embryo Research: Yes or No?* London: Tavistock Publications, for the CIBA Foundation, 1986. Reprinted in *BioEssays* 6 (1987).

Comments on Amartya Sen's Tanner Lectures, 1985, in Amartya Sen, *The Standard of Living*. Cambridge: Cambridge University Press, 1987.

"Formal Structures and Social Reality." In *Trust: Making and Breaking Co-operative Relations*, edited by Diego Gambetta. Oxford: Blackwell, 1988. Reprinted in *Making Sense of Humanity*.

"Dworkin on Community and Critical Interests." *California Law Review* 77 (1989).

"Social Justice: The Agenda in Social Philosophy for the Nineties." *Journal of Social Philosophy* 20 (1989).

"Who Might I Have Been?" In *Human Genetic Information: Science, Law and Ethics*. CIBA Foundation Symposium 149. Chichester: John Wiley & Sons, 1990. Reprinted in a revised version, entitled "Resenting One's Own Existence," in *Making Sense of Humanity*.

"Making Sense of Humanity." In *The Boundaries of Humanity: Humans, Animals, Machines*, edited by James Sheenan and Morton Sosna. Proceedings of Stanford University Centennial Conference, 1987. Berkeley and Los Angeles: University of California Press, 1991. Reprinted in *Making Sense of Humanity*.

"Saint-Just's Illusion: Interpretation and the Powers of Philosophy." *London Review of Books*, August 29, 1991. Reprinted in *Making Sense of Humanity*.

"Must a Concern for the Environment Be Centred on Human Beings?" In *Ethics and the Environment*, edited by C.C.W. Taylor. Oxford: Corpus Christi College, 1992. Reprinted in *Making Sense of Humanity*.

"Who Needs Ethical Knowledge?" In *Ethics*, edited by A. P. Griffiths. Royal Institute of Philosophy Lectures, 1992. Cambridge: Cambridge University Press, 1993. Reprinted in *Making Sense of Humanity*.

"Censorship in a Borderless World." Faculty Lecture 16, Faculty of Arts and Social Sciences. Singapore: National University of Singapore, 1996.

"The Politics of Trust." In *The Geography of Identity*, edited by Patricia Yaeger. Ann Arbor: University of Michigan Press, 1996.

"Toleration: An Impossible Virtue?" In *Toleration: An Elusive Virtue*, edited by David Heyd. Princeton: Princeton University Press, 1996.

"Shame, Guilt and the Structure of Punishment." *Festschrift* for the Margrit Egner-Stiftung Prize. Zürich, 1997.

"Forward to Basics." In *Equality*, edited by Jane Franklin. (Discussions of the Report of the Commission on Social Justice, 1997.) London: IPPR, 1997.

"Moral Responsibility and Political Freedom." *Cambridge Law Journal* 56 (1997). Reprinted in *Philosophy as a Humanistic Discipline*.

"Tolerating the Intolerable." In *The Politics of Toleration in Modern Life*, edited by Susan Mendus. Edinburgh: Edinburgh University Press, 1999. Durham: Duke University Press, 2000. Reprinted in *Philosophy as a Humanistic Discipline*.

"Liberalism and Loss." In *The Legacy of Isaiah Berlin*, edited by Mark Lilla, Ronald Dworkin, and Robert Silvers. New York: New York Review of Books, 2001.

"The Human Prejudice." In *Philosophy as a Humanistic Discipline*.

OCCASIONAL JOURNALISM

"The Theological Appearance of the Church of England." *Prism*, June 1960.

"Personal View." *The Listener*, October 24, November 7 and 21, 1963.

Letter (with Michael Tanner) about G.E.M. Anscombe's "Contraception and Chastity." *The Human World*, November 9, 1971.

"Discussion with Hailsham." *The Listener*, July 11, 1974.

"Paul Johnson on the State of the Universities." *Times Higher Education Supplement*, November 21, 1975.

"Portrait of the Artist as Professional Lodger." *Times Higher Education Supplement*, September 5, 1980.

"Whistle Blowing in the Public Service." In *Politics, Ethics and Public Service*. London: Royal Institute of Public Administration, 1985.

"Necessity Disguised as Luxury." (Based on Raymond Priestley Lecture, Birmingham, November 1986.) *Times Higher Education Supplement*, January 23, 1987.

"Beyond Unconscious Britain." *Times*, February 10, 1987.

"What Hope for the Humanities?" The Raymond Priestley Lecture, Birmingham, November 1986. *Educational Review* 39, no. 3 (1987).

"Toleration: An Awkward Virtue." *Unesco Courier*, June 1992.

"Problems of Identity." (Condensed version of Herbert Spencer Lecture, 1992.) *Times Higher Education Supplement*, December 4, 1992.

Contribution to symposium on pornography. *Threepenny Review* 55 (Fall 1993).

"Social Justice." *Times*, October 24, 1994.

"Suppression and Restriction of Pornography: Long Spoons and the Supper of the Righteous." In *Reservoirs of Dogma*, edited by R. Collins and J. Purnell. London: Institute for Public Policy Research, 1996.

"De moraal van de schaamte." (Interview.): *Filosofie Magazine* (Holland), February 1996.

"On Hating and Despising Philosophy." *London Review of Books*, April 18, 1996.

"Scholarship, Authenticity, Honesty." In *Musicology and Sister Disciplines: Past, Present, Future*, edited by David Greer, with Ian Rumbold and Jonathan King. Oxford: Oxford University Press, 2000.

Selected Reviews

The Liberal Hour, by J. K. Galbraith; *Kennedy or Nixon?*, by Arthur Schlesinger, Jr. *Spectator*, November 4, 1960.

Morals and Markets, by H. B. Acton. *Guardian*, April 1, 1971.

Responsibility, by Jonathan Glover. *Mental Health* (1971).

Education and the Development of Reason, edited by R. F. Deardon, P. H. Hirst, and R. S. Peters. *Times Literary Supplement*, April 1972.

A Theory of Justice, by John Rawls. *Spectator*, June 22, 1972.

Beyond Freedom and Justice, by B. F. Skinner. *Observer*, March 1972.

The Socialist Idea, edited by Stuart Hampshire and L. Kolakowski. *Observer*, January 5, 1975.

Anarchy, State, and Utopia, by R. Nozick. *Times Literary Supplement*, January 17, 1975.

Ethics of Fetal Research, by Paul Ramsey. *Times Literary Supplement*, September 5, 1975.

"Where Chomsky Stands." *New York Review*, November 11, 1976.

Life Chances, by R. Dahrendorf. *Observer*, January 27, 1980.

Rubbish Theory, by Michael Thompson. *London Review of Books*, February 1980.

Lying, by Sissela Bok. *Political Quarterly* (1980).

Logic and Society and *Ulysses and the Sirens*, by Jon Elster. *London Review of Books*, May 1, 1980.

The Culture of Narcissism, by Christopher Lasch; *Nihilism and Culture*, by Johan Goudsblom. *London Review of Books*, July 17, 1980.

Religion and Public Doctrine in England, by M. Cowling. *London Review of Books*, April 2, 1981.

Offensive Literature, by John Sutherland. *London Review of Books*, March 17, 1983.

Critical Philosophy and *Journal of Applied Philosophy*. *Times Higher Education Supplement*, June 15, 1984.

Secrets, by Sissela Bok; *The Secrets File*, by D. Wilson. *London Review of Books*, October 18, 1984.

Choice and Consequence, by Thomas Schelling. *Economics and Philosophy* (1985).

Privacy: Studies in Social and Cultural History, by Barrington Moore, Jr. *New York Review of Books*, April 25, 1985.

Ordinary Vices, by Judith Shklar; *Immorality*, by Ronald Milo. *London Review of Books*, June 6, 1985.

The Right to Know, by Clive Ponting; *The Price of Freedom*, by Judith Cook. *Times Literary Supplement*, October 4, 1985.

Taking Sides, by Michael Harrington. *New York Times Book Review* [mid-1980s?].

A Matter of Principle, by Ronald Dworkin. *London Review of Books*, April 17, 1986.

Whose Justice? Which Rationality? by Alasdair MacIntyre. *Los Angeles Tribune*, 1988.
    Reprint: *London Review of Books*, January 5, 1989.

Contingency, Irony, and Solidarity, by Richard Rorty. *London Review of Books*, November 1989.

Sources of the Self, by Charles Taylor. *New York Review of Books*, October 1990.

Political Liberalism, by John Rawls. *London Review of Books*, May 13, 1993.

Inequality Reexamined, by Amartya Sen. *London Review of Books*, November 1993.

REPORTS BY PUBLIC BODIES ON WHICH BERNARD WILLIAMS SERVED

The Public Schools Commission: First Report. Chairman: John Newsom. Her Majesty's Stationery Office, 1968.

Royal Commission on Gambling: Final Report. Chairman: Victor Rothschild. Her Majesty's Stationery Office, 1978.

Report of the Committee on Obscenity and Film Censorship. Chairman: Bernard Williams. Her Majesty's Stationery Office, 1979. Also published by the Cambridge University Press, with a new introduction by Bernard Williams.

Social Justice: Strategies for National Renewal. The Report of the Commission on Social Justice. Chairman: Gordon Borrie. Vintage, 1994.

Drugs and the Law: Report of the Independent Inquiry into the Misuse of Drugs Act 1971. Chairman: Ruth Runciman. The Police Foundation, 2000.

Index

miliar with, or
al approach to
g introduction.
y original voice
d a searching
ection of liberal
ty-five years.

ude *Truth and*
king Sense of
d the Limits of
sity; and *Moral*
n 2003, he was
, University of
a Professor of
University of

(continued from front flap)

and wit. Those who are u
unconvinced by, a philosop
politics, will find this an enga
Both will encounter a thorou
in modern political theory
approach to the shape and
political thought in the past

Bernard Williams's books
Truthfulness (Princeton); *N
Humanity; Morality; Ethics
Philosophy; Shame and Nec
Luck.* At the time of his dea
Fellow of All Souls Colle
Oxford. Geoffrey Hawthorn
International Politics at
Cambridge.